Expansionary Fiscal Contraction

The Thatcher Government's 1981 Budget in Perspective

In its 1981 Budget, the Thatcher government discarded Keynesian counter-cyclical policies and cut Britain's public sector deficit in the depths of the worst UK recession since the 1930s. Controversially, the government argued that fiscal contraction would produce economic growth. In this specially commissioned volume, contributors examine recently released archives alongside first-hand accounts from key players within No. 10 Downing Street, the Treasury and the Bank of England, to provide the first comprehensive treatment of this critical event in British economic history. They assess the empirical and theoretical basis for expansionary fiscal contraction, drawing clear parallels with contemporary debates on austerity in Europe, the United States and Japan in the wake of the recent global financial crisis. This timely and thoughtful book will have broad appeal among economists, political scientists, historians and policy makers.

Duncan Needham is Associate Director of the Centre for Financial History at Newnham College, Cambridge, and a Research Fellow of Darwin College, Cambridge. Before returning to academia, he worked as a credit trader at J. P. Morgan and then as a credit portfolio manager at Cairn Capital. Dr Needham lectures in economic history and teaches undergraduate and graduate courses in history, economics and politics.

Anthony Hotson is a Research Associate of the Centre for Financial History, Cambridge, and a member of Wolfson College, Oxford. He has worked at the Bank of England and as a market practitioner. More recently Dr Hotson was a Research Fellow of the Winton Institute for Monetary History in Oxford. He is a non-executive Director of Cenkos Securities plc.

Expansionary Fiscal Contraction

The Thatcher Government's 1981 Budget in Perspective

Edited by

Duncan Needham

and

Anthony Hotson

CAMBRIDGE
UNIVERSITY PRESS

CAMBRIDGE
UNIVERSITY PRESS

University Printing House, Cambridge CB2 8BS, United Kingdom

Cambridge University Press is part of the University of Cambridge.

It furthers the University's mission by disseminating knowledge in the pursuit of education, learning and research at the highest international levels of excellence.

www.cambridge.org
Information on this title: www.cambridge.org/9781107042933

© Cambridge University Press 2014

First published 2014

Printed in the United Kingdom by Clays, St Ives plc

A catalogue record for this publication is available from the British Library

Library of Congress Cataloging-in-Publication Data
Expansionary fiscal contraction : the Thatcher government's 1981 budget in perspective / edited by Duncan Needham, Anthony Hotson.
  pages cm
ISBN 978-1-107-04293-3 (hardback)
1. Budget – Great Britain – History.   2. Fiscal policy – Great Britain – History.
3. Great Britain – Economic policy – 1979–1997.   4. Thatcher, Margaret.
I. Needham, Duncan.   II. Hotson, Anthony.
HJ2095.E97 2014
336.94109′048–dc23
                                                                    2014001828

ISBN 978-1-107-04293-3 Hardback

Contents

List of figures	*page*	vii
List of tables		viii
List of contributors		ix
Foreword by Geoffrey Howe		xi
Note on the text		xiii
Definitions of UK monetary aggregates		xiv
List of abbreviations		xv

1 The 1981 statement by 364 economists
ROBERT NEILD — 1

2 The 1981 Budget: how did it come about?
TIM LANKESTER — 10

3 The London Business School and the 1981 Budget
ALAN BUDD — 37

4 The 1981 Budget: a view from the cockpit
ADAM RIDLEY — 56

5 The Bank of England and the 1981 Budget
CHARLES GOODHART — 83

6 1981 and all that
WILLIAM KEEGAN — 97

7 The origins of the Budget in 1980
CHRISTOPHER COLLINS — 102

8 The 1981 Budget and its impact on the conduct of economic policy: was it a monetarist revolution?
ANTHONY HOTSON — 123

9 The 1981 Budget: 'a Dunkirk, not an Alamein'
DUNCAN NEEDHAM — 148

10 Macroeconomic policy and the 1981 Budget:
    changing the trend
    RAY BARRELL   181

11 The Keynesian twin deficits in an inflationary context
    ROBERT Z. ALIBER   204

12 The long road to 1981: British money supply targets
    from DCE to the MTFS
    MICHAEL J. OLIVER   210

    List of names   229
    Chronology of events   232
    Official sources   238
    Bibliography of secondary sources   239
    Index   246

Figures

5.1 Retail prices index, effective exchange rate, nominal
    interest rate and broad money (£M3), 1979–83   *page* 85
8.1 The end of Bretton Woods: the dash for growth and
    fiscal deficits   125
8.2 Financing the PSBR: from underfunding to
    overfunding   125
8.3 The credit counterparts: DCE and M3   134
8.4 The credit counterparts of £M3   135
10.1 Productivity per person-hour relative to the United
    States   183
10.2 Trend growth in the United Kingdom   188
10.3 Real oil prices   190
10.4 Output growth around the 1981 Budget   197

Tables

1.1	Cyclically adjusted budget deficit as a percentage of GDP	*page* 6
4.1	Quarterly index of real GDP at factor cost, 1978–83	76
4.2	Shorter leading cyclical indicator	76
4.3	Trends in the PSBR as a percentage of GDP	76
5.1	Sectoral surplus or deficit, 1979–83	86
5.2	Exchange rate and interest rate movements, May 1979–September 1981	87
9.1	Unpublished and published DCE, M3 and £M3 objectives, 1968–79	150
10.1	UK growth in comparison	186
10.2	The United Kingdom in figures, 1979–90	192
10.3	First-year multipliers from a 1 per cent of GDP permanent consolidation	201

Contributors

LORD HOWE of Aberavon was Chancellor of the Exchequer in 1981.

ROBERT NEILD was Professor of Economics at the University of Cambridge in 1981 and an originator of the 364 economists' letter to *The Times*.

SIR TIM LANKESTER was the Prime Minister's Private Secretary for Economic Affairs in 1981.

SIR ALAN BUDD was Director of the Centre for Economic Forecasting at the London Business School in 1981.

SIR ADAM RIDLEY was Special Adviser to the Chancellor of the Exchequer in 1981.

CHARLES GOODHART was Chief Adviser at the Bank of England in 1981.

WILLIAM KEEGAN was Business Editor of *The Observer* in 1981.

CHRISTOPHER COLLINS is the Editor of margaretthatcher.org. He writes here in a personal capacity.

ANTHONY HOTSON was a Bank of England economist in 1981. He is currently a Research Associate of the Centre for Financial History, Cambridge, and a member of Wolfson College, Oxford.

DUNCAN NEEDHAM is Associate Director of the Centre for Financial History, Cambridge, and a Research Fellow of Darwin College, Cambridge.

RAY BARRELL is Professor of Economics at Brunel University.

ROBERT Z. ALIBER is Professor Emeritus of International Economics and Finance at the University of Chicago.

MICHAEL J. OLIVER is Professor of Economics at ESC Rennes School of Business.

Foreword

Geoffrey Howe

It is striking how much the 1981 Budget continues to fascinate economists and excite historians and political commentators. One cannot but assume that something quite important happened as a result of it! In recent years those interested in reading about it have been offered a great deal of interpretation and second-hand, subjective comment but relatively little history, though I would make exceptions of Nigel Lawson's fascinating autobiographical *The view from No. 11* and the first volume of Charles Moore's *Margaret Thatcher: the authorized biography*. So we should all welcome Cambridge University Press's splendid initiative and the hard work of Duncan Needham and Anthony Hotson in editing this richly informative collection of papers and essays. As a Cambridge man I am not, of course, totally surprised by the origin of this initiative.

Since it is vital to balance the subjective material – of which we already have plenty – with some real facts and an accurate record, I particularly appreciate the careful narrative work of (in alphabetical order) Messrs Budd, Collins, Goodhart and Lankester; and the filling out of the background undertaken by Robert Neild (who led the '364 economists'), Duncan Needham and my Special Adviser at the Treasury, Adam Ridley. I also enjoy the unavoidably arcane debates of the economists, even if their arguments are at times way over the head of a mere ex-Chancellor of the Exchequer.

That said, the book is dealing with some very important questions. This is not the time or place for me to speculate in detail about what went right or wrong; many of my own thoughts are to be found in my memoirs. But there are some points I should like to make now with the advantage of many years of hindsight, enlightened by this stimulating collection.

Today, the Medium-Term Financial Strategy we launched in 1980 may seem rather ephemeral – indeed, pointless, or even perverse. At the time, however, it was invaluable in reorientating radically the broad lines of British economic policy; or perhaps I should say in consolidating the earlier reorientation initiated in 1976 in one of his wise phases as the Chancellor of the Exchequer by my friend Denis Healey. Look at what happened to output, inflation and so much else in the fifteen years after 1981.

Some critics try to dismiss all these successful developments by referring to the fact that, after 1981, employment did not recover, or at least unemployment did not fall as quickly or to such low levels as it had done in periods of growths in the 1950s and 1960s. They disregard the sad fact that, by 1981, such an old-style recovery was no longer on offer.

All of which brings me, with a certain smile, to the famous 364 economists who wrote so trenchantly to *The Times* to attack the Budget in March 1981. In its aftermath, they (and many others) were ferocious in their criticism, constant in their predictions of continuing recession and strident in proclaiming that there were better alternatives to the policies we pursued. Looking back, we can be relaxed about the ferocity of their criticism, puzzled at their failure to suggest alternatives and amused at the inaccuracy of their prophesies, which were almost instantly disproved by the performance of the economy from the moment I sat down after my Budget speech. As we know, like the savage 1976 IMF Healey measures and the brutal Jenkins post-devaluation strategy of 1968, the vicious 1981 Budget was followed by years of unusually strong GDP growth.

Today, some thirty years later, there are two features of this period that stand out. As Alan Budd notes, those involved in political life or in 'high policy' are often marked by a 'searing experience'. For older generations, the searing experience was the depression and unemployment of the 1930s. For those active in the 1970s, it was the inflation, depression and unemployment following the first oil crisis. After the banking crisis of 2007–8 it will be the depression and unemployment that it unleashed. Each episode leaves society divided between those desperate not to repeat the mistakes of the previous crisis and those who recognise that we live in new times and must not unthinkingly follow standard orthodoxy.

Finally, I recall a little wistfully that the Conservative government elected in 1979 lived through a great deal of sound and fury. There was an exceptional emotional intensity about our politics at that time. This was as it should have been. There were massive issues at stake. It all made for a splendid spectacle for the historians. But it also made for some erratic history and unreliable memories, in which passions and emotions now need to be matched by a careful examination of the facts. Read on!

Note on the text

In this volume, '1972/73' means the fiscal year ending April 1973. '1972–73' means the two calendar years 1972 and 1973. This may differ in quotations from primary sources.

Fractions are used to denote a number to the nearest one-quarter, as opposed to decimals, which denote greater precision.

Citations from the Thatcher Foundation website are given in the following format: MTFW [unique document ID]. Documents can be found either by typing this number into the search box on the website or by appending it to the URL margaretthatcher.org/document. For example, MTFW 107590 can be found at www.margaretthatcher.org/document/107590.

Appendices 5.1 and 5.2 to chapter five reproduce Bank of England archive documents in full. We acknowledge the kind permission of The Governor and Company of the Bank of England in including them in this volume.

Definitions of UK monetary aggregates

M0   Currency in circulation with the public and held by banks, comprising Bank of England notes, current coin issued by the Royal Mint, and the fiduciary note issue of the Scottish and Northern Irish banks, plus UK banks' deposits with the Bank of England, often referred to as bankers' balances.

M1   Currency in circulation with the public and UK residents' sight deposits with UK banks.

M3   Currency in circulation with the public, plus UK residents' sterling and foreign currency deposits with UK banks. Deposits include time deposits and certificates of deposit.

£M3   Currency in circulation with the public, plus UK residents' sterling deposits with UK banks. Deposits include time deposits and certificates of deposit.

PSL1   Private Sector Liquidity 1: M1, plus private sector time deposits with a maturity of up to two years, plus private sector holdings of money market instruments.

PSL2   Private Sector Liquidity 2: PSL1, plus private sector building society deposits, excluding terms shares and Save As You Earn (SAYE) holdings, and National Savings, excluding longer-term savings, minus building society holdings of bank deposits and money market instruments.

Abbreviations

BEQB	*Bank of England Quarterly Bulletin*
BOE	Bank of England Archive
BSA	Building Societies Association
CBI	Confederation of British Industry
CCC	Competition and Credit Control
CPRS	Central Policy Review Staff
DCE	domestic credit expansion
EFC	expansionary fiscal contraction
EMS	European Monetary System
ERG	Economic Reconstruction Group
ERM	Exchange Rate Mechanism
FSBR	*Financial Statement and Budget Report*
GDP	gross domestic product
HMG	Her Majesty's government
HMT	Her Majesty's Treasury
IMF	International Monetary Fund
LIBOR	London Interbank Offered Rate
LBS	London Business School
LTV	loan to value
MBC	monetary base control
MLR	Minimum Lending Rate
MTFS	Medium-Term Financial Strategy
MTFW	Margaret Thatcher Foundation Website
NAFA	net acquisition of financial assets
NHS	National Health Service
NIC	National Insurance Contributions
NIF	national income forecast
OECD	Organisation for Economic Co-operation and Development
ONS	Office for National Statistics
OPEC	Organization of the Petroleum Exporting Countries
PSBR	public sector borrowing requirement
RPI	Retail Price Index

SAYE	Save As You Earn
SLA	US savings and loan associations
SSD	supplementary special deposits (the 'corset')
TFP	total factor productivity
TNA	the National Archives
TUC	Trades Union Congress
VAT	value added tax

1   The 1981 statement by 364 economists

Robert Neild

In 1981 my colleague Frank Hahn and I wrote a letter criticising Sir Geoffrey Howe's Budget. We intended to send it, signed by the two of us, to *The Times*, but it grew into a 'statement' signed by 364 economists that created rather a stir when it was published. I here recount how that came about and how I now see the episode in retrospect. At eighty-seven, my memories, filtered by age, are clear but of course subjective. I refer to documents and statistics of the period to the best of my ability.

The monetarist debate

The statement was a climax in the Keynesian/monetarist debate, the nature of which it is worth briefly recalling.

Keynes' great contribution to economics was a causal explanation of why aggregate demand in an economy may not match its productive potential with the consequence that there is unemployment – or inflation. In *The general theory*, published in 1936, he thus led us to understand why unemployment had plagued the world in the interwar years.[1] Then in *How to pay for the war*, published in 1940, he estimated how much civilian demand would need to be restrained by budgetary means if war expenditure was to be met without inflation.[2] In doing so, he pioneered the use of national income accounts in macroeconomic management.

With few exceptions, economists accepted his theory. It is logically coherent; it relates to measurable variables (in the national income and expenditure accounts); and it recognises the importance of psychology, in particular the 'animal spirits' of entrepreneurs: it is rational and realistic.

For twenty-five years after World War II budgetary policy was based on demand management using Keynesian analysis: the probable course of

---

An earlier version of this chapter appeared in the *Newsletter of the Royal Economic Society* in October 2012. It is reprinted with kind permission from the Royal Economic Society.

[1] J. M. Keynes, *The general theory of employment, interest and money* (London, 1936).

[2] J. M. Keynes, *How to pay for the war: a radical plan for the Chancellor of the Exchequer* (London, 1940).

aggregate demand was forecast, and the balance in the budget was set so as to bring aggregate demand towards the full employment level. The technique was far from perfect but the result was low unemployment, moderate inflation and real growth of 2 per cent a year.

This period of relative economic harmony was shattered in the 1970s when inflation exploded, triggered by sharply higher prices for oil, and by the reaction of the trades unions to the consequent squeeze on real wages. The annual rate of inflation hit a peak of 24 per cent in 1975 and averaged 14 per cent a year in that decade.[3] British governments, reluctant to reduce aggregate demand so as to cause unemployment to the point at which money wages were checked, tried negotiating incomes policies with the trades unions and employers. They had little success: there were strikes and social unrest.

It was against this background that monetarist doctrine was adopted by Sir Keith Joseph and other Conservatives in the 1970s and became part of the policies that were evolved in that period and applied to the economy when Margaret Thatcher came to power in 1979. The dominant evangelist of the doctrine was Milton Friedman. His message, like that of other evangelists, was wonderfully simple. Unions were not to blame for inflation, nor were oil sheiks. It was all the result of excessive expansion of the money supply: '[I]nflation can be mastered. The technical instruments of controlling the money supply are available. The obstacle is lack of political will.'[4] The policy would involve high unemployment only temporarily since the economy, being self-regulating, would soon return to the 'natural rate of unemployment'. The message was supported by a graph or graphs showing that, over time, prices and the money supply move approximately together.

The doctrine had two flaws. First, demonstrating that the money supply and prices move together is no better than showing that the length of life and the number of meals a person has eaten move together: a simple association between two variables tells one nothing about causation. Second, the causal explanations that Friedman offered did not bear scrutiny.

At the beginning of 1980 Frank Hahn and I criticised monetarist doctrine on these grounds in an article in *The Times*, entitled 'Monetarism: why Mrs Thatcher should beware'.[5] We quoted Friedman's view that unemployment would revert to a natural rate, which 'is the level that would be ground out by the Walrasian system of general equilibrium equations, provided there is embedded in them the actual structural characteristics of the labour and commodity markets, including market imperfections', and explained that:

---

[3] Office for National Statistics, long-term price series CDKO.

[4] M. Friedman, cited by R. R. Neild, 'The meaning of monetarism' ('Economic notebook'), *Guardian*, 30 September 1974.

[5] F. H. Hahn and R. R. Neild, 'Monetarism: why Mrs Thatcher should beware', *The Times*, 25 February 1980.

(1) in the previous decade mathematical economists had shown that, even if there were no market imperfections, the Walrasian equations could not be expected to produce a general equilibrium with full employment;

(2) the idea that they would do so in the presence of market imperfections, which abound in reality, was even more far-fetched.

We concluded:

There are neither theoretical foundations nor empirical support for the monetarists' proposition that the real economy is self-regulating and that activity and employment can be relied upon to recover automatically from the present fiscal and monetary squeeze.

It is not our purpose to propound or debate alternative policies here. Indeed we have held different opinions about policy in the past and might well do so again were we to debate it now. Our common concern is that the Government's policy, as well as analysis and debate of alternatives, should not be based on a misleading notion of how the economy works.

In a rather aggressive reply a week later, Friedman accused us of writing about the 'Phillips curve', to which we had made no reference. After this diversion, he went on to say: 'We can know that a bird flies and have some insight into how it is able to do so without having a complete understanding of the aerodynamic theory involved.' He then listed a series of points, to the effect that there was an historical association between money and prices, with variable time lags. Without offering any better causal explanation than that, he reasserted in remarkably strong terms his view that the economy would recover automatically from the monetary squeeze: '[R]educed monetary growth, such as Mrs Thatcher's government is trying to achieve, may increase unemployment temporarily, to be rewarded by a much sharper reduction in unemployment later.'[6]

That was the doctrinal background to our letter. The economic background was that unemployment was rising to levels not seen since the interwar years. Since the war the central objective of economic policy had been full employment, which had come to mean a rate of unemployment of 3 per cent or less, and that had been pretty well maintained until the 1970s. When unemployment rose to 7 per cent in 1980 and to 10 per cent in 1981, I certainly felt morally indignant that the great achievement of modern economics – the creation of full employment in place of the mass unemployment and the misery of the pre-war years, which I could remember – was being betrayed. I believe most economists felt the same. The feelings of the 364 economists were surely roused by the introduction of further fiscal tightening in the 1981 Budget when unemployment was already so high.

There was a further contributory cause, but I hesitate to mention it since it is personal. I do so because it is germane to understanding what

[6] M. Friedman, 'Monetarism: a reply to the critics', *The Times*, 3 March 1980.

happened. It is that Milton Friedman, who was very clever and made original contributions to economics, was an exceptionally artful debater, whose rhetorical skills in the advocacy of monetarism were such that some politicians embraced him as a saviour offering a painless escape from inflation, while some economists saw him as a charlatan.[7]

At this time I was invited by the BBC to debate monetarism with him live on television. I was forewarned by my next-door neighbour, Elaine Sofer (a sociologist, daughter of Benjamin Graham, the father of modern equity investment theory), that Friedman was a dangerous opponent in debate. She, when helping as a student to organise debates at the University of Chicago, had found that he was a most brilliant and enthusiastic debater. He did not mind being asked at short notice to take part in a debate, and typically would consent before asking what the subject was. If told that it was, say, capital punishment, he would say 'Great! Which side?' and perform brilliantly whichever side he was on. Although forewarned, I found the way he avoided saying what caused the historical association between money and prices, by means of prevarication and mockery, so maddening that I lost my temper with him on the live programme. The shame I felt at making a public exhibition of myself imprinted the episode in my memory.

The relative importance of these three strands of opinion – that monetarism was theoretically incoherent, that unemployment was already shamefully high and that Friedman was behaving as a charlatan – will have differed from person to person; and other considerations may also have been in their minds. But, as I remember those days, these were the dominant reasons why so many economists signed the statement. How it came into being was this.

The statement

After the Budget, Frank Hahn and I, over coffee at the Faculty of Economics (at the University of Cambridge), set about drafting a joint letter to *The Times* criticising its monetary foundations. Others wanted to join in and add their names, until they were so numerous that I telephoned *The Times* to see how many signatures they would publish. Since the number wanting to sign exceeded the limit, the alternative somehow evolved of turning the letter into a statement and inviting economists in all the universities in the country to sign it. I was amazed at the huge response.

The statement, which in essence repeated what Frank and I had said a year beforehand in *The Times*, read as follows.

---

[7] Paul Samuelson's obituary in *The New York Times* recounted that 'Mr Samuelson said he always had fear in his heart when he prepared for combat with Mr Friedman, a formidably engaging debater. "If you looked at a transcript afterward, it might seem clear that you had won the debate on points," he said. "But somehow, with members of the audience, you always seemed to come off as elite, and Milton seemed to have won the day." M. M. Weinstein, 'Paul A. Samuelson, economist, dies at 94', *New York Times*, 13 December 2009.

EMBARGOED 2400 HOURS 29.3.81

UNIVERSITY OF CAMBRIDGE

FACULTY OF ECONOMICS AND POLITICS

TELEPHONE (0223) 358944

SIDGWICK AVENUE
CAMBRIDGE CB3 9DD

Statement on Economic Policy

The following statement on economic policy has been signed by 364 university economists in Britain, whose names are given on the attached list:

"We, who are all present or retired members of the economics staffs of British universities, are convinced that:

a) there is no basis in economic theory or supporting evidence for the Government's belief that by deflating demand they will bring inflation permanently under control and thereby induce an automatic recovery in output and employment;

b) present policies will deepen the depression, erode the industrial base of our economy and threaten its social and political stability;

c) there are alternative policies; and

d) the time has come to reject monetarist policies and consider urgently which alternative offers the best hope of sustained economic recovery."

Analysis

Those who signed include:

a) 76 present or past professors

b) a majority of the Chief Economic Advisers to the Government since the war: Professor James Meade, Lord Roberthall, Sir Alec Cairncross, Sir Bryan Hopkin and Sir Fred Atkinson

c) the President, 9 of the Vice-Presidents, and the Secretary-General of the Royal Economic Society.

The statement was circulated as university terms were ending. The rates of response have therefore been influenced by when term ended, by how dispersed is the community of university teachers in the vacation, as well as by the climate of economic opinion in each university.

Origins

The statement was sent by us to one member of each university on 13 March with a covering letter which said:

"We believe that a large number of economists in British universities, whatever their politics, think the Government's present economic policies to be wrong and that, for the sake of the country – and the profession – it is time we all spoke up. We have therefore prepared the attached statement, cast in terms which we hope will command wide agreement."

A copy of the letter is attached.

F H Hahn
R R Neild

The aftermath

In March 1984, the third anniversary of the statement, I was one of six of the signatories who were asked to say what they now thought about the statement. The rate of unemployment was then at 12 per cent, which proved to be the peak; it remained above the figure of 10 per cent until the end of 1987. Inflation had fallen from a peak of 18 per cent in 1980 to 5 per cent in 1984. Similarly, the rate of increase in wage rates had fallen from 18 per cent in 1980 to 6 per cent in 1984. A key link in this turnaround was a fall in commodity prices consequent on the decline in demand from the United States, Britain and other industrialised countries as they applied their monetarist deflationary policies.[8] My comment was this:

> I see no reason to modify my view about how the economy works. The levelling-out in activity has been in large part induced by the government relaxation of controls on consumer credit. That's exactly what happened in earlier post-war stop-go cycles. The American recovery, induced by a budget deficit, has helped us too. I suspect that if you disentangle the figures the Chancellor's budget is expansionary.[9]

Today we can judge the budgets of that period by looking at the historical estimates of the cyclically adjusted budget balance, also called the 'structural budget balance', produced by the ONS (see Table 1.1). We can now see that the Budget was expanded by an amount equivalent to 1.5 per cent of GDP between 1981/82 and 1983/84, a significant but not extreme change.

The extent of the tightening that went before is extreme, however. Between 1978/79 and 1981/82 (which reflects the first-year impact of the 1981 Budget) the Budget was tightened by no less than 6.3 per cent of GDP. By far the greater part of that tightening (an amount equal to 4.9 per cent of GDP) was introduced in the 1981 Budget.

Table 1.1 *Cyclically adjusted budget deficit as a percentage of GDP*

1978/79	1979/80	1980/81	1981/82	1982/83	1983/84
4.8	4.0	3.4	−1.5	−1.4	0.0

---

[8] I am indebted to Wilfred Beckerman for reminding me of the importance of the fall in primary prices.

[9] F. Williams, 'The economic mirage – by "rebel" professors', *The Times*, 30 March 1984.

The statement in retrospect

Paragraphs (a) and (c) were statements about economic theory. They said that there was no basis in economic theory or supporting evidence for the government's monetarist belief in an automatic recovery, and that there were alternative policies. These, I believe, remain irrefutable propositions.

Paragraph (b) made the prediction that present policies would deepen the depression, with adverse economic and political consequences. In fact, unemployment remained above 10 per cent of the workforce for six years and, as noted above, reached a peak of 12 per cent in early 1984. The depression did not deepen as much as we had predicted; nor did the economy recover within a period consistent with any reasonable interpretation of Friedman's 'variable time lags'. In a vulgar political debate over the consequences of monetarism, the participants might call 'Quits'. Paragraph (d) followed from the others and requires no comment.

To get a better understanding of what happened in this period, economic historians will need to trace causation from the exogenous variables in macroeconomics, the most important of which are actions taken by the government (including the central bank) that influence the level of demand, and changes in demand and commodity prices in the world economy, through to the responses of the economy as recorded in the national income accounts, the monetary statistics and the statistics of unemployment and prices. They will never achieve a perfect explanation but they should be able to do better than I can now.

A few points are worth noting now.

(1) It is clear that, after 1979, many changes in policy were made in pursuit of two aims that were sometimes in conflict: the desire to check inflation and the desire to liberate market forces in the credit markets and other parts of the economy. The expansion of consumer credit that helped to sustain demand in this period is an example.

(2) The Employment Acts of 1980 and 1982 and the Trade Union Act of 1984, which cut the power of the trades unions, must have contributed to the rapid decline in inflation.

(3) The monetarist doctrine of Friedman has now been abandoned in favour of trying to use interest rates to control inflation, not the money supply. It seems to be recognised, implicitly at least, that the money supply is endogenous, not exogenous; a passive indicator of how the demand for loans is going, not a policy instrument. This is a view for which there is ample backing.[10]

---

[10] This view was implicit in the report of the *Committee on the working of the monetary system* (Radcliffe), Cmnd 827 (London, 1959), paras. 381–98. But the classic explicit statement is by N. Kaldor, 'Evidence to the Treasury and Civil Service Committee', July 1980,

Conclusion: the veil of monetarism

I now see that monetarism, despite its fallaciousness, served a useful purpose: it provided a veil for the severe deflation that was needed to stop the inflationary spiral of the 1970s.

That the pursuit of full employment might lead to inflation was widely foreseen. For example, William Beveridge, in his 1944 book *Full employment in a free society*, wrote: 'There is a real danger that sectional wage bargaining, pursued without regard to its effect upon prices, may lead to a vicious spiral of inflation.'[11] And, in the same year, the White Paper entitled *Employment policy* warned that '[a]ction taken by the Government to maintain expenditure will be fruitless unless wages and prices are kept reasonably stable... [I]t will be essential that employers and workers should exercise moderation in wage matters.'[12]

When inflation struck in Britain the necessary response was (1) a short, hard dose of deflation and (2) a radical reform of the trades unions. A hard-headed Keynesian analysis, or common sense, would have led to that conclusion. But before 1979 Labour and Conservative governments jibbed at such harsh policies, and so did the great majority of economists – of whom I was one.

Much as I abhor the social philosophy of Margaret Thatcher (and her follower, Tony Blair), I now give her credit for having introduced these two controversial policies that were necessary to check inflation – though I deplore the fact that monetarism so blinded the government that it pressed home deflation too hard and too long.

Monetarism served as a veil for politicians and central bankers in that it permitted them to avoid saying that they were imposing deflation, and therefore causing unemployment, so as to check inflation. Instead, they could say that their aim was to check the money supply so as to stop inflation, with or without the rider that they believed – with Friedman – that temporary unemployment would correct itself. I believe that the Conservative politicians who directed economic policy in Britain at this time spoke to this effect with complete sincerity, since they appear to have been converts to Friedman's faith. But that was not true universally. In the important case of the United States, there is strong evidence that Paul Volcker, who, as Chairman of the Federal Reserve, dominated monetary policy, adopted monetary targets cynically as the only means of getting

reproduced in N. Kaldor, *The scourge of monetarism* (Oxford, 1982), 45–8. See also J. C. R. Dow and I. D. Saville, *A critique of monetary policy: theory and British experience* (Oxford, 1988), 219–22.

[11] W. H. Beveridge, *Full employment in a free society* (London, 1944), 199.

[12] *Employment policy*, Cmnd 6527 (London, 1944), para. 49.

away politically with the big increases in interest rates needed to check inflation. A fascinating, detailed account by William Greider of how he did this was published in *The New Yorker* in 1987. Greider reports that, when Henry Wallich, a member of the board of the Federal Reserve, was told by Volcker that he proposed to adopt money supply targets, he accused him of making a pact with the devil, to which Volcker replied: 'Sometimes you have to deal with the devil.'[13] A little later in the article, Greider writes: 'The monetarist alternative offered a clever solution to Volcker's internal political dilemma: it would serve as a veil to cloak the tough decisions.'[14] A biography of Volcker published in 2004 gives the same interpretation of his tactics.[15]

---

[13] W. Greider, 'Annals of finance', *New Yorker*, 9 November 1987, 103.   [14] Ibid., 104.

[15] J. B. Treaster, *Paul Volcker: the making of a financial legend* (Hoboken, NJ, 2004), 149, passim. See also W. Greider, *Secrets of the temple: how the Federal Reserve runs the country* (New York, 1987).

2   The 1981 Budget: how did it come about?

Tim Lankester

The 1981 Budget has a mythological status in the history of Margaret Thatcher's premiership. It was highly controversial at the time because its contractionary stance went in the face of the conventional view that, in a deep recession, fiscal policy should be relaxed, not tightened. No fewer than 364 academic economists wrote to *The Times* arguing just that. Yet, on the surface at least, the critics were proved wrong. The economy started to recover in the quarter following the Budget announcements. Consequently, the improvement in Mrs Thatcher's political fortunes from 1981 onwards is often seen as stemming from this Budget. Whether in reality the Budget was responsible for the economic turnaround and recovery, or whether they happened in spite of the Budget, as has been argued, is addressed elsewhere in this volume.

The aim of this chapter is not to argue the merits and demerits of the Budget but to examine how it came about. What were the views of the key players in the run-up to the Budget – the Prime Minister and her advisers, and the Chancellor, his ministerial team, Special Advisers and top officials – and how were these played out?

The answers to these questions are of interest because they throw light on decision making at the highest level at a critical moment in the Thatcher premiership, and on the clash of economic ideas prevalent at the time. They can also illuminate an old debate about the Budget's 'paternity': who among the principal players can claim primary responsibility for the main Budget decisions?

The case for revisiting the 1981 Budget process

The 1981 Budget has already been the subject of many accounts. Several of the key participants have published their recollections of what happened: Margaret Thatcher herself, Sir Geoffrey Howe and Nigel Lawson in their respective memoirs; and Thatcher's two key advisers in the No. 10

Policy Unit, Alan Walters and John Hoskyns.[1] There have also been accounts by others, notably by Thatcher's biographers, Hugo Young, John Campbell, and Charles Moore, and by economic journalist William Keegan.[2]

The case for this further examination of the 1981 Budget process is twofold. First, many of the relevant papers, which were not available to earlier writers, are now in the public domain. Neither Howe nor Lawson would have had access to papers prepared by Thatcher's advisers, nor to their diaries, which are now in the Thatcher Foundation archive; and Thatcher, Walters and Hoskyns would not have had access to many of the Treasury papers. Second, all five were writing from their own particular perspective, and it is legitimate to ask whether their accounts are biased. Other writers had the disadvantage of not being directly involved, and only Moore had access to most of the papers.

I was the Prime Minister's Private Secretary for Economic Affairs at the time, on secondment from the Treasury. My job, amongst others, was to coordinate the briefing and advice that Mrs Thatcher received from the Treasury and from others in and outside government on economic and financial matters. I was the note taker at her meetings with Howe in the run-up to the 1981 Budget, and I was in close touch with the No. 10 Policy Unit advisers and with the Treasury team – ministers, their Special Advisers, and officials. I was thus in a good position to observe how the thinking on the Budget developed. Moreover, I had – and have – no particular axe to grind. My first loyalty was to the Prime Minister, but I also had an allegiance to the Treasury insofar as the latter was my 'home' department, and it was my responsibility to ensure that the Treasury's views were properly understood and considered by Thatcher.

I was in the middle ground in terms of economic philosophy. Originally trained as an economist with a definite Keynesian bias, by 1981 I was well conscious of the limitations of fiscal policy as a tool of demand management, particularly in times of high inflation. I had learnt this from having worked on macroeconomic policy at the Treasury in the mid-1970s, at the time of Britain's request for assistance from the International Monetary

[1] M. H. Thatcher, *The Downing Street years* (London, 1993); R. E. G. Howe, *Conflict of loyalty* (London, 1994); N. Lawson, *The view from No. 11: memoirs of a Tory radical* (London, 1992); A. A. Walters, *Britain's economic renaissance: Margaret Thatcher's reforms 1979–84* (Oxford, 1986); J. A. H. L. Hoskyns, *Just in time: inside the Thatcher revolution* (London, 2000).

[2] H. J. S. Young, *One of us: a biography of Margaret Thatcher* (London, 1989); J. Campbell, *Margaret Thatcher*, 2 vols. (London, 2000, 2003); C. H. Moore, *Margaret Thatcher: the authorized biography*, vol. I, *Not for turning* (London, 2013); W. J. G. Keegan, *Mrs Thatcher's economic experiment* (London, 1984).

Fund. Equally, while acknowledging that control of the money supply was necessary if inflation were to be contained, I was no believer in the sort of crude monetarism that posited a one-for-one link between the growth of one or other monetary aggregate and price inflation, or that the short-run impact of a monetary squeeze could be principally on prices with only a minimal effect on real activity. I was therefore well positioned to understand, and present, the different views on macroeconomic policy making that partly underlay the different views on how the Budget should be constructed. To the extent that my own views counted – which was not a lot compared with Walters and Hoskyns and the Treasury team – I tended to the more cautious line of the Treasury 'doves'.

But the differences were considerably less than has sometimes been described – especially by Walters and Hoskyns. Howe and Moore correctly aver that, at the political level (i.e. between Margaret Thatcher and Geoffrey Howe) the Treasury and No. 10 were never far apart; and there were at least two senior officials at the Treasury, Terry Burns and Peter Middleton, whose thinking was close to that of Walters. To the extent that differences of view did exist, they were as much within the Treasury, and within No. 10, as between the two. Moreover, the views of several of the key participants switched during the course of the ongoing discussions – not least Thatcher and Howe themselves.

Previous accounts

The most detailed account of what happened is provided by Hoskyns. It draws heavily on his diary and makes for fascinating reading. But it is inevitably one-sided – as well as incomplete, because, when he wrote his book, he did not have access to key Treasury papers. Hoskyns writes that 'the top Treasury officials were totally opposed to what we were suggesting'.[3] He goes on to say that 'the shape of the Budget first emerged at an advisers' meeting in my office on 21 January – and in the end, Margaret and Geoffrey took the outsiders' advice rather than Whitehall's'.[4] Thatcher in her account tends to support Hoskyns' view that it was due to pressure from the advisers and herself that the public sector borrowing requirement in the Budget came out in the way it did.

By contrast, according to Howe and Lawson, the Treasury were working towards a similar PSBR goal as the Prime Minister's advisers throughout the Budget process; and the final Budget decisions were Howe's, albeit endorsed by the Prime Minister. If he and the Treasury team

---

[3] Hoskyns, *Just in time*, 283.   [4] Ibid., 285.

approached the final decisions less single-mindedly and with greater caution, it was because they weighed the pros and cons – both political and economic – more carefully. Hoskyns essentially takes the view that Howe and Lawson altered the story with the benefit of hindsight so that they could take principal credit for a successful Budget.

At the same time, it can be asked whether there is not an element of hindsight in the Hoskyns/Walters accounts. After the Budget decisions had finally been taken, Walters argued that the budgeted reduction in the PSBR was inadequate. In his book, he skates over this. In a footnote, he does say that he 'would have preferred to have a figure [for the PSBR] below £10 billion'.[5] But then he goes on to say: 'I am convinced that the total thrust of the 1981 Budget was substantially right.'[6] Possibly he changed his tune because the Budget was seen in retrospect to have been a success, and because the PSBR outcome for 1981/82 came out £2 billion lower than in the Budget forecast.

Moore provides the best-rounded account. He captures well the sense of crisis and gloom at No. 10 in the months preceding the Budget, and he gives a good idea of just how exceedingly difficult the discussions were. This was in part because of Thatcher, who found it hard to understand how and why, under her overall direction, things had gone so badly wrong. Although he was one of her closest political allies, she was starting to lose confidence in her Chancellor – though this was as nothing compared with her relations with the Governor of the Bank of England, Gordon Richardson.[7] Thatcher's and Howe's methods were also very different. Howe liked to ponder long and hard about the trade-offs and risks he faced. Thatcher was more intuitive in her approach, and was more inclined to make snap judgements. These factors did not make for easy or coherent debate between the two.

In charting the discussions within No. 10, and between the Treasury and No. 10, in the weeks before the Budget, Moore's reading of what happened is largely correct. Yet in one critical respect (of which more below) he is wrong; and this leads him to attach greater importance to Thatcher's role in the final decision making than it deserves.

---

[5] Walters, *Britain's economic renaissance*, 87.   [6] Ibid., 88.

[7] Thatcher's relations with Richardson by this time were at rock bottom. She blamed him for failing to keep the money supply under control – albeit with only limited justification: the chosen aggregate, £M3, was notoriously difficult to control over the short term; the target for 1981/82 turned out to have been set far too low in view of structural changes affecting broad money (i.e. the ending of the 'corset'); and the £M3 overrun was partly due to the government's failure to meet its PSBR target and the lower than forecast level of activity. She also blamed him for being slow to accept the case for monetary base control. In addition, she had a general mistrust of the Bank of England, as an institution too close to its City clients and too far from her control.

Mrs Thatcher's advisers

Moore also fails to capture quite how fraught the relations between Thatcher and her advisers could be. On this, Hoskyns is a better guide – while Thatcher provides little sense of it at all. She rarely saw fit to ask for their views. Instead, it was they who constantly had to take the initiative in drawing issues to her attention and putting forward advice. Sometimes this was welcomed, at other times it was not. She blew hot and cold, on some occasions treating them as her closest confidants, at other times shutting them out altogether. The volatile nature of their relationship was all too evident in the 1981 Budget deliberations.

Hoskyns had worked with Thatcher in opposition as an occasional adviser, and after the 1979 election he became head of the Policy Unit at No. 10. Her relations with him were ambiguous. He was a former army officer and successful businessman, good-looking and charming. She had a high regard for his analytical capability, and for his economic vision and commitment to her cause. On the other hand, she found his thinking overly conceptual and systems-oriented, and insufficiently grounded in what she felt was practical. She didn't rate his political sense.[8]

Hoskyns, for his part, was frequently frustrated by her unwillingness to think strategically and logically, or to engage in serious debate. He saw the running of the country like the running of a very large company; she was less taken by the analogy. He was openly critical of her management and leadership style. She disliked the apocalyptic tone and rough language of some of his memos. She preferred the more guarded and respectful language of the civil service. And she didn't quite trust him and Walters to maintain her confidences. For all the devotion they showed to her personally, and their wish for her to succeed, she felt they shared too much information with colleagues outside No. 10. Hoskyns thought that her insistence on secrecy stifled useful debate.

Walters was a monetarist economist of great distinction, and his presence as adviser after January 1981 certainly accorded her ill-formed monetarist views greater weight and shifted the balance of power between No. 10 and the Treasury. Thatcher valued the clarity and freshness of his thinking, and his ability to take on the Treasury and the Bank of England. She also admired the fact that he had 'come a long way' – in some respects, a good deal further even than herself. His father, like hers, was a grocer, but – in stark contrast to Alfred Roberts – a communist.

---

[8] Hoskyns accepted that politics was not the Policy Unit's strong suit. In December 1980 he admitted that 'we are amateurs in the political field': J. A. H. L. Hoskyns, 'Government strategy', 19 December 1980, London, TNA, PREM 19/174, MTFW 113306.

Walters left school at age fifteen and initially worked as a machine oper-
ator in a shoe factory, before enrolling at his home-town university,
Leicester, while she went from grammar school in Grantham to privileged
Oxford. He later had a brilliant career as an academic economist in the
United Kingdom and the United States.

Walters had a disarming self-confidence, which helped to give Mrs
Thatcher renewed hope that a way forward to a sustainable recovery
could be found. On the other hand, she considered him politically and
bureaucratically naïve, and too much the academic economist, with
insufficient understanding – because of his years spent in America – of
the political problems she faced inside and outside her party.

One other adviser at No. 10 needs to be mentioned: political adviser
David Wolfson. Scion of the Wolfson retail family, he had also worked for
Thatcher in opposition. He worked closely with Hoskyns and Walters and
provided a practical, common-sense and calming influence when, at
times, calm and practicality were in short supply. Yet, as we will see, on
the 1981 Budget his influence was anything but calming.[9]

Policy challenges

In what follows, I review the key papers – including the records I made of
the Thatcher/Howe meetings – to see how the thinking of the two leaders
and their respective advisers developed. In doing so, I examine the question of whether she and her advisers were instrumental in achieving the
£10.5 billion PSBR in the Budget, or whether the Treasury team – ministers and officials – were heading for this level of PSBR anyway. The
detailed chronology, especially in the final couple of weeks, is important
for providing an objective answer to this question.

I focus principally on the Budget stance (i.e. the PSBR). But of course,
as in any budget, there were numerous decisions to be taken on the
composition of the measures to meet the chosen PSBR target, which in
the end involved a PSBR reduction package of £4 billion, roughly equivalent to 1¾ per cent of GDP. These were entirely made up of tax
increases, including substantial increases in indirect taxes and in income
tax; an additional tax on North Sea oil production; and a special levy on
bank deposits.[10] The discussions between the Treasury and No. 10

---

[9] Wolfson's official title was 'Chief of Staff'. This was misleading, as no staff at No. 10
reported to, or through, him.

[10] The additional tax on North Sea oil had in fact been announced in November 1980, so
there was an element of double counting to make the Budget package appear tougher than
it actually was.

regarding the particular tax increases were relatively painless, compared with the PSBR discussions. Agreement on most of them, including the controversial levy on bank deposits and the sizeable hike in indirect taxes, was reached without much difficulty. There was one exception: whether to raise the basic rate of income tax or whether to freeze the personal income tax allowances. The No. 10 advisers, with periodic support from Thatcher, strongly favoured the former; the Treasury team, after considerable internal debate, in the end favoured the latter.

There was one other particular theme running through the internal Treasury discussions throughout the winter months: the need to switch resources from wage and salary earners, who had been doing rather well through the recession provided they kept their jobs, to the increasingly loss-making corporate sector. This came to be known as the 'Burns–Middleton hypothesis'. The question was whether to use some of the revenue from increased personal taxes to help industry. In the end, it was decided not to give any significant breaks to the corporate sector and to use the bulk of the extra revenue to reduce the PSBR. (Companies did receive some help but this was limited to £200 million in stock relief.) Thatcher expressed a preference for giving priority to the PSBR reduction in view of the lower interest rates that she believed the latter would bring about and from which companies would benefit (though the Confederation of British Industry did not think much of this argument); but the issue did not feature prominently in their discussions. Basically, the issue was decided by Treasury ministers, albeit with Thatcher's support.[11]

To all the participants, it was clear by the second half of 1980 that economic policy was in a serious mess. The Medium-Term Financial Strategy, a four-year programme of gradual reductions in the PSBR and the growth of the money stock, had been launched with great fanfare as part of the 1980 Budget. Its aim was to provide a credible plan for bringing inflation down permanently and reducing the burden of government borrowing, and thereby create the conditions for restoring prosperity. By the autumn of 1980 it was abundantly clear that, in its first year, the MTFS was already seriously off track. The PSBR was running way over forecast, owing to extra spending on the nationalised industries, a disastrous public sector pay round and reduced revenues and higher social security payments resulting from worsening levels of economic activity.

---

[11] Amongst Treasury ministers, Lawson appears to have led the way in favouring a lower PSBR over tax breaks for the corporate sector. See, for example, his remarks in A. J. Wiggins, 'Note of a meeting held at No. 11 Downing Street on Tuesday, 27 January, 1981 at 9.30 am', 28 January 1981, private office files of Geoffrey Howe, MTFW 127452.

In the 1980 Budget, the PSBR had been forecast by the Treasury at £8½ billion. By November the forecast for 1980/81 was revised upwards to £11½ billion, an increase equivalent to 1½ per cent of GDP – and the eventual outturn was £13¼ billion. The monetary aggregate that the MTFS had chosen to target, £M3 (broad money), was running wildly over its target range owing to the ending of quantitative controls over the banks' deposit taking (the so-called 'corset') and other unforeseen factors, especially the overshooting of the PSBR. After peaking in May 1980, inflation was coming down; but other economic indicators were mainly negative. Company profits were being squeezed by high interest rates and by an impossibly high exchange rate; output was continuing to fall; and unemployment was rising inexorably. In the 1980 public spending 'round', the Treasury had been unable to rein back spending for 1981/82 and beyond on any significant scale. The government seemed unable to stem the haemorrhaging of taxpayers' money into the steel, coal and automobile industries. As a result, if the PSBR overrun in 1980/81 was to be reversed and brought back more in line with the MTFS in 1981/82, the main burden would have to be borne by tax increases – the opposite of what the government had been elected to deliver.

The policy challenges were therefore very considerable indeed. In particular, what could be done to revive the corporate sector's profitability? What could be done to bring down the exchange rate? And what could – and should – be done to restore the credibility of the MTFS with respect to the money supply and the PSBR?

The November 1980 mini-Budget

The Treasury did not wait until the 1981 Budget to address these issues. On 24 November 1980 Howe announced revenue increases amounting to £2 billion (about ¾ per cent of GDP), roughly half from an increase in employees' national insurance contributions (NICs) and the other half from an increase in petroleum revenue duty. (Denis Healey for the Labour opposition said that Howe should *increase* the PSBR by £7 billion in 1981/82.)[12] On the same day the Bank of England's Minimum Lending Rate was reduced by two percentage points in an attempt to assist industry and reduce the upward pressure on the exchange rate – and this despite the risk that it might further inflate £M3 and make gilt sales more difficult.

Both practically and philosophically, the November measures can be seen as a precursor of the 1981 Budget. Despite major concerns about the

---

[12] House of Commons debate (hereafter 'HC Deb.', as reported in Hansard), 24 November 1980, vol. 994, c209.

ongoing recession, action was taken to rein back the budget deficit rather than increase it, and one of the purposes was to make possible a cut in interest rates so as to restrain the upward pressure on the exchange rate.

Initially, there was no appetite among ministers for fiscal action ahead of the 1981 Budget. The Conservatives had come to power highly critical of Labour's frequent resort to mid-year fiscal corrections, or 'mini-budgets'. The Prime Minister and Treasury ministers alike were keen to see monetary growth brought under control, as well as a drop in the exchange rate. But they did not regard early action to reduce the PSBR as a priority. Thus, at a meeting on 22 September between Treasury officials and ministers to discuss the overall economic situation, Lawson is recorded as noting that tax increases might be necessary in the 1981 Budget, but that it would be 'undesirable for the Government to take hasty and perhaps inappropriate action now'.[13] Any announcements in his view should focus on other measures to reduce monetary growth – possible funding initiatives and even controls on credit. Howe did not show any enthusiasm for early fiscal action either, though he did authorise discussions to take place on a contingency basis for an increase in employees' national insurance contributions.[14] And there was no push from the Prime Minister or from the No. 10 Policy Unit for the early announcement of action to reduce the PSBR. Instead, as a way of directly curbing the upward pressure on sterling, Thatcher showed a passing interest in re-imposing exchange controls, only to be rebuffed by Howe.[15]

Treasury officials took a different view. At the 22 September meeting, the Permanent Secretary, Sir Douglas Wass, and the Second Permanent Secretary, Bill Ryrie, both argued that an early reduction in interest rates would be credible only if it was accompanied by the announcement of measures to reduce the PSBR.[16] It was this view – a clear foretaste of the logic behind the 1981 Budget – that in due course prevailed in Howe's 24

---

[13] A. J. Wiggins, 'Note of a meeting held in the Chancellor of the Exchequer's room, HM Treasury at 9.30 am on Monday, 22 September 1980', TNA, T386/544, MTFW 128330.

[14] Ibid.

[15] See chapter by Christopher Collins, 'Origins of the Budget in 1980', in this volume.

[16] A. J. Wiggins, 'Note of a meeting held in the Chancellor of the Exchequer's room, HM Treasury at 9.30 am on Monday, 22 September 1980', TNA, T386/544, MTFW 128330. It is ironic that the call for fiscal action came from two of the Treasury's so-called 'doves'. Neither Wass nor Ryrie ever found favour with Mrs Thatcher. She considered Wass tainted by his association with Labour's policies and by his lack of enthusiasm for the MTFS. As for Ryrie, she had clashed with him when she visited Washington as leader of the opposition in 1977 and he was the Treasury representative in Washington at the time. At a briefing meeting, he contradicted her on her analysis of American economic policy. They had another unsatisfactory meeting when she visited Washington as Prime Minister in 1979. When Ryrie returned to London in 1980 she undoubtedly held these two encounters against him, and as a result his career in the civil service effectively stalled.

November mini-Budget. Following the 22 September meeting, Ryrie told Kit McMahon, Deputy Governor of the Bank of England, that 'officials were more concerned about the PSBR and the necessity of fiscal action than ministers'.[17]

Howe naturally discussed the November measures with Thatcher, but, in contrast to the period immediately running up to the Budget, her advisers played no significant role. Alan Walters had not yet arrived at No. 10, and before his arrival the No. 10 Policy Unit did not get closely involved in macroeconomic policy. (Its main concerns prior to Walters' arrival were overall government strategy, public spending, the nationalised industries, and the trade unions and employment law.)

The Treasury's internal forecast of the PSBR for 1981/82 just prior to the November measures was 4½ per cent of GDP (about £11 billion), compared with 3 per cent (about £7½ billion) in the MTFS.[18] With the November measures, the PSBR forecast ought to have reduced to around £9 billion. By the middle of December, however, the forecast had deteriorated again to around £10½ billion.[19] So, unless there were to be a substantial adjustment to the MTFS projection to allow for cyclical factors, there would need to be further action in the upcoming Budget if the PSBR path was to be made consistent with the MTFS.

Donald Derx, an exceptionally knowledgeable official at the Department of Employment, suffered a similar fate, after clashing with her on the details of trade union law. See Moore, *Margaret Thatcher*, 424. (Thatcher was not averse to challenge; in fact, she enjoyed an argument. But it had to be on her terms, and preferably with individuals she already knew and trusted.) Both Wass and Ryrie were brilliant civil servants, loyal to the governments they served, and it was unfortunate and unfair that Thatcher never adequately appreciated them. Wass nonetheless saw out his term as Permanent Secretary. Ryrie took early retirement from the civil service and went on to serve with great distinction as head of the World Bank's private sector arm, the International Finance Corporation.

[17] C. W. McMahon, 'Treasury thinking on economic policy', 25 September 1980, London, BOE, 7A134/16, MTFW 113082.

[18] The PSBR forecast, prior to the November measures, is taken from a draft paper, 'The economic prospect and implications for policy', that the Treasury had intended to send to Thatcher around the end of October. A copy later found its way into Alan Walters' files at Churchill College, Cambridge. The paper argued for a PSBR reduction of £2.5 billion (compared with the £2 billion reduction achieved in the November measures). It explicitly ruled out a reduction – around £4 billion – of the size that would have been needed to get the PSBR back in line with the MTFS's 3 per cent of GDP, on the grounds that this would be too much in the light of the worsening recession. HM Treasury, 'Economic prospects and implications for policy', October 1980, Cambridge, Churchill Archives Centre (hereafter 'Churchill'), WTRS 1/1.

[19] The mid-December forecast assumed a PSBR of £9 billion for 1981/82 (3¾ per cent of GDP) with a fiscal adjustment of £1 billion at 1978/79 prices (roughly £1.5 billion at 1981/82 prices) to achieve it: T. Burns, 'Medium term prospects and the fiscal adjustment', 16 December 1980, private office files of Geoffrey Howe, MTFW 127437.

Views of ministers, officials and advisers

This was the situation that faced the Treasury when Budget discussions started in earnest in January 1981. During January Walters arrived as Thatcher's economic adviser, and he immediately brought an additional consideration to bear. Bolstered by advice from Professor Jürg Niehans from Berne, he was convinced that the £M3 overrun was giving an entirely misleading impression of monetary laxity, and that monetary policy – as indicated by the high exchange rate and the slow growth of narrow money (M0 and M1) – was too tight.[20] The point was not entirely new: the Bank of England had been making it for months. But Walters' championing of it gave it immediate traction at No. 10. The priority had to be to get interest rates down further. This in Walters' view further strengthened the case for a tight budget, since an MLR cut would be credible to the markets only if the PSBR was brought back under control.

At this point, there was no one amongst the top Treasury officials who believed there was any option but to reduce the PSBR. They had already shown this by taking the initiative in proposing the revenue package in November. But, not surprisingly, there were differences of opinion as to how much it should be reduced. Too much of a reduction could put an excessive squeeze on economic activity at a time when the economy was still in deep recession and there was no certainty of an upturn; and inflation was already falling quite rapidly, so there was little need for further downward pressure. Too small a reduction would fail to impress the markets, make it impossible to reduce MLR, risk a funding crisis and make it difficult to restore credibility to the MTFS. It was a fine judgement where to draw the line, bearing in mind also what was politically feasible. Howe needed to hear both sides of the argument – and he did. As he says in his memoirs, the Treasury was not a monolith.[21]

The balance of opinion amongst the top Treasury officials was on the side of caution (i.e. what Hoskyns described as 'underkill'). Wass and Ryrie were in this camp, as were Brian Unwin, the Under Secretary in charge of budget coordination, and Howe's Principal Private Secretary, John Wiggins. These officials may have had personal doubts – and Wass certainly did – about the monetarist philosophy as embodied in the MTFS; but the record suggests that they repressed those doubts and provided the best possible advice, as they saw it, within the framework

---

[20] Niehans was brought in as a consultant on Walters' advice and paid for by private Conservative supporters.
[21] Howe, *Conflict of loyalty*, 200.

of the MTFS. If they showed caution, it was because – with the key MTFS targets quickly proving untenable – they were worried about the impact on the real economy of trying to re-establish them too quickly.

There were two prominent officials who took a more hawkish line on the PSBR, however. The Chief Economic Adviser, Terry Burns, was one of the intellectual architects of the MTFS from his time as professor at the London Business School, and he was close to Walters in terms of monetarist philosophy. Peter Middleton, the Deputy Secretary in charge of monetary policy (and later to succeed Wass as Permanent Secretary), was of a more pragmatic bent, seeing a significant lowering of the PSBR as an essential precondition for getting the money supply back under control and for lower interest rates.

But the views of the 'doves' and the 'hawks' among Treasury officials on what the PSBR for 1981/82 should be were never very far apart. Judging from the Treasury papers, they never diverged by more than £1 billion, less than ½ per cent of GDP, even as the PSBR forecast worsened. In short, the differences within the Treasury official team were not that significant, and were well within the margin of error in forecasting the PSBR.[22] By the same token – insofar as the 'hawks' in the Treasury held similar views to Walters' – the differences between the 'doves' in the Treasury and the No. 10 advisers, except in the latter's more excitable moments, were not very significant either. Conceptually, the relatively small differences essentially turned on how much adjustment should be made to the MTFS projection to allow for the worse than previously projected economic outlook. Even Walters accepted that a significant adjustment needed to be made – which is why his views were not that different from the official Treasury view.

At the start of the Budget discussions, the range of views amongst the Treasury political team was rather greater. Shortly before Christmas 1980 Howe asked his ministerial colleagues and Special Advisers for their first 'sighting shots' on the Budget. They came back with a range of answers. At one end were the Economic Secretary, Peter Rees, and the Treasury minister in the Lords, Arthur Cockfield, who suggested little or no fiscal adjustment at all. In the middle were the Chief Secretary, John Biffen, the Financial Secretary, Nigel Lawson, and Special Adviser Adam Ridley, who suggested an adjustment so as to bring the PSBR down to around 3½ per cent of GDP, half a percentage point above the MTFS number. At the

---

[22] The average error in forecasting the PSBR one year ahead in the 1970s was about 1.5 per cent of GDP (£3.5 billion in 1981 prices). See *FSBR 1981–82* (London, 1981), 28, tab. 10.

other extreme was Special Adviser Peter Cropper, who suggested a PSBR of 2½ per cent of GDP – well below the MTFS number.[23]

Howe was famously collegiate in terms of wanting to hear and ponder the views of his Treasury colleagues and advisers. To others outside the Treasury, including Thatcher, his decision making seemed unnecessarily tortuous – especially if it meant shifting his position from one day to another, as happened with the 1981 Budget. What it did mean, however, was that – once he had made up his mind – every possible angle had been covered.

Among his ministerial colleagues, Howe relied more than any other on Lawson. Lawson, who would succeed Howe as Chancellor of the Exchequer in 1983, was only a Minister of State, whereas Biffen was a member of the Cabinet. But Biffen, though a Thatcherite politically, had been opposed to the MTFS, and in his role as Chief Secretary he was held partly responsible for failing to curb public spending. Moreover, in early January 1981 he was moved sideways to become Secretary of State for Trade. His successor as Chief Secretary, Leon Brittan, though a close friend and confidant of Howe, had limited financial experience or expertise. Lawson, by contrast, could rightly consider himself the political progenitor of the MTFS, and he had a strong track record as an advocate and exponent of neoliberal economics in opposition and then as a Treasury minister. Not surprisingly, when it came to the 1981 Budget, he was consistently hawkish on the PSBR.

Like others, Lawson saw the reduction in the PSBR as essential for restoring credibility to the MTFS, and thereby to improving market expectations with regard to inflation and private investment. All the participants in the Budget discussions believed that a lower PSBR, assuming the reduction was large enough, should allow a reduction in interest rates. Lawson subsequently wrote that the link between the PSBR and interest rates was overstated.[24] He has also claimed that he didn't think much of the argument at the time. In fact, it is not obvious from the Treasury records that his view was different from the consensus Treasury view – namely that, while a lower PSBR would not

---

[23] Principal Private Secretary John Wiggins advised the Chancellor that 'I doubt the merits of going for a notably tighter fiscal policy next year than our current stance would suggest': A. J. Wiggins, '1981 budget', 18 December 1980, private office files of Geoffrey Howe, MTFW 127445.

[24] Lawson writes that 'short term interest rates…are determined not by the scale of the PSBR but by the needs of the government's anti-inflation policy'. He goes on to argue that, 'as the capital market was becoming increasingly a single global market, the public borrowing of any one country – with the important exception, because of its sheer size, of the United States – had a correspondingly diminished effect': Lawson, *The view from No. 11*, 90.

automatically lead to lower interest rates, a lower PSBR was more likely to be compatible with lower interest rates than a higher PSBR. Thus, in a post-Budget statement, he said of Labour's spending plans that, with unchanged monetary targets, 'the effect of borrowing more would be higher interest rates'.[25] Nonetheless, insofar as he understood these things better than most, he may well have been concerned that Thatcher and Howe were placing too much emphasis on the PSBR/interest rate link per se, rather than the effect of a lower PSBR on expectations more generally.[26]

At No. 10, Walters and Hoskyns, along with Wolfson, were consistently on the side of 'overkill'. They were partly influenced by what they saw as the Treasury's consistent tendency to underestimate the PSBR. This was certainly true of 1980/81, though in the 1970s the Treasury had in fact as often overestimated as underestimated it.

Hoskyns viewed the PSBR through the lens of the systems analyst as a 'stabilisation' issue: he believed that without a serious reduction in government borrowing, and preferably its eventual elimination, the economy would never stabilise. He wanted to maximise the PSBR reduction so as to impress the markets and restore credibility to the government's economic strategy and stability in the economy.

Walters approached the problem as a macroeconomist. With the level of PSBR in prospect, he believed that the confidence effect for the private sector of a very tight Budget, along with lower interest rates, would outweigh any direct deflationary impact. As prescribed in the MTFS, there had to be a progressive reduction in the structural deficit; but he was prepared to accept some adjustment to the PSBR projections in the MTFS to take into account cyclical factors.[27] For both Hoskyns and Walters, the link between a lower PSBR and lower interest rates and a lower exchange rate was crucial. They were less interested in the link between the PSBR and £M3 because the latter, in their view, was largely discredited as a monetary indicator.

Mrs Thatcher was drawn instinctively to their general point of view, though she attached more importance than they did to the link between

---

[25] N. Lawson, 'The Budget Judgement', 12 March 1981, Oxford, Christ Church College, Lawson MSS, MTFW 128044.

[26] The distinction was slightly academic, for, while there was no mechanistic link between the PSBR and interest rates except under very restrictive conditions, an improvement in market expectations brought about by a reduced PSBR was likely to result in lower interest rates.

[27] Walters writes that 'the policy of increasing the 1980 projected deficits by some 1.25 to 1.75 percent [of GDP] does not seem outrageously perverse. On the contrary, it appears to be in the appropriate ballpark.' Walters, *Britain's economic renaissance*, 82.

the PSBR and £M3, which – despite her interest in monetary base control – she was not ready yet to jettison. She and her Chancellor had invested too much political capital in the control of broad money as a means of controlling inflation.

There was also Robin Ibbs, head of the Central Policy Review Staff in the Cabinet Office. Ibbs was a senior executive at Imperial Chemical Industries (ICI), one of Britain's largest trading companies, on secondment to the government. He had a better idea than anyone else with access to Thatcher of the damage that the high exchange rate was doing to business. He was not part of the inner circle dealing with the Budget; but he nonetheless took every opportunity to argue that action had to be taken in the Budget to help the company sector and, in particular, to bring the exchange rate down. He doubted whether a reduction in interest rates made possible by the Budget would reduce the level of sterling sufficiently. The situation was so urgent that he favoured targeting the exchange rate and 'flexing' the monetary target as necessary.[28] Thatcher sympathised with his view that sterling had to come down, but a switch to targeting the exchange rate was anathema to the prevailing monetarist philosophy. Ibbs' was a lone voice in government on this issue at the time, and his proposal received no serious consideration.

Countdown to the Budget

On 17 January 1981 Thatcher held a special meeting with her advisers and with Howe and Burns and others from her inner political circle at Chequers. At this meeting, Howe warned of the worsened prospects for the PSBR (£11 billion, with the real possibility of further upward revision), and the need for a tough budget.[29] Walters and Hoskyns believed that the PSBR forecast would only get worse, which – unless it was dealt with – would produce a major economic crisis and in due course electoral

---

[28] In a letter to Howe dated 6 February 1981, Ibbs argued that a 10 per cent depreciation of sterling was needed – to bring the rate back to where it had been in early 1980. He suggested 'a system of monetary targets which could be temporarily flexed to eliminate unacceptable exchange rate changes whilst still retaining confidence in the basic monetarist approach'. It is doubtful whether commentators or the markets would have seen this as consistent with 'the basic monetarist approach': J. R. Ibbs, 'The 1981 Budget', 6 February 1981, TNA, PREM 19/438, MTFW 113992.

[29] I was not present and there were no minutes of the meeting. Hoskyns and Howe describe the discussion in broad outline. The PSBR forecast of £11 billion mentioned here is the figure mentioned by Burns at the meeting with the Governor of the Bank of England on 22 January: A. J. Wiggins, 'Note of a meeting held at 11, Downing Street at 8.30 am on Thursday, 22 January, 1981', 22 January 1981, BOE, 7A133/3, MTFW 117373; Hoskyns, *Just in time*, 260–1; Howe, *Conflict of loyalty*, 200–2.

defeat. From that moment they made it their principal goal to ensure a budget that would bring about the maximum possible reduction in the PSBR.

Howe met with the Governor of the Bank of England on 22 January. He revealed the same worsening story on the PSBR and the need for contractionary action in the Budget. The Governor told Howe that the Bank were more pessimistic than the Treasury about the economic outlook and 'questioned whether – in the light of the recessionary prospect – it would be appropriate to tighten both fiscal and monetary [sic] policy'.[30] At this and other meetings in the run-up to the Budget, Richardson and his Bank of England colleagues were clearly on the side of the 'doves'.[31]

On 27 January Howe held a meeting with his ministerial team plus officials and Special Advisers. Wass started the meeting by telling Howe that 'officials were generally agreed that a net contraction of around £1.5 billion would be sensible'.[32] The aim would be to deliver a PSBR of between 4 and 4½ per cent of GDP (around £10 billion), and thus a downward path from the 5½ per cent of GDP now likely for 1980/81. Lawson is recorded as saying that the markets would be very pleased with a figure of £10 billion provided they believed it. Howe concluded that the PSBR reduction should be a minimum of £1½ billion.[33]

Howe followed this meeting up with a note to the Prime Minister on 5 February. He reminded her that the PSBR forecast (which assumed full indexation of personal tax allowances and specific duties plus the £2 billion of revenue measures announced in November) was about £11 billion, compared with around £7½ billion implied in the MTFS. 'Taking into account the extent of the recession,' he wrote, he would be aiming for a PSBR 'somewhat below £10 billion' with a PSBR reduction package amounting to £1 to 1½ billion.[34] On seeing this note, Walters advised the Prime Minister that it would be better to plan on a PSBR reduction of £2 billion rather than £1½ billion, in order to reduce the

---

[30] There is no mention of anyone at the meeting suggesting a tightening of monetary policy: A. J. Wiggins, 'Note of a meeting held at 11, Downing Street at 8.30 am on Thursday, 22 January, 1981', 22 January 1981, BOE, 7A133/3, MTFW 117373.

[31] Howe says no one ever explained to him why the Governor failed to provide his customary 'Budget judgement' letter. With their views so out of line with the views of the Treasury team, Howe perhaps should not have been surprised that the Governor did not bother to send in formal advice on the 'Budget judgement'. Richardson met him again and again in the weeks running up to the Budget; Howe was hardly left in the dark as to what he thought. Howe, *Conflict of loyalty*, 204.

[32] A. J. Wiggins, 'Note of a meeting held at No. 11 Downing Street on Tuesday, 27 January, 1981 at 9.30 am', 28 January 1981, private office files of Geoffrey Howe, MTFW 127452.

[33] Ibid.

[34] 'R. E. G. Howe to Prime Minister', 5 February 1981, TNA, PREM 19/438, MTFW 113990.

funding burden further and improve the prospects for bringing down interest rates and the exchange rate.[35]

On 10 February Howe had the first of five meetings with Thatcher in which they discussed the Budget stance and the PSBR. Wass and Burns were also present for the Treasury, and so were Walters and Wolfson. Howe revealed that the PSBR forecast had now jumped to £13 billion, so, to bring the PSBR back to below £10 billion would be extremely difficult. Burns said it would be hard to defend a PSBR any higher than £10 to 10½ billion. They discussed the main options for bringing in more revenue. Howe had ruled out the practical feasibility of expenditure cuts at this late stage for 1981/82 and the political feasibility of an increase in income tax rates. (This would have meant putting into reverse one of the main planks of his first Budget, in 1979.) He had to rule out any increase in tax on the corporate sector (apart from the oil producers) because of its poor financial state; if anything, he would wish to offer the sector some tax reliefs. The main options he was left with, bearing in mind that he was already intending a special levy on bank deposits and the additional tax on North Sea oil production announced in the November mini-Budget, were increasing indirect taxes by more than inflation and limiting the increase in personal income tax allowances to perhaps only 6 per cent, compared with over 15 per cent if there were to be full indexation.[36]

Thatcher responded that the greatest priority was to improve industrial activity, which meant reducing the PSBR to enable a reduction in interest rates and the exchange rate.[37] Walters followed up with a note to Thatcher warning that the PSBR forecast could well rise further, and that therefore there was a real risk that the Budget measures would be inadequate – requiring a mini-Budget later or leading to a funding crisis.[38] He and Hoskyns and Wolfson met with Thatcher later that night to ram home the point. They thought they had succeeded. But then, the next day, Hoskyns was dismayed to hear that she scarcely seemed to remember what they had discussed.[39] In the wake of this, Hoskyns, Walters and Wolfson sent Thatcher another note warning of the dangers ahead and

---

[35] 'A. A. Walters to Prime Minister', 6 February 1981, TNA, PREM 19/438, MTFW 113994.

[36] Following the 1977 so-called Rooker–Wise amendment, personal allowances were automatically indexed to inflation unless countermanded by Parliament.

[37] T. P. Lankester, 'Note for the record', 10 February 1981, TNA, PREM 19/438, MTFW 113996.

[38] A. A. Walters, 'The Budget, etc.', 10 February 1981, TNA, PREM 19/438, MTFW 113997.

[39] Hoskyns, *Just in time*, 269–70.

pressing again for a tough budget. They later found she hadn't bothered to read it.[40]

In briefing Thatcher for her next meeting with Howe, on 13 February, I advised that the PSBR forecast had risen yet again – to £13¾ billion. I suggested that it would be necessary to get the PSBR down to £10 billion to justify any reduction in MLR; but I also warned that the 'short-term effect [of such a large PSBR reduction] may arguably be too deflationary. We need to consider carefully the trade-off between the deflation caused by interest rates not falling, and the deflation which would come from what the Policy Unit call "over-kill".'[41]

At the meeting itself, Howe told Thatcher that he did not think it would be possible, given the new PSBR forecast, to reduce the PSBR below £11¼ to £11½ billion. Ideally, it might be desirable to reduce it below £11 billion, but he did not believe it was politically feasible. Walters intervened to say that the markets would be disappointed by a PSBR of £11 billion, and therefore there was the strong likelihood that Howe's measures would be insufficient. He didn't believe a PSBR of £10 billion would be any more deflationary than a PSBR of £11 billion, because the latter would be worse for expectations. He urged that consideration be given to raising the basic rate of income tax by one or two percentage points. Although no final decisions were taken, Thatcher indicated that she agreed with Howe that the package he was proposing was the most that was politically sustainable.[42] It was after this meeting that, according to Walters, she screamed at him: 'You are just an academic and you don't know what the political implications [of tax rises] are.'[43]

Hoskyns and Walters were sufficiently shocked by this turn of events that they began seriously to consider resigning. They felt that Howe and Thatcher were in 'self-denial' and that their advice was having no effect.[44]

But the story was by no means over yet. Four days later, on Tuesday 17 February, Howe came to see Thatcher again. I was the only other person present. Howe said that he was now seriously thinking of raising the basic rate of income tax by one percentage point and raising the personal allowances by 10 per cent rather than the 6 per cent he had earlier suggested. This combination would be fairer and would bring in some additional useful revenue. Thatcher said she was now 'veering towards the view that a PSBR of less than £11 billion was essential'; and, if there was extra

---

[40] Ibid., 271–3.
[41] T. P. Lankester, 'Meeting on the Budget', 13 February 1981, TNA, PREM 19/438, MTFW 114003.
[42] T. P. Lankester, 'Note for the record', 13 February 1981, TNA, PREM 19/438, MTFW 114002.
[43] Moore, *Margaret Thatcher*, 625.   [44] Hoskyns, *Just in time*, 273.

revenue in his new proposals, she was willing to contemplate a basic rate increase.[45]

For some reason, Hoskyns and Walters were unaware that this meeting was taking place. Possibly Thatcher had already told me that they were no longer to be invited to her Budget meetings (see below), or it may have been because it was unscheduled, taking place immediately after an important statement in the House of Commons on the coal industry (the government had just caved in to the demands of the miners' union), which both Thatcher and Howe would have been present for.

My record of the 17 February meeting is dated that same day, and it was copied to Walters and Hoskyns.[46] But, for some reason, they ignored it; or perhaps they didn't fully appreciate the shift in Thatcher's and Howe's position from reading my note. Walters' diary records hearing about the meeting for the first time from me orally on 23 February.[47] I told him they had reached a provisional understanding on the need for an increase in the basic rate. I also, according to the diary, reported that Thatcher had told Howe that he had to get the PSBR below £11 billion, or 'you are for the chop'. The following day, 24 February, Walters passed on this information to Hoskyns, who described in his diary what he heard as 'an amazing *volte face*' on the part of Thatcher. He wrote: 'So our onslaught bears fruit at last?'[48]

The volte-face Hoskyns is talking about is clearly with reference to the Thatcher/Howe meeting on 17 February. Moore confusingly links it to the next meeting between Thatcher and Howe, on 24 February – in relation to which the remark makes no sense (as we shall see below).

My report that Thatcher had instructed Howe to reduce the PSBR or else he was for the 'chop' has become part of the 1981 Budget folklore.[49] I was likely exaggerating, or Walters was putting his own spin on what I said, for there is nothing in my record of the meeting to give any inkling – even allowing for the sanitised language of an official note – that she threatened him in this way: the essence is that they were both moving towards a PSBR of less than £11 billion. If she did use the word 'chop',

---

[45] T. P. Lankester, 'Note for the record', 17 February 1981, TNA, PREM 19/438, MTFW 114007.

[46] Ibid. Their names are shown as copy recipients. At some point Walters clearly read it, since there is a manuscript 'Wow' in the margin of his copy in his personal files at Churchill College. T. P. Lankester, 'Note for the record', 17 February 1981, Churchill, WTRS 1/5.

[47] A. A. Walters, 'Diary entry', 23 February 1981, Churchill, WTRS 3/1/1, MTFW 128827.

[48] Hoskyns, *Just in time*, 276–7.   [49] See, for example, Howe, *Conflict of loyalty*, 203.

which would have been uncharacteristic, it was probably out of exasperation with the political dilemma they both faced.

In the light of Thatcher's meeting with Howe on 17 February, she might have expected a note from Hoskyns and his colleagues acknowledging hers and Howe's change of heart on the PSBR and the basic rate. Instead, she got the opposite. On Friday 20 February the three advisers sent her a roughly worded memo warning that 'the present budget strategy leads to disaster'.[50] They pressed once again for a 'tough budget' – to include an increase in income tax rates, which would be seen as 'fair and honest in hard times', in preference to holding down the personal allowances. The memo didn't make clear how tough a Budget they now had in mind. Walters had been arguing for a PSBR in the region of £10 billion. Even if they still believed that Howe was aiming for a PSBR of around £11 billion, the difference was hardly sufficient to justify the memo's apocalyptic language. Or were they now suggesting an even tougher Budget?

Judging by her scant jottings on the memo, Mrs Thatcher wasn't pleased.[51] She must have been even less pleased when the advisers, having received no response to their Friday memo, sent her a further memo after the weekend with a copy of their earlier memo attached, warning that 'this is the eleventh hour, but it is still possible to choose a budget that gives some chance of success'.[52]

While Hoskyns and his colleagues, in apparent ignorance of the Thatcher/Howe meeting of 17 February, were firing off their singularly inappropriate weekend missiles, Howe was in fact changing his mind yet again. On the evening of Monday 23 February he sent Thatcher a note outlining his latest thinking: no increase in the basic rate after all, increasing personal allowances by only half the rate of inflation (i.e. by about 8 per cent), raising indirect taxes (other than value added tax) by twice the rate of inflation, and a PSBR of £11¼ billion.[53] In other words, this was a complete reversal of the position he had proposed on 17 February, and a reversion more or less to where he had been on 13 February.

Thatcher and Howe met again the following day (24 February), with only Wass and me in attendance. Implausibly, Thatcher writes in her memoirs that Walters was absent because he was 'engaged on some

[50] A. A. Walters, D. Wolfson and J. A. H. L. Hoskyns, 'Budget strategy', 20 February 1981, TNA, PREM 19/439, MTFW 114016.

[51] Ibid.

[52] 'A. A. Walters, J. A. H. L. Hoskyns and D. Wolfson to Prime Minister', 23 February 1981, Churchill, WTRS 1/3.

[53] 'R. E. G. Howe to Prime Minister', 23 February 1981, TNA, PREM 19/439, MTFW 114018.

other business'.[54] The truth is that I had been instructed by her not to invite him. I did not know precisely why at the time. I knew she was getting tired of Hoskyns' and Walters' pressuring her but I wasn't aware of their 20 and 23 February memos (which hadn't been copied to me) and how badly she must have taken them. These memos, and the fact that she felt that she was well aware of the economic arguments, and that the decisions were now essentially political, were almost certainly the reasons why she didn't want Walters or Hoskyns at the meeting. The fact that she allowed Howe to bring Wass with him made their exclusion all the more galling. Hoskyns writes despairingly of the secrecy that had overtaken the No. 10 deliberations.

At the meeting, she said she was dismayed that Howe was proposing once more a PSBR as high as £11¼ billion. She pressed for a PSBR of £10½ billion, which she suggested was the maximum figure that could justify any reduction in MLR. She argued that an increase in the basic rate could be justified on account of the increased spending on the National Coal Board and the British Steel Corporation, which somehow had to be paid for. Howe responded that he and his ministerial colleagues at the Treasury had concluded that an increase in the basic rate was not politically feasible.

My record of the meeting says that she 'remained concerned at the risks that the Chancellor was taking, but she was prepared to accept his political judgement that an increase in the basic rate was not possible'.[55] They then went on to discuss various suggestions from Thatcher on how to raise more revenue from indirect taxes, none of which were feasible. Although the record does not explicitly say so, my clear memory is that the meeting finished with Thatcher assenting – albeit reluctantly – to a PSBR of £11¼ billion. She did not believe she could push Howe any further. Moore writes that 'her point about the lower PSBR stood'.[56] But in what sense did it stand? Both Howe and Thatcher wanted a lower PSBR, but Howe did not think it possible and Thatcher did not insist on it.

I informed Hoskyns, Walters and Wolfson of what had happened. They were pleased that Thatcher had at least attempted to persuade Howe of the need for a PSBR below £11 billion, and of the case for an increase in the basic rate, but they were equally disappointed that she had not prevailed. Walters called on her early the following morning to double-check. According to Walters, she told him that she had told Howe that he had to take £3.5 billion off the PSBR (i.e. to reach a figure of £10.5 billion); and,

[54] Thatcher, *The Downing Street years*, 136.
[55] 'T. P. Lankester to A. J. Wiggins', 24 February 1981, TNA, PREM 19/439.
[56] Moore, *Margaret Thatcher*, 626.

when he pressed whether she was sure, she answered: 'Of course I'm sure. That's what you want, isn't it?'[57] The account in her memoirs is consistent with this when she writes: 'I told him [Walters] that I had insisted on the lower PSBR he wanted. But I still did not quite know how Geoffrey would react.'[58]

The reality, as my official record of the meeting shows, is that she did not tell Howe he had to take £3½ billion off. She had reluctantly gone along with a smaller reduction. She was either too upset or too embarrassed to tell Walters what had really happened.

After hearing the disappointing outcome of the 24 February meeting, Wolfson drafted what was, for him, an uncharacteristically brutal memo to Thatcher, in which he accused her of 'self delusion'.[59] He wrote that the 'political judgement is your own', that she would be held responsible by 'the City, the Country and the Colleagues' if there were a funding crisis, and that failure to act would be bordering on 'Criminal Liability' if the country were a company.[60] 'Does the Chancellor really hope to fool all of the people all of the time? Do you?'[61] The tone was so rough that Mrs Thatcher's principal Private Secretary, Clive Whitmore, who had not been much involved in the discussions to date, felt he had to intervene and show it to her in private. When she read it she was so incensed she tore it up. She had had enough of her advisers: she was not going to press their views on Howe any further.

While this was going on at No. 10 on the morning of 25 February, Howe had called an early meeting with his ministerial colleagues and senior officials at the Treasury. He said he had thought further overnight and had decided it was too risky to go for a PSBR of £11¼ billion, especially if the object was to reduce MLR by two percentage points. Perhaps he was influenced by Sir Keith Joseph, the Secretary of State for Industry, who had been briefed by Hoskyns the evening beforehand and had, according to Hoskyns, gone on to see Howe later.[62] In any event, Howe was now minded to go for a PSBR of £10.5 billion after all.

The ensuing discussion focused on two issues. First, officials suggested that Howe had a choice: he could either go for a PSBR of £11¼ billion and an MLR reduction of one percentage point, or a PSBR of £10½ billion and an MLR reduction of two percentage points. Treasury officials were divided: Ryrie and Unwin argued for the former on the grounds that it

---

[57] Ibid. [58] Thatcher, *The Downing Street years*, 136.

[59] 'D. Wolfson to Prime Minister', 25 February 1981, Churchill, HOSK 2/273, MTFW 127996.

[60] Ibid. [emphasis in original]. [61] Ibid.

[62] Howe has no recollection of meeting Joseph: telephone interview with Lord Howe, 6 August 2013.

would be less deflationary, Burns and Middleton for the latter (the opinion of Wass is not recorded). The other ministers and Howe's Special Adviser, Ridley, favoured £10.5 billion. This is what Howe decided – and, subject to further discussion with the Bank of England, a two percentage point MLR cut. Second, they had to decide how to finance this further PSBR reduction. Other options having been ruled out by now, there were only two possibilities: increasing the basic income tax rate by 1p or freezing the personal allowances. The former was less regressive (i.e. the burden would be spread more evenly and would be better from the point of view of making it worthwhile for people at the bottom end to seek work), but politically more difficult. All the ministers present, with Wass's support, agreed that freezing the allowances was easier to present than raising the basic rate; the latter would patently be seen as a tax rise whereas, with the former, nominal taxes would not be affected.[63] Lawson's preference in favour of freezing the allowances over any increase in the basic rate may have particularly influenced Howe, since it was he (Lawson) who from the Conservative benches had strongly supported the Rooker–Wise amendment in 1977; and he would therefore be especially prone to criticism if the allowances were not raised in line with inflation.

With the Treasury meeting concluded, Howe asked to see the Prime Minister, so that he could inform her before she left for the United States in the afternoon. He came over in the late morning. It was a strange meeting. Thatcher's mind was on other things: a speech she had to make at lunchtime to the Parliamentary and Scientific Committee, and her preparations for America and her first meetings with President Ronald Reagan following his recent election. Howe told her of his decisions on the PSBR and on the income tax allowances. She neither congratulated him on the former nor demurred on the latter. The official record (by me) simply says that she 'was content'.[64] It seemed she almost no longer wanted to know: it was now his Budget, despite the fact that she had been deeply engaged in Budget discussions with him for weeks. Perhaps she wanted ownership of the Budget now to be entirely his – even though no one would believe it – in case it all went badly wrong.

Mrs Thatcher instructed me not to tell her three advisers of this final turnaround.[65] She probably didn't want any further argument with them;

---

[63] A. J. Wiggins, 'Note of a meeting held in the Chancellor of the Exchequer's room, HM Treasury on Wednesday, 25 February 1981 at 9.30 am', 25 February 1981, TNA, T388/231, MTFW 127482.

[64] T. P. Lankester, 'Note for the record', 2 March 1981, TNA, PREM 19/439, MTFW 114024.

[65] Although I informed them orally, this probably explains why – unusually – I did not write a note of the meeting until several days later.

for, although the PSBR had come out more or less their way, they weren't going to be happy with the decision to freeze the allowances. And by this time she was becoming paranoiac about keeping the Budget decisions secret: she was worried they would leak the information to like-minded colleagues in yet another effort to secure what they wanted.

I ignored her instruction and told them. To deny them the information after all their involvement to date seemed to me ridiculous; it wasn't the way they should be treated; and it would have made our working relations in the office, which to date had always been friendly and harmonious, impossible.

Hoskyns' and Walters' reaction was ambivalent. After hearing from me what Howe had decided, Hoskyns still believed there was a good chance there would be a funding crisis within six months.[66] The following week, though, he writes, 'It was now, to our great relief, becoming clear that the Budget was going to be as tough as we had hoped it would be.'[67]

In his diary on 25 February, Walters wrote that 'at least the PSBR will be about right'.[68] Yet, in the same diary entry, he described the Budget decisions as 'stupid politically, indefensible morally and economically'. On that same day, after a lunch in the City, he wrote to Howe that, for the City, a 'really satisfactory figure for the PSBR would be £7 billion'.[69] And, on the following day, he wrote to Wass in the following terms: 'I have seen neither evidence nor arguments to suggest that the present proposals are not very much a case of too little and the wrong kind. The consequences are likely to appear in crisis measures after a few months.'[70] He went on to say that, 'with this Budget, I would think it desirable not to move MLR at all'.[71] If MLR had to be reduced, the reduction should not be more than one percentage point.[72] In his diary, he wrote that he had told Middleton that he thought the Budget had 'all the seeds of disaster'.[73]

The Treasury team were put out, if not baffled, by Walters' late démarche. It was an intensely worrying time at the department: no one could be absolutely confident that they had got the Budget right. To have Walters sniping from the wings, after Howe and Thatcher had now agreed

---

[66] Hoskyns, *Just in time*, 278.   [67] Ibid., 280.
[68] A. A. Walters, 'Diary entry', 25 February 1981. Churchill, WTRS 3/1/1, MTFW 114204.
[69] Howe, *Conflict of loyalty*, 203.
[70] 'A. A. Walters to D. W. G. Wass', 26 February 1981, TNA, PREM 19/439, MTFW 114026.
[71] Ibid.   [72] Ibid.
[73] A. A. Walters, 'Diary entry', 26 February 1981. Churchill, WTRS 3/1/1, MTFW 114204.

on a budget stance more or less in line with his previously stated views, was hardly helpful.

What were the reasons for these contradictory signals from Hoskyns and Walters? For Hoskyns, it seems to have taken a little time for him to realise that the Budget had come out more or less as he had wanted. Or perhaps he was worried that Howe would do yet another about-turn just ahead of Budget day? As for Walters, one possible explanation for his contradictory posture and colourful language is that he was thoroughly fed up with the final twists and turns, and with his exclusion from the final discussions. Another possibility is that he was genuinely torn between what he believed would be acceptable to the markets and what he thought was right in terms of macroeconomic theory. The figure of £7 billion he had mentioned to Howe after his lunch in the City was approximately the figure implied by the MTFS. It was this figure that less sophisticated market practitioners had their eye on, whereas the figure of around £10 billion, which he had been supporting in the Budget discussions, was consistent with allowing for a 1¼ per cent cyclical adjustment – an upward revision that, in his book, he later wrote was 'in response to the deep recession, and was entirely consistent with the medium term framework'.[74] In objecting to the Budget decisions on moral and political grounds, he was presumably referring to the freezing of personal allowances in preference to an increase in the basic rate. Considering that the distributional impact was not vastly different, calling the decision 'stupid politically' and 'indefensible morally' was perhaps the sort of hyperbole for which a diarist can be forgiven. Yet unlike many economists of a Conservative persuasion, perhaps reflecting his own personal background, Walters did care about equity.

Following Howe's meeting with Thatcher on 25 February, the main elements in the Budget were fixed. There then followed within the Treasury considerable debate on how to present the figures. It was decided – so as to make it the more credible with the financial markets – to make the Budget look even tougher than it actually was. This was achieved by the unusual ploy of including in the Budget arithmetic the revenue from the supplementary petroleum duty announced in November 1980. The latter, up until then, had been included in the pre-Budget revenue forecast. By taking it out, the pre-Budget PSBR forecast went up to £14.5 billion, and the total Budget measures could be presented, with some

---

[74] Walters, *Britain's economic renaissance*, 81. In his post-Budget statement referred to earlier, Lawson had taken a similar line. He justified the £10.5 billion PSBR on the grounds that the MTFS target for the PSBR required an adjustment of £3 billion on account because of the 'extra severity of the recession': Lawson, 'The Budget Judgement'.

other minor adjustments, as amounting to a PSBR cut of £4 billion.[75] It is doubtful whether many market practitioners were taken in by this presentational gambit. What they were most interested in was the post-Budget PSBR forecast of £10.5 billion and whether there were steps in place to achieve it. As it turned out, there were: the actual PSBR for 1981/82 came out at £8.5 billion.

The Budget's paternity

We come back to the question: how much was the final Budget judgement due to Thatcher and her advisers at No. 10?

There is no doubt at all that the No. 10 advisers pressed consistently for a low PSBR, and that their voice had influence both with the Prime Minister and with the Treasury. Hoskyns certainly thought he and Walters had influenced Howe. After Howe's final meeting with Thatcher on 25 February before she left for America, Hoskyns wrote in his diary: 'I think Geoffrey came because our barrage of notes is affecting him'.[76] But it was not their voice, nor the Prime Minister's, that ultimately determined the Budget stance. As the Treasury papers show, the official Treasury was by no means monolithic on the Budget. Burns and Middleton were effectively in the same camp as Walters; and so were Lawson and Howe's own Special Advisers, Cropper and Ridley; and, when it came to Howe's final meeting with officials on 25 February, the 'doves' among the Treasury officials were only £¾ billion apart from the 'hawks' – a relatively small amount given the margin of error in the forecasting. Howe himself wanted a tough Budget. If he – and, indeed, Thatcher – appeared at times less hawkish than the No. 10 advisers, it was because they were more mindful of the political difficulties of imposing a really tight Budget.

Thatcher, as I have shown, did not force Howe to accept a £10.5 billion PSBR. She certainly pressed him in that direction over several meetings; but, like Howe, she also veered backwards and forwards on whether this was politically feasible. At their penultimate meeting, on 24 February, she went along with his judgement that £10.5 billion was impossible. The volte-face the next day was his decision and was not due to renewed pressure from her. It is straining the record for Moore to write, as he does, that she 'found ways to get Howe to accept it'.[77]

---

[75] This was net of £320 million of extra spending on the nationalised industries, which was decided in early March 1981. Full details of the Budget measures, their costings and their impact on the PSBR can be found in the *FSBR 1981–82*.

[76] Hoskyns, *Just in time*, 277.   [77] Moore, *Margaret Thatcher*, 627.

On the composition of the Budget measures, Mrs Thatcher and her advisers were unsuccessful. They – and she, intermittently – would have preferred an increase in the basic rate instead of freezing the allowances. (Quite why she preferred the former was something of a puzzle – since she had not shown much interest in the fairness or unfairness factor in Howe's previous Budgets, and raising the basic rate was clearly worse in presentational terms. Probably, it was out of deference to Walters.) Howe decided to freeze the allowances; and Thatcher did not attempt to get him to change his decision.

Finally, there is the question of who called the shots on the related decision on whether the Budget should be accompanied by a reduction in MLR. The Treasury team, with the possible exception of Lawson (see above), believed that an important rationale for a tight Budget was to achieve a cut in MLR. Thatcher was determined to achieve a reduction; it was the pay-off that made a tough Budget politically feasible. The markets were expecting it. The Governor of the Bank of England supported it. Walters did not; although he believed in the link between the PSBR and interest rates, his view was that a PSBR of £10.5 billion wasn't low enough to justify a reduction.

MLR was reduced by 2 percentage points on Budget day to 12 per cent, and this helped to temper the political and media row that inevitably followed the Budget announcements. But, as Walters had warned, the reduction proved excessive. In the autumn of 1981, amid worries that sterling was falling too far and that private credit demand was rising too rapidly, MLR was allowed to climb back to 15.125 per cent. Walters thought they had overreacted, putting at risk the fragile recovery. Not for the first or last time, Walters found himself at odds with the Treasury.[78]

---

[78] Walters, *Britain's economic renaissance*, 148. His most famous falling-out with the Treasury was in 1989, when he got into a public spat with Lawson over exchange rate policy, leading first to Lawson's resignation and then his own.

3   The London Business School and the 1981 Budget

Alan Budd

Lord Lawson has commented, on more than one occasion, that academic economists have less influence on policy than they suppose.[1] Despite this comment, the truth of which I do not dispute, this chapter seeks to describe some academic ideas, particularly those propounded by economists at the Centre for Economic Forecasting at the London Business School, which provided an explanation of and justification for the measures introduced in the 1981 Budget.[2]

The background

The economic ideas described here were a response to policy decisions and their consequences for much of the post-war period and particularly from the early 1970s. I have referred elsewhere to the idea of the 'searing experience', which has a profound effect on those who are affected by it and can explain later attitudes to policy.[3] When I first joined the Treasury, in 1970, the senior economists had experienced the effects of the Great Depression. That was their searing experience. As I have said, the dole queues of the 1930s still wound their way through the corridors of the Treasury in the early 1970s, and the senior economists were determined that there would never again be high unemployment.[4] The searing experience for myself and some of my colleagues was the policy experiment

---

I am grateful to Geoffrey Dicks for comments on an earlier draft.

[1]   For example, D. J. Needham, M. J. Oliver and A. Riley (eds.), 'The 1981 Budget: facts and fallacies', transcript of witness seminar held at Lombard Street Research, 27 September 2011, 22, available at www.chu.cam.ac.uk/archives/exhibitions/1981_Budget.pdf.

[2]   'LBS' is used as a convenient label throughout but it is not implied that the views described were shared by all members of the LBS, or, for that matter, of the Centre for Economic Forecasting.

[3]   A. P. Budd, 'The development of demand management: comments', in F. A. Cairncross (ed.), *Changing perceptions of economic policy: essays in honour of the seventieth birthday of Sir Alec Cairncross* (London, 1981), 55.

[4]   A. P. Budd, 'Fiscal policy in the United Kingdom', in I. McLean and C. Jennings (eds.), *Applying the dismal science: when economists give advice to governments* (London, 2006), 44.

37

that produced what was known as the 'Barber boom' and its painful aftermath. The ideas associated with the 1981 Budget were a reaction to that experiment, and it is worth sketching some of the features of the policies introduced by Anthony Barber as Chancellor of the Exchequer. Later experience may have changed one's views of what happened and why, but I describe here the conclusions that some of us drew at the time.

Barber, who became Chancellor in 1970, inherited a tradition in which fiscal policy was seen as the main instrument of demand management. The policy objective pursued by the Treasury can be defined as the minimisation of unemployment subject to a balance of payments constraint. The balance of payments was the constraint since policy was conducted under a fixed exchange rate regime. Excessive balance of payments deficits threatened an unsustainable loss of foreign currency reserves. In the early post-war years fiscal policy was mainly directed to offsetting what was expected to be excess demand, but thereafter there were the normal attempts to offset cyclical fluctuations in demand.

The pound had been devalued in 1967 since it was believed that an overvalued currency was restricting growth. The evidence for this view was the tendency for the balance of payments constraint to become effective at ever higher levels of unemployment. The Labour government had tightened domestic demand to make room for the hoped-for boost to net trade following the devaluation, and the Conservative government inherited a slowing economy with rising unemployment. By 1971 unemployment was threatening to exceed 1 million, an unacceptably high level at the time, and there were expansionary Budgets in 1972 and 1973 that were intended to bring unemployment below 500,000 by the end of 1973.

I have said that fiscal policy was the main instrument of demand management, and it may be useful to recall how fiscal policy was conducted in practice. At the core of the process there was the Treasury's pre-Budget forecast. The Treasury's short-term macroeconomic model had been computerised, though the ideas it embodied, and the conduct of the forecasting round, reflected an earlier approach based on (pre-computerised) spreadsheets. The main forecast was known as the national income forecast (NIF). It was primarily an exercise in forecasting real variables. It included forecasts of prices and nominal earnings but the construction of a full current price forecast happened at a later stage (and was not fully conducted in the Treasury), and the balance of payments forecast was also a separate exercise, though linked to the NIF. The forecast of monetary variables, including the money supply, was also conducted separately. In principle it was possible to adjust the NIF, including the inflation forecast, in response to the monetary forecasts, but this rarely happened in practice. Earnings forecasts depended partly on the level of unemployment, and there was assumed to be a simple downward-sloping Phillips curve. Prices were a variable mark-up on costs.

The first step in forming the Budget judgement was to examine the forecasts for growth, unemployment and the balance of payments and to determine whether the prospects were acceptable. If, subject to the balance of payments constraint, the prospects for unemployment were unacceptably high, a package of fiscal measures would be devised to expand demand. The opposite would happen if the forecast balance of payments deficit was unacceptably large. A menu of options was provided by the 'Brown Book' (because of the colour of its cover), which was a volume showing the effects on growth, unemployment and the balance of payments of various fiscal measures. Ministers could choose a package that produced the desired outcome.

The measures selected for the 1972 Budget involved the largest fiscal expansion of the post-war period. In 1971 the conduct of monetary policy had been changed (as set out in Competition and Credit Control) to give banks greater freedom over their choice of financial assets. As a result, banks greatly increased their advances, and the money supply grew rapidly. In 1972 sterling was allowed to float. There was further relaxation of fiscal policy in the 1973 Budget. This combination of actions, together with a strong growth of world output, produced rapid growth in the United Kingdom, and unemployment did indeed fall below 500,000.

One might ask whether this rapid growth was expected to produce higher inflation. The official answer was 'No'. In 1971 there was a combination of rising unemployment and rising inflation. That was inconsistent with the accepted shape of the Phillips curve. There were a number of possible explanations. One general approach implied that inflation was not primarily an economic phenomenon, and explanations were sought in social changes. London was 'the swinging city' and inflation was seen as evidence of a breakdown in social discipline. An explanation with slightly more economic content relied on the growing political consciousness of the trades unions, which had been defeated in 1926 and compliant (mainly) during World War II. Inflation was the outward sign of the struggle between labour and capital for a share of GDP. Union pressures pushed up wages, and firms, in response, pushed up prices to preserve profits. A slightly different version of this idea was that workers had a target for their increase in real wages. If they failed to achieve it, because inflation was higher than expected, they increased their claims in the next round. An important implication of this theory was that faster growth of real wages could reduce pay claims and hence inflation. In addition, there was the familiar phenomenon that labour productivity tended to rise in periods of rapid growth.

The Phillips curve, it was said at the time, had been stood on its head. In his 1972 Budget speech, Barber said:

I do not believe that a stimulus to demand of the order I propose will be inimical to the fight against inflation. On the contrary, the business community has repeatedly said that the increase in productivity resulting from a faster growth of output is one of the most effective means of restraining price increases.[5]

As described above, the Budgets of 1972 and 1973 achieved their immediate objective of raising the rate of growth and cutting unemployment. But the longer-term consequences were highly unfavourable. In 1975 inflation approached 30 per cent (partly as a result of the quadrupling of oil prices) and unemployment reached what was at the time a post-war record (it was exceeded later). The rapid acceleration of inflation occurred in spite of (and arguably because of) the introduction of prices and incomes policies of ever-increasing complexity. For some of us involved in advising or commenting on economic policy, that was a searing experience.

A new approach

The inflation and recession did not come as a surprise to everyone. Unsurprisingly, some of us paid close attention to those who had anticipated the disasters of 1975. The first group included the small coterie of monetarists, particularly at the University of Manchester. The Treasury model provided no transmission mechanism linking changes in the money supply to inflation, although a judgemental adjustment could have been made. The monetarists had drawn attention to the rapid growth of the nominal money supply from 1971 and to the fall in the real money supply from 1973. These moves anticipated the rapid growth of GDP, the rise of inflation and the recession of 1974–75.

The monetarists could also explain the combination of rising unemployment and rising inflation. Milton Friedman had criticised the downward-sloping Phillips curve and introduced the idea of the 'natural rate of unemployment' in his 1967 presidential address to the American Economics Association.[6] These ideas are now part of mainstream economics, but in the early 1970s they were minority views in policy-making circles. The apparent upward-sloping Phillips curve could be explained by shifts in short-run curves in response to changing expectations of inflation

[5] HC Deb., 21 March 1972, vol. 833, c1353.
[6] M. Friedman, 'The role of monetary policy', *American Economic Review*, 58, 1 (March 1968), 1–17.

following the devaluation of 1967. The natural rate of unemployment also embodied the idea of a supply constraint, in contrast to the simple Keynesian approach, in which there appeared to be no lower limit for unemployment.

Monetarist ideas were also being expounded in *The Times*, through its economics editor, Peter Jay, and Tim Congdon. Alan Walters, who later became Margaret Thatcher's economic adviser, was specialist adviser to the Expenditure Committee (General Sub-Committee) of the House of Commons, which took on the role of investigating macroeconomic policy. It can be seen as a precursor of the Treasury Select Committee. The committee members included Nicholas Ridley and Jock Bruce-Gardyne, who became proponents of monetarism. The session of 8 July 1974, at which Treasury officials (including me) gave evidence, presents a classic example of the confrontation between the Treasury approach to forecasting and the ideas reaching the committee from the monetarists. At one point there was the following exchange.

Mr Bruce-Gardyne:	What I find riveting about the first two paragraphs of your memorandum and also about some of your earlier evidence is that inflation seems to be treated as the residual in all these assessments. It was what you were left with at the end of the day. I notice that in your memorandum you say that 'The primary objective of the Treasury's short-term forecasting system for the domestic economy was to assess the outlook for employment and unemployment'. You go on to say in paragraph 3 that it has become more sophisticated and now you can elaborate the financial and monetary aspects of the forecasts. However, the impression I get is that inflation, in fact, is the residual which you are left with at the end of the day and something which does not come into your calculations?
Miss Brown	[Under Secretary (Economics), HMT]: No. The object of the exercise is demand management.[7]

As mentioned above, the adviser to the Expenditure Committee (General Sub-Committee) was Walters, who can be said to have introduced its members to the ideas underlying monetarism. His predecessor was Wynne Godley, who had developed ideas based on the inter-sectoral flow of funds. He examined the behaviour of the three main sectors – public, private and overseas. By accounting identities, the financial surpluses (then known as the net acquisition of financial assets) had to sum to zero. In brief, he argued that the private sector (households plus companies) tended to have a fairly stable financial surplus. It followed that

---

[7] 'Ninth report from the Expenditure Committee', 1974, 134, HC328.

any change in the NAFA of the public sector had to be balanced by an equal and opposite change in the NAFA of the overseas sector. Godley's work was important in drawing attention to financial stocks and flows, and in particular to the public sector borrowing requirement. (I can remember being asked for the forecast of the current price value of the budget deficit during the OECD examination of the United Kingdom in 1973 and wondering why the question had been raised. To me, only its real value mattered.)

In the event, the deterioration in the balance of payments after the fiscal expansions of 1972 and 1973 was not as large as a simple application of the Godley approach would have suggested. The reason was a significant rise in the household sector's savings ratio, which was explained by the attempt by households to maintain the real value of their financial assets. The inflation was unexpected, and indexed assets did not appear until much later. The idea of a positive relationship between inflation and the savings ratio was an important building block in the policy approach being developed at the LBS.

There remained the question of the transmission mechanism between the money supply and inflation. The LBS focused on the role of the exchange rate. The so-called 'Swedish model' assumed that competition in the market for traded goods would ensure that they converged on a single price. Thus a fall in the exchange rate in the United Kingdom, for example, would be followed by a rise in the sterling price of UK traded goods. This rise would in turn be transmitted to domestic labour costs, through wage increases, and to the prices of non-traded goods. From a starting point of equilibrium, changes in the nominal exchange rate would have no long-term real effect. In a fixed exchange rate system, changes in monetary growth would affect the balance of payments. In a floating exchange rate system, changes in monetary growth would be followed by changes in inflation via a change in the exchange rate. (This approach was labelled as 'international monetarism' by some commentators.)

The final element in the LBS approach to fiscal policy was provided by the conditions imposed on the United Kingdom by the International Monetary Fund following the loan to the country in the autumn of 1976. The Letter of Intent from the UK government to the IMF set out ceilings for the PSBR and domestic credit expansion for 1977/78 and 1978/79. The use of DCE emphasised the link between the PSBR and the money supply through the monetary identities.

The core of the ideas developed at the LBS at the time can thus be summarised in the following (oversimplified) version. Changes in the growth of the money supply could have significant short-term effects on the growth of demand and GDP but would, in the longer term, mainly change the rate of inflation. A fiscal expansion would at best have only temporary effects on the level of output. If the expansion were wholly financed by additional sales of government securities to the non-bank private sector (i.e. without any accompanying monetary expansion), the result was likely to be a rise in real interest rates, which would discourage expenditure, particularly on business investment. If it were funded by an increase in the money supply, the result – under a floating exchange rate – would be a rise in inflation, which would cause a rise in the savings ratio and a contraction of consumer spending. A policy directed at reducing inflation would require a reduction in the growth of the money supply. If unfavourable effects on investment were to be avoided, such a contraction should be accompanied by a reduction in the PSBR.

A proposal for a 'financial plan'

In the October 1977 issue of the London Business School's *Economic Outlook*, Budd and Burns published an 'Economic viewpoint' article entitled 'How much reflation?'.[8] The policy response to the IMF crisis had been followed by a significant improvement in financial conditions. Interest rates had fallen, particularly at the short end, and the exchange rate had strengthened. The indicators also suggested a recovery in real economic activity. The core of the article was the proposal that fiscal policy should be set within a medium-term framework. The argument was set out as follows:

The kind of confused discussion that is taking place over the suggested November measures can only be avoided if we have a major change in the nation's financial planning and budgeting procedures and the amount of public information that is provided. In addition to an annual budget which contains a detailed description of components of tax revenue and expenditure there should be a medium-term outline budget or financial plan which would contain estimates of tax receipts, expenditure and the borrowing requirement on the basis of existing policies with a set of targets for monetary aggregates, domestic credit expansion and reserve changes. This needs to be set within the outlook for the 'real' economy but this should not cause problems as long as targets are not overambitious. At the moment we have the outline of such a system set out in the Letter of Intent to the IMF. The danger is that amidst the euphoria caused by the reserve gain we may be tempted to abandon the financial targets beyond April 1978 and substitute nothing in their place. If a financial planning debate was introduced, debate on macro-economic policy could then proceed on two levels.

---

[8] A. P. Budd and T. Burns, 'How much reflation?' ('Economic viewpoint'), London Business School Centre for Economic Forecasting, *Economic Outlook*, 2, 1 (October 1977), 7–11.

First, there would be a discussion of appropriate targets for monetary and fiscal indicators, including the appropriate path for the money supply (and for the exchange rate if it is to be pegged). Second, there would be a discussion of whether spending and taxation proposals and the forecasts for output and inflation are consistent with the guidelines.[9]

Budd and Burns provided an illustrative set of targets for the years to 1980. The path for the growth of the money supply allowed an acceleration from an expected growth of 11 per cent in 1977 to 16 per cent in 1978 and then a slowdown to 10 per cent in 1980. DCE was to be held at £8 billion from 1978 onwards. These figures were expected to be consistent with a fall in inflation to 6.7 per cent (from 14.6 per cent in 1977) and average growth of GDP of 2.5 per cent a year. They considered whether financial planning was feasible and concluded as follows:

An immediate objection to this approach will no doubt be that the margins of error in financial forecasting are so large that the exercise will be worthless. We can suggest three replies. The first is that forecasting, difficult as it may be, would be only part of a longer-term budgetary control. The financial director of any company knows that his control over the environment is extremely slight; but that does not reduce the need for forecasts as part of his system of financial and budgetary management. Second, the striking success of the Letter of Intent in restoring financial confidence should suggest that, even in the present state of the art, such attempts at producing a financial plan are extremely valuable. Finally, it can be suggested that the difficulty of making such forecasts in the past mainly reflects the low priority which has been given to financial targets in the pursuit of short-term goals for the real economy.[10]

Later in the same month the Conservative Central Office published *The right approach to the economy*.[11] It included the following:

Recognition of the key role of monetary policy has been a major factor in the success of other countries. We must follow these examples. The general principle of monetary policy must be the steady and gradual reduction in the rate of growth of the money supply... So – strict control of the money supply, firm cash limits on public expenditure: these are the vital factors which can influence the pay climate and which – properly and continuously explained, as the Government has so far failed to do – can help to ease the return to realistic collective bargaining.[12]

One of those who helped produce the report commented that it had been conceived with the LBS financial plan in mind.

[9] Ibid., 8.   [10] Ibid., 10.
[11] R. E. G. Howe, K. S. Joseph, J. M. L. Prior and D. A. R. H. Howell, *The right approach to the economy* (London, 1977).
[12] Ibid., 14.

In its *Forecast Release* of November 1978 the LBS commented on ways in which the Labour government's economic policy, with Denis Healey as Chancellor of the Exchequer, had changed in ways that could be said to be consistent with the LBS approach.[13] One source for this view was Healey's 19 October Mansion House speech. The *Forecast Release* recalled that the LBS had emphasised five arguments in the previous eighteen months:

(1) The exchange rate plays a critical role in any attempt to control inflation, whilst devaluation has little long-term effect on competitiveness.

(2) Control of monetary aggregates is an important aspect of controlling inflation and a key to stability of the exchange rate.

(3) Fiscal policy must be consistent with monetary policy.

(4) Higher inflation rates exercise a strong downward impact upon private sector expenditure.

(5) Incomes policies play, at best, only a subsidiary role in controlling inflation.[14]

It argued that Healey appeared to accept all these points except for the last. Words from his speech included the following:

Fiscal and monetary policy both contribute towards the control of the monetary aggregates and this in itself provides the essential foundation for price stability. . . The Government is no less determined to control the growth of public expenditure so that the fiscal policy is consistent with the monetary stance.[15]

After the election of Thatcher's Conservative government in May 1979 and the introduction of its first Budget, Budd and Burns wrote an article entitled 'Should the PSBR be cut next year?'.[16] They commented:

There is considerable economic theory and empirical evidence to support a strategy of reducing inflation by cutting monetary growth although the same evidence suggests that squeezing the inflation out of the system in this way could be painful in the short term. But it is unlikely that there is any other way of reducing inflation. We are concerned here with the policies required to achieve this objective but it is clear that the other objectives impose important constraints on policy. To make the problem more difficult the Government seems to have imposed two further objectives on itself – to reduce the Budget deficit each year and to cut income tax each year. These constraints may be dangerous. First, it is not necessary reduce the PSBR in each and every year to reduce monetary growth and

---

[13] 'The lessons of the Mansion House', London Business School Centre for Economic Forecasting, *Forecast Release*, 3, 2 (November 1978), 1–4.

[14] Ibid., 1.   [15] Ibid., 2.

[16] A. P. Budd and T. Burns, 'Should the PSBR be cut next year?', London Business School Centre for Economic Forecasting, *Economic Viewpoint*, 3, 11 (August 1979), 1–4.

second, cutting taxation at the same time as reducing inflation may require very large cuts in public spending.[17]

They emphasised the distinction between the cyclical deficit and the structural deficit and argued that the government's objective for the PSBR should take account of the cyclical position of the economy:

Although the aim of reducing inflation requires a gradual reduction in the budget deficit as a percentage of output it is not necessary to achieve this in each year. A recession normally leads to an increase in the PSBR through the operation of the automatic stabilisers in the economy; tax receipts are lower than they otherwise would be and some social security expenditures will be higher. At the same time it becomes easier to finance a given level of the PSBR.[18]

They concluded that the PSBR in 1980/81 could safely be raised to £10.5 billion compared with the ceiling of £8.3 billion in 1979/80. Their final words were:

We are entering a period when it would be characteristic of policy to be more contractionary than intended. It is mistakes of this kind which lead to excessive reactions later (as in 1972/3). The Conservative Government has officially discarded attempts to stabilise the economy. That may be realistic but if they are to adopt a policy of rapid monetary deceleration rather than a gradual path it would be better to be conscious of risks they are running now rather than be shocked by them later.[19]

The Medium-Term Financial Strategy

In January 1980 Burns moved to HM Treasury as Chief Economic Adviser. In the February issue of the LBS *Economic Outlook*, Budd and Dicks presented an 'Economic viewpoint' article entitled 'The Budget, the PSBR and the money supply'.[20] Much of the paper was devoted to the relationship between the PSBR and the money supply. They argued that, while there might be little or no short-run relation between the two, the longer-term relationship was inescapable. Their main proposals for the Budget were:

Briefly, we argue that the monetary target for 1980–81 should be a growth of M3 of about 8 per cent. On our forecast that would require a PSBR of £10b [slightly higher than the expected outcome for 1979–80]; but the PSBR can be higher if the recession is more severe than we expect. There is no scope for a relaxation of fiscal policy.

---

[17] Ibid., 1.   [18] Ibid., 3.   [19] Ibid., 4.
[20] A. P. Budd and G. R. Dicks, 'The Budget, the PSBR and the money supply' ('Economic viewpoint'), London Business School Centre for Economic Forecasting, *Economic Outlook*, 4, 5 (February 1980), 13–17.

We have emphasised on previous occasions that these decisions should be set within a medium-term financial framework as an essential step towards a stable environment in which economic agents can operate without fears of a sudden recurrence of rapid inflation.[21]

The 1980 Budget was presented by Sir Geoffrey Howe on 26 March. It appears that he was not convinced by the argument that the PSBR should be allowed to rise in response to the recession. The Budget involved net cuts of £810 million, mainly through public expenditure cuts. The PSBR for 1980/81 was projected to be £8.5 billion, equivalent to 3.75 per cent of GDP, compared with 4.75 per cent in 1979/80. The *FSBR* stated:

In the short term the reduction in public expenditure is likely to reduce economic activity slightly. This is probably also true of the net effect of reducing direct and raising indirect taxes. But these measures are a necessary step in the medium-term strategy of reducing the burden of public sector borrowing and improving incentives. They will therefore be beneficial to sustainable economic growth.[22]

The 1980 Budget also introduced the Medium-Term Financial Strategy. It set out a path for the growth of broad money, £M3, and for the PSBR. £M3 growth was to fall from 7 to 11 per cent in 1980/81 to 4 to 8 per cent in 1983/84. The PSBR was to fall from 4.75 per cent of GDP in 1979/80 to 1.5 per cent in 1983/84. The MTFS was explained in the following terms:

The Budget is a further stage in the Government's medium-term policy of reducing inflation and improving the supply side of the economy. The central feature of the anti-inflation policy is the gradual reduction of monetary growth. To achieve this reduction without intolerably high interest rates public sector borrowing will be reduced over the medium term.[23]

The concluding paragraph of the section on the MTFS issued the following stern warning:

To maintain a progressive reduction in monetary growth in these circumstances it may be necessary to change policy in ways not reflected in the above projections. The Government would face a number of options for policy changes to achieve this aim, including changes in interest rates, taxes and public expenditure. But there would be no question of departing from the money supply policy, which is essential to the success of any anti-inflationary strategy.[24]

In the LBS *Economic Outlook* of June 1980, Budd and Dicks wrote an 'Economic viewpoint' on the MTFS.[25] They commented on the widely

---

[21] Ibid., 13.   [22] *FSBR 1980–81* (London, 1980), 4.   [23] Ibid., 3.   [24] Ibid., 19.
[25] A. P. Budd and G. R. Dicks, 'The Medium-Term Financial Strategy', London Business School Centre for Economic Forecasting, *Economic Outlook*, 4, 9 (June 1980), 12–15.

discussed issue of the path for public expenditure set out in the Budget documents. They wrote:

> The government's first Public Expenditure White Paper, published last November, started with the memorable statement: 'Public expenditure is at the heart of Britain's present economic difficulties.' We have always emphasised that the case for a medium-term financial plan does not depend on that view of public expenditure. What matters is the size of the Public Sector Borrowing Requirement. That is not to deny that the question of public expenditure is extremely important as far as the structure of the British economy is concerned. The government believes that excessive public expenditure has obstructed economic growth. The intention to cut public expenditure steadily must be seen as part of the government's supply side policy rather than as a necessary part of its financial strategy.[26]

Perhaps a brief digression may be permitted at this point. Budd and Dicks quoted part of Healey's speech in the House of Commons in a debate on the White Paper:

> There is no relationship between money supply and the percentage of public expenditure... There is no relationship between the level of public expenditure and the public sector borrowing requirement... There is no relationship between the level of public expenditure and interest rates.[27]

Budd and Dicks included the following footnote:

> Mr Healey's speech was interrupted by Mr Nigel Lawson, the Financial Secretary to the Treasury, who said:
> If the right hon. Gentleman is asserting that there is no relationship between the public sector borrowing requirement and the rate of interest and that there is no relationship between the public sector borrowing requirement and the rate of monetary growth, why was his first action on becoming Chancellor to seek to reduce the public sector borrowing requirement?[28]

At that stage Healey had made no such assertion about the PSBR. It therefore seems that the obvious reply would have been to point out that he had been talking about public expenditure, not the PSBR. Instead, he replied with a traditional parliamentary combination of evasion and abuse. Since Healey is a notably skilled debater, one must assume that he realised that the obvious reply would (1) have emphasised that all his previous points related to public expenditure and not to the PSBR and (2) have immediately drawn another question asking what his views about the PSBR were. He avoided the awkward intermediate steps and was thus able to plunge on with the rest of his speech. It is perhaps a pious hope that the new House of Commons committees will be able to circumvent this kind of tactic and to persevere with a line of questioning until it has been

[26] Ibid., 12.   [27] Ibid.   [28] Ibid.

fully answered. This is not to criticise debates but to point out that they are not always a useful way of resolving economic problems. It is open to question whether that pious hope has been justified.

To return to the MTFS, Budd and Dicks explained that it was not designed as an exercise in demand management but as the necessary framework for a policy of reducing inflation through cutting the growth of the money supply.

Budd and Dicks asked whether the MTFS was feasible in relation to two questions. First, would the proposed underlying path for the PSBR achieve the money supply targets? Second, was the underlying path for the PSBR feasible? They concluded on the basis of rules of thumb and the use of the LBS model that the underlying path for the PSBR would broadly achieve the money supply targets. They also concluded, subject to recognition of the considerable uncertainty attached to fiscal forecasts, that the PSBR path was feasible.

They argued against those who asserted that fiscal policy would have to be tightened if growth turned out to be lower than expected. The MTFS included figures for a 'fiscal adjustment' in later years. The figures showed the extent to which taxes could be cut or public expenditure increased if the economy and the public finances proceeded as expected on the basis of announced policies. They argued that the fiscal adjustments would be sufficient to avoid the need for fiscal tightening for a plausible range of outcomes for GDP growth. They added:

> The LBS model suggests a further reason for rejecting the view that the strategy is threatened if the growth of GDP is low. A low growth of GDP with a given fiscal structure generates a lower growth of the money supply. Thus low growth of output does not threaten the monetary targets. (However, if the underlying growth of output were lower, the government would, presumably, adjust its monetary targets.)[29]

These final words seem strangely familiar at a time when a government is seeking to meet fiscal objectives in a rather different context.

Budd and Dicks concluded their article as follows:

> The feasibility of the strategy is concerned only with the Government's targets for the growth of the money supply. But the money supply is not a policy objective in its own right; it is an intermediate target which is only relevant to the extent that its control has beneficial effects for the economy. The primary objective of the government's monetary policy is to reduce the rate of inflation. We have no doubt that the government's policy will achieve this objective though the process is slow. It has been argued that obsession with a single objective is causing unnecessary harm to the economy in terms of loss of output, jobs and investment.

---

[29] Ibid., 15.

That argument cannot simply be ignored. The Government's policy is based on the view that either the costs are unavoidable or that they are worth paying. We have always argued that in current conditions the control of inflation must be regarded as a primary aim of policy. We do not believe that it is worth paying any price to achieve it; that is why we persistently argued against a reduction in the level of the PSBR in this year's Budget. We have also argued that it is wrong to load so much of the burden of adjustment to the lower rate of inflation onto the company sector. However, if the rate of inflation is to be brought down by monetary means it is essential both to persevere with the policy and to show that the monetary objectives are feasible. The Medium-Term Financial Strategy shows that they are.[30]

The June 1980 issue of the *Economic Outlook* also included an article by Michael Beenstock and Andrew Longbottom entitled 'The statistical relationship between the money supply and the public sector borrowing requirement'.[31] The authors produced evidence to support the existence of a long-term relationship between the money supply and the PSBR. They argued that the critics had examined only the flow relationships between the two and had missed the long-term stock relationship. The lags in the relationship emphasised that control of the PSBR could be regarded only as a medium-term instrument for money supply control, as it was in the MTFS.

The 1981 Budget

The LBS published two articles on the 1981 Budget ahead of its presentation by the government. In the October 1980 issue of the *Economic Outlook*, Budd and Dicks wrote 'Bringing counter-inflation policy back on course'.[32] At that point it looked as if the money supply (£M3) would grow by 16 to 18 per cent during 1980/81, compared with the MTFS range of 7 to 11 per cent. They assumed that the base would be adjusted upwards by four or five percentage points but that growth in 1981/82 would be clawed back by about two percentage points. The range for 1981/82 would thus be 4 to 8 per cent, compared with the MTFS range of 6 to 10 per cent. Their assessment was that, on unchanged policies, the PSBR in 1981/82 would be about £9.5 billion, about 3.75 per cent of GDP. The figure in the MTFS for 1981/82 was 3 per cent. They estimated that, if the LBS forecast

[30] Ibid.

[31] M. Beenstock and A. Longbottom, 'The statistical relationship between the money supply and the public sector borrowing requirement', London Business School Centre for Economic Forecasting, *Economic Outlook*, 4, 9 (June 1980), 27–31.

[32] A. P. Budd and G. R. Dicks, 'Bringing counter-inflation policy back on course', London Business School Centre for Economic Forecasting, *Economic Outlook*, 5, 1 (October 1980), 17–22.

was adjusted for the slower growth of GDP compared with the MTFS forecast, the PSBR would be about 3.5 per cent of GDP. The PSBR would therefore need to be cut by at least £1 billion to meet the government's target.

It followed that it would be extremely difficult for the (adjusted) money supply target for 1981/82 to be met on the basis of unchanged policy. The forecast assumed, however, that the growth of the money supply would be reduced to around 6 per cent during 1981/82. They warned against policy relaxation in 1983, when the economy would be growing more strongly and inflation would be falling: 'It may seem premature, at a time when the economy is still deep in recession and inflation is still at 16 per cent, to talk of the possible problems of success. But the whole point of the Medium-Term strategy is that it is intended to provide a policy commitment over many years and it cannot be too early to warn of the dangers of departing from it in the future.'[33]

In the February 1981 *Economic Outlook*, Budd and Beenstock wrote 'Tightening the fiscal and monetary controls'.[34] By then the monetary targets had been drastically exceeded, and the PSBR was expected to be far above its original ceiling. £M3 was expected to be about ten percentage points above the centre of the original target range. Four percentage points of the excess could be explained by the removal of the 'corset'. The PSBR in 1980/81 was expected to be £13.5 billion, compared with the 1980 Budget forecast of £8.5 billion. On unchanged policies, the PSBR was expected to be about £12 billion in 1981/82. Budd and Beenstock emphasised that it was important to try to determine how much of the overrun was due to lower than expected growth. They estimated that about half the overrun was due to the unexpected depth of the recession, leaving an excess of about £2.5 billion, which was due to a combination of overspending and an unexpected shortfall of revenue. They proposed that the government should reverse the overrun and set a PSBR ceiling in 1981/82 of £10 billion, a cut of £2 billion compared with unchanged policies.

Howe presented the 1981 Budget on 10 March. The opening paragraph of the FSBR stated:

The Budget represents a further step towards the achievement of the Government's medium-term objectives of bringing down inflation and creating the conditions for sustainable growth of output and employment. In order to permit its monetary objectives to be met at tolerable interest rates, the

---

[33] Ibid., 22.
[34] A. P. Budd and M. Beenstock, 'Tightening the fiscal and monetary controls', London Business School Centre for Economic Forecasting, *Economic Outlook*, 5, 5 (February 1981), 21–7.

Government's aim is to contain public sector borrowing to a real level well below that of 1980–81.[35]

The net direct effect of the Budget was to reduce the PSBR in 1981/82 by £3.3 billion (from a non-indexed base). The PSBR was projected to be £10.5 billion, 4.25 per cent of GDP. The targets for monetary growth for the years 1981/82 to 1983/84 were unchanged from the 1980 version of the MTFS. The final paragraph of the section on the MTFS reflected the experience of the previous year and embodied a less severe tone:

The projections shown above fall within a very wide range of possible outcomes. They should be taken as no more than illustrative of one particular evolution of the economy. If the economy were to evolve in a different way, the projection of public finances could be substantially affected. The policy response to such changes would depend on their nature, but although the revenue and expenditure figures could change substantially, the intention would be to hold firmly to the main thrust of the financial strategy – which is to bring about a progressive reduction in the growth of the money supply and inflation over the medium term.[36]

The projected PSBR of £10.5 billion in 1981/82 looked very close to the figure of £10 billion proposed by Budd and Beenstock, although the announced fiscal tightening was larger. The LBS *Forecast Release* of March 1981 consisted of an article by Budd and Dicks entitled 'The 1981 Budget'.[37] They argued that the 1981 Budget was, in fact, neutral. Although taxes had been raised, they questioned the forecasts for public spending in current prices and nationalised industry profits. On public spending, they believed that the official forecasts for pay and prices in the public sector were too low. They concluded that the PSBR would be about £12.5 billion. They welcomed the growing use of direct cash controls on public spending and the innovations in techniques for controlling the money supply. In the event, Budd and Dicks were too pessimistic, and the outturn for 1981/82 was close to £8.5 billion. On the most recent calculations, the PSBR was reduced by the equivalent of about 2.5 per cent of GDP between 1980/81 and 1981/82. The cyclically adjusted PSBR was reduced by nearly 5 per cent of GDP.

The economists at the LBS were not invited to sign the letter of the 364. In June 1981 they received some attention for their economic forecast, which showed GDP growth of 2.8 per cent in 1982, largely because of a slowdown in the rate at which stocks were being run down.[38] Preliminary

[35] *FSBR 1981–82*, 4.   [36] Ibid., 19.

[37] A. P. Budd and G. R. Dicks, 'The 1981 Budget', London Business School Centre for Economic Forecasting, *Forecast Release*, 5, 6 (March 1981), 1–4.

[38] 'Forecast summary', London Business School Centre for Economic Forecasting, *Economic Outlook*, 5, 9 (June 1981), 3.

estimates suggested that the forecast was too optimistic, and the LBS revised down its subsequent forecasts, but the most recent figures (which are not strictly comparable) suggest that GDP started to grow in the second quarter of 1981 and grew by 2.25 per cent between 1981 and 1982, followed by growth of 3.8 per cent and 2.9 per cent in 1983 and 1984, respectively, though unemployment continued to rise until 1986.

It must be admitted, however, that the fiscal tightening did not, on the face of it, produce the promised fall in interest rates. Base rate was cut from 14 per cent to 12 per cent on 11 March 1981 but was then raised, from August onwards, to 15 per cent. It might, of course, have been even higher in the absence of the fiscal tightening.

After 1981, some reflections

This chapter is not presented as a contribution to the rather sterile debate of whether the 1981 Budget was 'right' or 'wrong'. As described at the beginning, it is an account of the development of ideas among a small group of economists working at the London Business School (including Sir James Ball, who founded the Centre for Economic Forecasting). With the exception of *The right approach to the economy*, referred to above, I have not claimed that these ideas had any direct effect on government policy. The LBS economists were among those who were responding to the events of the 1970s in a similar way. Their number included Nigel Lawson. In *The view from No. 11*, he writes:

I do not, of course, claim intellectual paternity of the idea of a medium-term financial strategy. Several economists (including Terry Burns and Alan Budd in the October 1977 London Business School *Economic Outlook*) had suggested something similar. But I was responsible both for introducing the idea into the political arena and for getting it past the watering-down instincts of permanent officials.[39]

This is fair enough. Former civil servants are, or should be, the first to recognise the crucial role of ministers in selecting, fighting for and implementing new policies.

While I decline the task of judging the 1981 Budget, it is reasonable to ask what survives of the ideas that LBS developed or supported in the lead-up to it. I quoted above five principles listed in an article published in November 1978:

(1) the exchange rate plays a critical role in any attempt to control inflation, while devaluation has little long-term effect on competitiveness;

---

[39] Lawson, *The view from No. 11*, 69.

(2) the control of monetary aggregates is an important aspect of controlling inflation and a key to exchange rate stability;

(3) fiscal policy must be consistent with monetary policy;

(4) higher inflation rates exercise a strong downward impact on private sector expenditure; and

(5) incomes policies play, at best, only a subsidiary role in controlling inflation.

It is important to recall that the list was presented at a time when inflation was around 10 per cent and had, in recent memory, come close to 30 per cent. Some of these ideas are less salient at a time when inflation is in low single figures.

The first principle would now seem to be generally accepted, since the United Kingdom is an open economy, trading in a competitive world. The second can be seen as a moderate statement of the monetarist position. After 1981, evidence suggested (though not to all observers) that quantitative targets for the money supply (under various definitions) did not provide a sufficiently reliable intermediate target, and there was a quest for alternative nominal anchors, including the shadowing of the deutschmark, membership of the Exchange Rate Mechanism and, finally, inflation targets. The instrument for the conduct of monetary policy also shifted from quantitative targets for the money supply to interest rates.

The third principle can be defined in a narrow sense as a statement about the quantitative link between the PSBR and the growth of the money supply; but it can be extended to include three further ideas about fiscal policy: the first is that discretionary fiscal policy is ineffective, except possibly in the short term, as a means of regulating aggregate demand; the second is that it is important to distinguish between cyclical and structural changes in the fiscal stance; the third is that fiscal policy should be set within a medium-term framework. All these ideas are linked. As far as the narrow sense of the third principle is concerned, there has been a shift away from the emphasis on the PSBR and the growth of the money supply, which has accompanied the downgrading of the importance of the money supply itself.

The question of the effectiveness of discretionary fiscal policy remains open, despite the confidence with which some economists make claims on one side or another of the debate. What has been true is that the use of discretionary fiscal policy as an instrument of demand management was abandoned from 1979 onwards and was not reinstated until 2008 (briefly), and the task (within a framework of inflation targets) was shifted to monetary policy. The fact that the economy recovered after the 1981 Budget gave comfort to those who believed that economic growth and fiscal tightening could occur simultaneously, and possibly played some part in the adoption of the successful period of fiscal tightening from 1992 onwards under the chancellorships of Norman Lamont and Kenneth Clarke. (At that time Budd was Chief Economic Adviser and Burns was Permanent Secretary at HM Treasury.)

The discussion of the effectiveness of fiscal policy requires a reference to the fourth principle. The links in the causal chain were between the PSBR, the money supply, inflation and the personal sector's savings ratio. The last step has disappeared from the debate as inflation has fallen back from the high rates of the 1970s.

To return to the third principle, the distinction between structural and cyclical deficits is now commonplace, although, alas, the measurement of the cyclical element has become no easier, particularly at a time of wide divergences in views about the sustainable rate of GDP growth. It is worth pointing out that the importance that the LBS placed on the distinction was to avoid unnecessarily tight policy (e.g. in 1980). But the channel for the excessive tightness – and the threat to the growth of GDP – was through its effect on the money supply.

From 1980 onwards successive governments accepted the necessity of placing fiscal policy within a medium-term framework. The Conservative government's MTFS was followed by the Labour government's adoption of the 'golden rule' and the prudent investment rule, with its target for the debt/GDP ratio. These, in turn, were followed by the medium-term fiscal targets of the present government. The role of the framework shifted from the task of supporting monetary targets to ensuring the sustainability of the public finances but it is, perhaps, the most enduring legacy of the ideas developed during the 1970s. Finally, incomes policies were not tried again after 1979.

In conclusion, those whose experience of policy debate coincided with the broad policy consensus that had emerged by the time of the Labour victory in 1997 and who enjoyed the Great Moderation may find it hard to imagine the passion and bitterness generated by the debates of the 1970s and early 1980s. The current debates are mild by comparison and cover a much narrower range of disagreement. It was also a time when the foundations of long-held beliefs seemed to have been swept away. That so much has survived from that turbulent time may, perhaps, justify a (modest) sense of satisfaction.

4   The 1981 Budget: a view from the cockpit

Adam Ridley

The 1981 Budget was probably the most decisive episode in the eighteen years of Conservative governments between 1979 and 1997. Had it failed – economically or politically – a major change of both leadership and strategy would have been hard to avoid. It was shaped by a variety of developments over the previous decade: the collapse of the Bretton Woods exchange rate system; the troubled record of the Labour government after 1974, culminating in the party's loss of office in 1979; and, in the wider world, the rise of the ayatollah in Iran, followed swiftly by the second oil crisis. These would have confronted any government elected in 1979 with extreme challenges. At least partly for these reasons, the Conservative government's economic strategy did not meet its own objectives in 1979 and 1980. Such failures made the 1981 Budget critical.

The end of Bretton Woods

The end of the Bretton Woods system of fixed exchange rates in August 1971, the Smithsonian agreement and the travails of the European currency 'snake' (from 1972 onwards) changed macroeconomic management in ways that few people understood for many years, and some still do not appreciate.[1] The new system of floating exchange rates necessarily gave a much greater influence to the markets in international currencies, credit and securities. Once unfettered, they immediately made every Western economy much more vulnerable to the interests, beliefs and concerns of market participants. These attitudes could, and did, change substantially – indeed, sometimes mercilessly – in days and even hours. Under Bretton Woods, larger countries had been able to defend their currencies, interest

I am grateful to Lord Howe, Lord Lawson, Sir Alan Budd, Sir Tim Lankester and Sir Peter Middleton for their helpful comments on earlier drafts of this chapter.
[1] The European currency 'snake' was established in April 1972 to enhance currency stability by limiting variations between the major European currencies to within a 2.25 per cent band.

rates or other policy objectives by intervening in the market in various ways, sometimes helped by relatively modest loans from multilateral bodies such as the IMF. In this new world, the markets swiftly established the upper hand, to the dismay and disbelief of many observers.[2]

Until the 1970s adjusting the balance between income and spending – Keynesian demand management – had been the principal way of influencing the balance of payments, inflation and unemployment. But, in the new world, such policies were much less predictable, and frequently – and increasingly – quite ineffective. At the same time, like it or not, monetary developments and monetary policy exercised an increasingly powerful influence on spending, production and international financial relationships. In this new world, there was no avoiding the role of market expectations, market efficiency and the operation of supply-side influences. Their central importance in long-term economic growth needed to be recognised by governments and combined with fiscal and monetary policy in a structure that was coherent, credible and stable.

The Labour governments, 1974–76

The leaders and policies of the successive Labour governments of March to October 1974 and October 1974 to April 1976 showed little understanding of this new world. Their public policy statements were often inconsistent. Even the Treasury ministerial team of the Chancellor, Denis Healey, found it hard at times to support their own department's position.[3] From the outset public spending and borrowing grew rapidly and were subject to increasingly ineffectual control, against the backdrop of an unprecedented wage explosion and the sustained exercise of trades union political muscle, militancy and 'industrial action'.[4]

Despite a belated recognition in 1975 that the wage explosion had to be checked, the government's market credibility and the policies that relied

---

[2] This was vividly illustrated by the large inflow of capital that occurred in 1977 as the authorities sought to maintain export competitiveness by capping the sterling exchange rate. Despite lowering interest rates from 14 per cent to 5 per cent to deter these increasingly unwelcome inflows, the authorities were forced to remove the cap in October 1977, upon which sterling immediately rose by 5 per cent against the dollar.

[3] Edmund Dell was a junior Treasury minister (Paymaster General) between 1974 and 1976, during which period he made a number of speeches that were released by the Treasury. Some of these were critical of government policy and were frequently quoted by opposition spokesmen in order to embarrass the Chancellor and his colleagues.

[4] One measure of the degree to which expenditure is under control is the extent of the 'supplementary estimates', voted after Parliament has approved the 'estimates' for each financial year. The 'supplementary estimates' normally add only a few percentage points to total relevant expenditure. In 1975/76 they totalled over 30 per cent of the expenditure initially approved.

upon it both collapsed suddenly in late 1976, culminating in an immediate request for massive and conditional IMF assistance.[5] The markets had lost confidence twice over: first, in a disorganised government with a tiny majority and weak leadership; second, in policies that attached little importance to controlling public spending, borrowing, inflation and the money supply. The suddenness of the collapse in market sentiment and the unavoidable haste of Healey's appeal to the IMF were not an accident. Rather, they demonstrated clearly the volatile way in which critical markets would henceforward work – and, clearly, still work today – in the new post-Bretton-Woods world.

The IMF negotiation and agreement relaunched Labour's economic policies at the end of 1976 in a radically different framework. The IMF's programme – which can be viewed as a precursor of the 1980 Medium-Term Financial Strategy – was based on tight and increasingly restrictive targets for public borrowing and spending; major improvements in the way in which public spending was controlled; and commensurately tough targets for slower growth in money and credit. This unprecedented programme worked extremely well, because it was well designed; because of the happy coincidence that North Sea oil production grew dramatically over the period in question; and because the IMF's involvement and the government's undertakings to honour the conditions of the IMF's assistance together endowed the United Kingdom's policies with credibility it could no longer achieve on its own.[6]

Once the programme had succeeded, Healey waved the IMF a picturesque public farewell in the summer of 1978 on what he more than once called 'Sod-off day'. This unguarded, not to say hubristic, *envoi* to an institution that had just saved his government's bacon still appears psychologically significant. It was perhaps the candid comment of an unbelieving monetarist who implemented the IMF's painful measures only because it was publicly expedient to do so, and who welcomed them in private only because he and his colleagues could not muster the collective willpower to introduce them on their own.[7] It indicated that, even after

---

[5] See S. F. J. Fay and H. J. S. Young, 'The day the pound nearly died', *Sunday Times*, 14 May 1978, 21 May 1978, 28 May 1978.

[6] On 15 December 1976, the day the government announced its agreement with the IMF, I noted in an internal assessment for the Conservative Party leadership that the package contained 'a clear new synthesis of doctrines about the causes and remedies for inflation round which we can unite': A. N. Ridley, 'Containing inflation', 15 December 1976, Churchill, RDLY 2/1/2/3.

[7] The term 'unbelieving monetarist' has been used since the middle of the 1970s to denote those politicians and officials who, while not accepting the theory of monetarism, advocated the expedient pursuit of monetarist policies such as targets for the growth of the money supply because that was what the markets wanted. See, for example, D. W. Healey,

four crisis-ridden years as Chancellor of the Exchequer, he had still not embraced deep down some of the fundamental changes in the techniques of economic management that the end of Bretton Woods had ushered in in 1971. On the other hand, the policy debate, both internally in Whitehall and the Bank of England and in the world outside during the early 1970s and the year and a half of the fourth Wilson government (October 1974 to April 1976), hints at a different story.[8]

There was a growing realisation of the need for reforms in the planning of public spending and an increasingly lively debate about the importance of monetary institutions and policies, and the need for monetary discipline and, perhaps, targets. Labour ministers also espoused a plan to 'tunnel through' the next few years of budgetary trouble as best they could, by relying on heavy borrowing until the revenue from North Sea oil could rescue them. Their public spending reforms were too late, however, and the 'tunnelling through' required an implausible degree of patience and generosity on the part of the markets and the world outside.

Whatever the true story, both at home and abroad the markets undoubtedly saw in the 'IMF measures' of 1976 a set of benchmarks for sound policies in the new world of floating currencies. Henceforward they would naturally apply these criteria to the United Kingdom with alacrity and vigour.

As it happened, Labour's self-discipline and virtue were abandoned shortly after Healey said farewell to the IMF. The autumn of 1978 saw the union movement's rejection of the 5 per cent wage limit proposed by the government, growing criticism from the Trades Union Congress and, by early 1979, the unusually eye-catching and widespread public sector strikes of the 'winter of discontent'. The public sector unions' dominant concern was to mobilise their members to fight to raise their pay levels to 'catch up' with higher pay in the private sector after years of public sector wage restraint. In the middle of all this disorder, public spending was relaxed. The government, with at best a tiny and unstable majority in the House of Commons, became demoralised.[9]

This loss of economic virtue raised the fear that the United Kingdom might be reverting to 'the bad old days' and the unsuccessful policies of

---

The time of my life (London, 1989), 433–4. Fay and Young suggest the final package could not have been adopted without US and IMF pressure: S. F. J. Fay and H. J. S. Young, 'How the Cabinet embraced the IMF', *Sunday Times*, 28 May 1978.

[8] Steve Ludlam has described some of the work undertaken up to 1976 in the Bank of England and the Treasury on cash limits, public spending and money supply, including monetary targets: S. Ludlam, 'The gnomes of Washington: four myths of the 1976 IMF crisis', *Political Studies*, 40, 4 (December 1992), 713–27; see also D. J. Needham, *UK monetary policy from devaluation to Thatcher, 1967–1982* (Basingstoke, 2014), and the discussion below in the section 'What might have been?'.

[9] B. Donoughue, *Downing Street diary: with James Callaghan at No. 10* (London, 2009).

Labour's early years. In addition, there was a new and sinister fear. People began to ask whether the country was becoming ungovernable. In 1978/79 many observers were particularly unsettled by the sight of a union movement that was prepared to strike against a Labour government's principal policies and, thus, to risk bringing its own government down.

Conservative policy making, 1978–79

The Conservatives' economic strategy and the 1979 election manifesto were largely developed in 1978, for the election that Callaghan nearly called that autumn. In the policy planning undertaken from the summer of 1976 to 1978, much detailed work was undertaken in most key areas of economic policy, such as public spending, taxation and social security. In other areas, however, rather less was done, most notably exchange control, monetary policy and privatisation – and that for a variety of reasons.

British exchange controls had become complicated and bureaucratic by the middle of the 1970s. The regulations and procedures were well understood only by a small group of specialists, mostly in the Bank of England, most of whom were by then sceptical of their relevance. Moreover, no one could predict the constraints and possibilities bearing on exchange control policy that would face an incoming government, such as volatile flows across the exchanges, the influence of commodity prices, and the rest.

In opposition, a normal practice when confronted with such challenging policy areas is to settle for a general policy statement, leaving the detailed work on precise options to be undertaken by officials, both before and after the election. A senior opposition spokesman will typically make a clear, authoritative public statement well in advance to permit the necessary work to be done. When the issue involves special sensitivity (as with exchange controls), he will tactfully and discreetly make the party's wishes and attentions known to relevant senior officials in the key departments. Accordingly, in the autumn of 1978 the shadow Treasury team advised the Bank of England that a future Conservative government would want to receive early on a full review of the case for reducing or scrapping exchange controls by stages. So, while the preferred direction of travel was clear, reinforced by a trenchant article by Nigel Lawson in *Financial Weekly* in April 1979 advocating total abolition, there was no formal commitment to an ultimate goal, be it abolition or partial retention.[10]

Monetary policy posed different challenges to opposition policy makers. Although in the world outside it was not generally appreciated at that

[10] N. Lawson, 'Safeguard balance of trade by relaxing exchange control', *Financial Weekly*, 20 April 1979.

time, or, perhaps, until very recently, there had been discreet work within both the Bank of England and the Treasury on analysing, predicting, controlling and targeting the growth of monetary aggregates as far back as the early 1970s. The Labour administration announced some tentative, and little-noticed, monetary targets in the Budget of 1976.[11] They assumed importance, however, only when the IMF package of that year required firm targets for both money, in the form of £M3, and for credit, in the cumbersomely named domestic credit expansion.

Once the IMF package was in place, it was self-evident that an incoming government would be likely to continue initially with such targets in pretty much their existing form, all the more so if it had urged the importance of monetary discipline in opposition, as had Margaret Thatcher and Sir Geoffrey Howe from an early stage. The markets were clearly comfortable with this default option, and there was no need or pressure to say more in public. In private, however, it was not easy to take forward detailed work on monetary policy. In particular, it would have been hard to orchestrate any definitive, collectively agreed advice on which aggregate to target, and over what period, how to control it, how to revise targets if things went wrong, or how fiscal policy should be married with the monetary target. Monetary specialists – both Conservative sympathisers and market experts in the City and elsewhere – held sharply differing views. For example, within monetarist circles, there were the following positions.

(1) Some believed that it was the 'monetary base' (M0) that should be controlled. Others said that introducing such controls would require major and disruptive modification of the institutions of monetary policy. Even if the modifications could be made, critics feared they might well lead to very big, sudden and disruptive interest rate changes while, contrary to hope and prediction, still not providing an effective system of stable monetary controls.

(2) Some suggested that it was 'broad' money, £M3, that really mattered. Movements in £M3 were believed to be a better predictor of inflation than a narrower measure. £M3 could be controlled relatively directly by public sector borrowing policies, at least in principle, without revolutionary institutional change, so targeting it would not precipitate major institutional disruption. Their critics warned, however, that £M3 was, at best, hard to target in principle and nearly impossible to control in practice.

---

[11] In his 1976 Budget, Healey announced that the growth of M3 would 'come more into line' with the growth of nominal GDP in 1976/77. Samuel Brittan assumed this to mean M3 growth of 'about 15 per cent., give or take a couple of per cent': 'Another gamble on incomes policy', *Financial Times*, 7 April 1976; HC Deb., 6 April 1976, vol. 909, c236.

It was clear that fundamental issues such as these needed careful, sustained, professional studies involving the Treasury, the Bank of England and outsiders such as could be undertaken only *after* an election. It was quite unrealistic to imagine that the shadow Treasury spokesmen, the Conservative Research Department and their heterogeneous informal technical advisers could come together in some kind of grand policy-making synthesis to resolve these issues authoritatively, with little or no access to the Treasury and the Bank of England, in the hectic run-up to an election whose date could not be predicted.

The preparation of privatisation policy fell into two parts. There was a clear commitment from successive Conservative industry spokesmen and the shadow Cabinet to return all companies recently nationalised by the Labour government to the private sector. Significant preparatory work was undertaken in opposition on at least some firms and industries that would be eligible for this return to private hands. On the other hand, the study of privatising the 'classic nationalised utility industries' such as telecommunications was not taken far. In part this reflected an implied recognition that developing a privatisation strategy for numerous large firms in complex industries, which accounted for over 10 per cent of GDP, might overwhelm the shadow industry spokesman and the single policy adviser supporting him in the Research Department. But it also recognised the fact that, however firm our intentions, such policies had to be developed and publicised cautiously, testing each new step in the light not just of expert opinion but also evolving public attitudes – both of which were initially often sceptical and hostile.

A fundamental underlying assumption, held universally until at least early 1979, was that after the next election both the world and the UK economy would continue to grow at normal rates over the coming four or five years. Even if Britain achieved only an unremarkable annual average rate of GDP growth of 2 to 3 per cent, this would still provide a sound platform for a strategy of holding public spending flat in real terms, thus permitting the fiscal growth dividend to be applied simultaneously to reductions in public borrowing, interest rates and levels of taxation. Equally importantly, in such circumstances the government could envisage building on most of the key features of the recent IMF measures, in particular prudent targets for public sector borrowing and the growth of money and credit. Given these sound foundations, one could then more easily remove or reduce controls and regulation of prices and incomes, and foreign exchange, and reduce interest rates and tax on incomes and enterprise. The 1979 manifesto was prepared for *fair weather* government.

In the event, what the new government confronted was extremely *foul weather* for years to come. Therefore, as the Labour government's position weakened in the autumn of 1978 onwards, the Conservative manifesto team devoted considerable efforts to reviewing – and at times revising – the party's election platform. This was hard to organise at a time when day-to-day politics and the imminent Scottish and Welsh devolution referenda absorbed such time and effort. But the task was unusually complicated on this occasion, for several more fundamental reasons.

Coping with Labour's legacy

By early 1979 it had become evident that mushrooming industrial disruption was holding back output, distorting the money supply, lowering the tax take (how far temporarily, how far permanently?) and damaging confidence. But, because some strikes affected the collection and publication of many critical statistics, there were fewer and fewer statistics available even within government, let alone to the public, until weeks or months after the general election, which took place on 3 May.

There were also clear signs that public spending was being relaxed. But it was hard to tell where or by how much. The White Paper on public expenditure for 1979/80 was published in January 1979, only weeks before the government fell. Since it was based on particularly ambitious GDP growth assumptions and, one surmised, inaccurate base figures, it did not constitute the usual comprehensive and reasonably reliable basis of information for planning public spending. In the short time available it was possible to trim several important spending commitments from the manifesto and, in general, to adopt more cautious language. But in some critical respects there was no opportunity to establish prudent, politically defensible positions.

This was particularly true of the policy towards the Clegg Commission, appointed in the last days of the Labour administration to provide an escape from the epidemic of public sector strikes.[12] From that point on, it was immediately evident that, during the election campaign, Conservative

---

[12] Callaghan announced the creation of a 'Standing Commission on Pay Comparability', to be chaired by Professor Hugh Clegg, in a statement to Parliament on 7 March 1979. Its tasks included 'the possibility of establishing acceptable bases of comparison, including comparisons with terms and conditions for other comparable work, and of maintaining appropriate internal relativities. Any further role for the Commission in each case will be a matter for agreement between the Government and the parties.' Further, 'the Commission will make recommendations which the Government and trades unions have undertaken to accept'. On the same day Callaghan announced that several large unions had already submitted claims to the commission, a clearly implied premise being that a valid process of comparability had already been established before the commission had even been appointed, let alone started work. Among the major groups were local authority and NHS manuals, two of the largest public sector groups: HC Deb., 7 March 1979, vol. 963, c1252.

spokesmen and parliamentary candidates were likely to be asked by Labour leaders, union representatives and numerous concerned voters what a future Conservative government would do about the Clegg Commission's awards.

The shadow Cabinet's first and only opportunity to consider systematically a policy towards the commission and its possible recommendations was at what turned out to be its last formal meeting, on 4 April. This was held only hours before Parliament was dissolved, and the manifesto was completed for printing over the weekend for launch the following Tuesday (10 April). A short statement, hurriedly circulated the next day, was all that could be agreed for use during the election.[13] It was dangerously threadbare, stating little more than that claims for which the Clegg Commission had made awards would be honoured, subject to cash limits on departmental spending. But there was no guidance as to how to answer the tricky questions, such as these.

(1) Which unions' claims were, and which were not, covered by this undertaking (little work had been done on this problem and there was no official guidance)?
(2) What was meant by the reference to cash limits?
(3) Was it proper for an incoming government to consider reneging on commission recommendations that its predecessor had quixotically undertaken to honour but that all other parties to the negotiations had undertaken to accept in good faith?

Only days later, on 12 April, just as the election campaign got underway, Callaghan put the simple question to Thatcher: would a future Conservative government honour any 'catch-up' awards that the Clegg Commission would be considering (or influencing) for the very wide range of public sector employees in central and local government, the nationalised industries, the National Health Service (NHS) and other public sector areas? With the pay increases of millions of public sector voters at stake, it was felt impossible not to state in general terms that all such awards would be honoured. Little was said in qualification about the impact of cash limits, or Clegg's supposed work on whether there was a valid basis of comparison to use in determining such claims. This decision alone added cumulatively – avoidably and, at least in part, unjustifiably – a vast sum to public spending over the coming two years.[14] The Clegg

---

[13] A. N. Ridley, 'Draft reply on public sector pay', 4 April 1979, private office files of Sir Adam Ridley.

[14] Between 1950 and the early 1970s the relationship between public and private sector pay to male manual workers was generally stable. The years 1970 to 1972 constitute a reasonable benchmark, being the last in which there was no incomes policy, formal or informal, and also a period in which the public sector was relatively favourably placed. By 1980, when

Commission's last report was not published until the spring of 1981, and many of the awards it made were implemented by stages extending into 1980 and later. Not knowing what might have happened if the position had been better handled makes it hard to estimate the 'excess' precisely. The unjustifiable, avoidable awards probably totalled at least 1 per cent of GDP per year, however – equivalent to the yield of several pence on the basic rate of income tax.

Releasing suppressed taxes, price increases and pay distortions

There were other less spectacular but equally significant legacies that confronted the victor of the 1979 election. Between 1974 and 1979 the outgoing Labour government's finances suffered progressively from a kind of suppressed inflation, which arose in several ways. At the heart of the difficulty was the political economy of the 'social contract', Labour's prices and incomes policy, which – whether formal or informal – was negotiated with the unions each year. To secure the consent of the unions to each successive year of wage restraint, ministers were pressed to 'do something' to restrain the growth of prices. In particular, they were urged not to uprate the specific duties (on alcohol, hydrocarbons, etc.) in line with inflation in each Finance Act (which they duly did not do in 1978). They were also urged to limit nationalised industry prices, which typically could not be increased much under a prices and incomes policy without ministerial, or at least departmental, approval.

Another related problem was pressure to moderate taxation to encourage lower pay claims. The government did so twice: with a two percentage point cut in VAT in the summer of 1974, and with exceptional increases in

many, if not all, of the Clegg awards had largely been implemented, the relationship of public sector manual earnings relative to private had improved substantially.

Public sector earnings as percentage of private sector

	1970–72	1980	Percentage change
Male manual workers	95	104	+9
Male non-manual workers	103	104	+1

Source: HC Deb., 5 February 1981, vol. 998, c201W (written answer by Sir Geoffrey Howe to Mr Beaumont-Dark), quoting *New earnings survey* (London, 1970, 1971, 1972, 1980).

income tax thresholds in the 1976 Budget, which were explicitly conditional on TUC support for a further year of wage restraint.[15]

This policy of seeking a year's wage restraint, not always successfully, year after year in exchange for lasting and accumulating reductions in direct taxes or the suppression of nationalised industry price increases was irresponsible. Admittedly, if pursued successfully for a very short time, against a clear and reliable undertaking that the distortions would be released quickly and without justifying any special wage increases to compensate, a case could just be made for it. But that was not the state of affairs by 1979. Whenever and however one released the price and tax increases that had been held back, they would inevitably provoke public irritation and would not be moderated by the slightest recognition of the reasons for which the restraint had been imposed in the first place. So the doctrine of 'unripe time' was sure to be deployed on the grounds of political expediency to induce the Treasury not to unwind very far or very quickly. Yet, in truth, the problem was not really the timing but the unappetising size of the unwinding required. Its scale, and the probable compensatory wage claims provoked by it, would only become greater and still less appetising the longer one delayed dealing with it. So the least bad course of action was to release it as soon as possible.

The Clegg Commission embodied in institutionalised form another harmful legacy of prices and incomes policies. Income restraint almost always bore unevenly on different sectors, occupations and unions. So it distorted wage relationships and created tensions, which normally released themselves later in extravagant and disorderly bargaining to restore relativities once the period of restraint ended.

Finally, there were also ominous developments in the international economy. Following the displacement of the shah of Iran by the ayatollahs, oil and commodity prices started to rise sharply through the world. Before long these increases threatened to be lasting rather than a short-term blip. In the run-up to the election, however, it was not fully appreciated that they would cause as much recession and inflation as the oil crisis of 1973–75. With uncertainty about energy prices in particular, it was very hard in early 1979 to form any reliable estimate of how much they might add to prices in a 'corrective' Budget in May/June. But one could envisage substantial and early increases in oil, energy costs and hence many nationalised industry prices arising directly from such developments in the international economy, coupled with the

---

[15] Healey, *Time of my life*, 397.

exceptional increases necessitated by the restoration of the real value of specific duties.

From the 1979 election victory to the 1981 Budget

Within a few days of the Conservatives entering office, and thanks to the end of the civil service strikes, the Bank of England was able to resume publishing statistics. The monetary growth figures were alarmingly large. A commensurately extreme policy response was required, as the Bank advised. Interest rates were put up to levels higher than even the pessimists had feared, and that within less than a month of the election, just as the final decisions on the first Budget were coming to a head.

In this Budget the government was, as is well known, able to cut taxes on incomes and enterprise and to effect a significant switch of taxation from direct to indirect taxes, by raising VAT to 15 per cent. From the start, Treasury ministers put forward rigorous targets for spending, borrowing and the money supply. But the outturn was consistently disappointing. Moreover, by early 1980 the publication of the four-year Medium-Term Financial Strategy provided a handsome list of government targets that could be missed year by year and, for that very reason, prayed in aid to criticise the government.

Both supporters and critics of the MTFS have for many years asked why it was brought in and, if it was needed, why it was introduced at such a difficult, not to say unsuitable, time. These are big issues, which cannot be dealt with exhaustively here. But the role and significance of the MTFS were outlined compactly by the minister responsible for its introduction, Nigel Lawson, in his memoirs.[16] His invaluable basic exposition is now being enriched as the relevant official archives are studied – as several valuable chapters in this volume demonstrate. In the present context, there are several features of the MTFS to note.

First, the new government was moving away from the Keynesian year-to-year fine-tuning of real demand towards managing nominal and monetary aggregates over a much longer period. It wanted to set a path of declining monetary growth targets, and hence nominal GDP growth, as a basis for bringing down inflationary expectations. In so doing, it wanted to avoid the expedient flexibility that had for decades been the lubricant of so much bad policy making in labour market and industrial policy. Such limits had to be respected and become credible if they were to account for anything at all. Such self-imposed rules, inevitably arbitrary, had to be

---

[16] Lawson, *The view from No. 11*, 66–75.

defended ferociously nonetheless if they were to be taken seriously. The critical issue was 'Rules rule: OK?', as Lawson had written in an important article in *The Times* in 1978.[17]

Since the monetary aggregates and public borrowing are connected significantly and intimately, if not simply, then it is advisable to integrate one's objectives for the two in a consistent way, and to chart the path they must together take to a better future. It is all the more advisable since, as and when such commitments are honoured and become more credible, interest rate expectations will be firmer and both inflationary expectations and the risk/uncertainty premium that interest rates normally embody will diminish. Since a central part of the government's strategy was to restrain the growth of the state and to lower taxes, it was also important that the MTFS set out a credible, consistent reduction in their burden. The seminal ideas behind the MTFS went back several years, not least to the work of Terry Burns and Alan Budd in 1977, at the London Business School.[18]

The underlying analysis and assumptions had taken shape in a *fair weather* world. When the internal Treasury team was set up in the autumn of 1979 to start work on the MTFS, it did not fully take into account the possibility that the imminent abolition of exchange controls that had just been promised might have an unexpectedly large and early impact on the monetary aggregates. Partly for these reasons, the monetary targets of the MTFS were regularly exceeded on a grand scale as the economy adjusted to the new freedoms. So, as 1980 drew to a close, the 'failure' of the MTFS was added to the initial grounds for criticism, and to the doubts as to whether the government's strategy was wise.

Even without this problem, the economy's general performance in 1980 was disappointing: record interest rates, sharply falling GDP, rising unemployment, little abatement of the growth in prices and wages, and continuing serious strikes in important industries. To cap it all, by the

[17] N. Lawson, 'The economic perils of thinking for the moment', *The Times*, 14 September 1978; Howe, *Conflict of loyalty*, 155.

[18] I also encountered a proposal not dissimilar to the MTFS in discussions in an EEC working group in Brussels in 1977. This was in the third report by the Centro d'Economia e di Politica Economica (Centre for Economics and Economics Policy), in 1976. In it, the authors Giorgio Basevi, Marcello de Cecco, Michele Fratianni and Giorgio La Malfa put forward a four-year 're-entry plan' to the Italian economy following the shocks of 1973–75. Its four basic components were: a path for public spending and the public deficit; a path for the money supply; a path for increases in labour costs; and a planned course for the lira exchange rate. The underlying thinking was close to that developed in the United Kingdom, save for the understandable local idiosyncrasy that the plan would be the object of negotiation between the 'social partners': Budd and Burns, 'How much reflation?'. See also Alan Budd, 'The London Business School and the 1981 Budget', in this volume.

autumn of 1980 Treasury ministers had to have recourse to an autumn mini-budget of the kind they had vigorously and reasonably criticised Healey for introducing year after year. Matters were made no easier by the presentational problems encountered by the Chancellor when announcing this package to Parliament.[19]

Such consistent failure to achieve the economic goals of the manifesto or the new MTFS, and to revive the economy, attracted trenchant criticism. Specialists in economic policy asked ever more insistently when (or often to predict that) the Thatcher government would be forced to follow Ted Heath's U-turn in 1972, and to switch to reflation and a prices and incomes policy agreed with the unions and the CBI. This scepticism was not universal, and certainly did not dominate sentiment in financial markets. But even sympathetic financial specialists were becoming acutely anxious about the government's apparent inability to pull off a strategy whose philosophy they strongly supported.

The political debate was not dissimilar. Within the Conservative Party, the committed 'wets' and 'dries' briefed furiously in both directions. There was sporadic, but not entirely frivolous, talk of leadership challenges. In the country at large, the government's standing in the opinion polls was very poor. Admittedly, the Labour Party offered ineffective opposition in Parliament under the leadership of Michael Foot and his former Cabinet colleagues. At the same time, however, the Social Democratic Party under Roy Jenkins and his team had already become a serious force for both major parties to reckon with.

The run-up to the 1981 Budget

The picture appeared yet more discouraging inside the Treasury, and deteriorated progressively throughout the financial year as deadlines for the final decisions on the March 1981 Budget approached. By early 1981 it was clear that there were two daunting obstacles to overcome.

The first was the worsening figures emerging for the 1980/81 outturn, which would strike every reader of the next Budget 'Red Book' who compared the expected outturn with the estimates in the previous year's Red Book. Thus the February 1981 internal Treasury forecasts revealed the following.
(1) The 1980/81 PSBR was projected at £14 billion, almost twice the 1980 Red Book forecast of £7.2 billion.
(2) Of that deterioration, less than £2 billion was attributable to revenue shortfalls; some £5 billion was overspending.

[19] See Christopher Collins, 'Origins of the Budget in 1980', in this volume.

(3) The overspending was not in programmes subject to cash limits, which had held up well. Nor was it in spending areas supported by the contingency reserve, though, had it been, that would have been no consolation, since the reserve was already exhausted.

(4) Nor was there any padding or unspent money left in remaining programmes.[20]

The challenge to ministers and officials was daunting, therefore. Given the sustained failure to meet targets, how could the markets be reassured that the over-/undershooting of key objectives, driven largely by public spending, would not continue in 1981 and afterwards?

Turning to the projections for 1981/82, the estimated PSBR on unchanged policies was £14 billion, for the second year running. To announce such a figure would be doubly risky. Of itself, it would leave the MTFS and the government's other economic targets alike with no remaining credibility in the market. That, in turn, would be a very serious blow to the government's whole programme, and to the leaders who had put it forward and been elected on it. The obvious conclusion was that the government should set a PSBR target for 1981/82 that could absorb another substantial in-year deterioration matching that of 1980/81 without leading to an unacceptable outcome. One should 'aim off' and work to achieve a PSBR of, say, £10 billion or a little more. Doing this would require several billion pounds of extra economies or revenue. Moreover, that addition would be on top of the substantial sums already earmarked to support two other critical policy objectives: correcting the major imbalances that had arisen between personal and corporate sectors in recent years, and cutting the deficit to clear the path to lower interest rates.

In the run-up to the Budget, several measures were considered, and either rejected or found inadequate, since they would save too little, too slowly or at too high a political cost to 'fill the gap'. The thinking was as follows.

(1) Spending control could be toughened (and was), mainly by extending the coverage of cash limits. This procedure was intrinsically unsuited to limiting important demand-determined programmes such as social security, in which the overspends were the most acute, however.

(2) The contingency reserve could be widened (and was); but, like cash limits, it could not sensibly be extended to cover such categories as debt interest, local government spending and some nationalised industry spending.

---

[20] A. N. Ridley, 'Public spending, the contingency reserve and the Budget', 12 February 1981, private office files of Sir Adam Ridley.

(3) Within each cash-limited programme, one could, in theory, carve out an extra element of uncommitted money to provide extra flexibility to meet unforeseen spending surges elsewhere. But, after two or more years of economies and unforeseen cost pressures, there was nothing left to squeeze.

(4) One could examine using the indirect tax 'regulator' introduced by Selwyn Lloyd, the then Chancellor, in 1961 to impose quick-acting in-year tax increases.[21] In the same spirit, one could also consider indexing the specific duties (i.e. on petrol, alcohol, tobacco, etc.) to inflation by adjusting them quarterly rather than annually. Both appeared to be unlikely to raise enough revenue to justify the political and administrative inconvenience involved.

More radical steps were clearly needed.

The Budget

The final decision was to hold the PSBR to £10.5 billion in 1981/82, which required reducing it by some £3.5 billion below its latest projected level. This was achieved mainly by *not* indexing the personal tax allowances for inflation; by above-inflation increases in indirect taxes; and by special one-off taxes on the banks and North Sea oil. This cut in the PSBR facilitated a two percentage point cut in interest rates, which reduced the upward pressure on the pound; significant measures to offset Stock Appreciation Relief against Corporation Tax for companies; and a material 'enterprise package' for new and small businesses. The Budget was also the occasion for the introduction of index-linked gilt-edged securities. This important innovation marked a new and adventurous phase in the techniques of monetary policy and debt management. It made it easier to initiate and maintain sales of public sector debt in difficult market conditions and thus reduced the government's chronic vulnerability to funding crises.

Both the objective importance of this Budget and the subjective fascination triggered by its dramatic and unexpected proposals provoked unusual interest from the start. Many commentators and observers pursued, and still pursue today, a somewhat extreme, 'tabloid newspaper' interpretation of events. They tend to describe the circumstances and decisions largely as a story of personalities and personal differences,

---

[21] The 'regulator' enabled the Chancellor, between Budgets, to (1) raise or lower indirect taxes by up to 10 per cent, with retrospective parliamentary approval needed within three weeks, and (2) add to employers' National Insurance.

laced with a touch of conspiracy here and there. This is misleading – indeed, in most respects incorrect. The path to the 1981 Budget was not a knock-out competition or a sporting championship, let alone a gladiatorial fight. It was the product of a rational debate, albeit a very tense one, within the normal restricted budget circle; of a collective discussion rather than the raw clash of a few dominant personalities.

When preparing a budget in the 1970s and 1980s, leading the budget team through the process was rather like organising a convoy. Treasury ministers and senior officials brought together a variety of specialists from the Inland Revenue, Customs and Excise and the Bank of England, as well as economists and tax specialists from within the Treasury itself. At any given time during the journey, some participants were in the lead, some behind, some on one flank and some on the other. But there was no furious controversy or separation into different antagonistic groups. The participants stayed in formation and arrived at their destination together.[22]

That the process was so smooth owed a great deal to the Chancellor's approach to policy making. As Lawson has stressed, Geoffrey Howe has always been committed to collegiate, consensual, collective decision making.[23] He stuck to this philosophy assiduously in the preparation of the 1981 Budget, whether in his relations with ministers, officials, Special Advisers and the budget team proper, or with the newly arrived economic adviser to the Prime Minister, Alan Walters, and John Hoskyns in the No. 10 Policy Unit. The principal concern of Treasury Special Advisers, Hoskyns and Walters alike, was that the PSBR figure finally adopted for 1981/82 should be realistically small. We freely shared our anxieties and views on what should be done to achieve this. While there was a spread of views amongst Treasury officials, they provided coherent and loyal support.

All that said, there was a special tension in the debate. The No. 10 advisers probably did not have a full or personal appreciation of the many daunting political problems that ministers had to resolve in the Budget's decisions and, most importantly, its presentation. Their subsequent accounts of the Budget process indicate a degree of frustration that was perhaps provoked by the politicians' need to respect these realities rather than an obstinate inability to follow the path of common sense.[24]

---

[22] On this point, and for further detailed discussion of the Budget measures, see Tim Lankester, 'The 1981 Budget: how did it come about?', in this volume.

[23] Lawson, *The view from No. 11*, 22, 94.

[24] Walters, *Britain's economic renaissance*, 86–91; Hoskyns, *Just in time*, 262–85.

The United Kingdom's experience in the late 1970s and early 1980s illustrates some important principles about how best to handle difficult economic and budgetary decisions. One is that in general the public reacts badly to sudden, unexpected and unpleasant surprises. In some cases – often very important ones – a government has no alternative to announcing a fait accompli, not least because earlier declarations of intent can have damaging side effects, or mobilise opposition to an irresponsible degree. In most cases, however, timely advance warning and explanatory initiatives can help greatly. They give time for measured discussion, calm contemplation and careful analysis of difficult challenges. At the same time they help banish the electorate's fear that 'the politicians' are rushing the country or that the politicians themselves are being rushed into hasty decisions before the issues can be properly discussed within a party or in Parliament. One should let people down gently and help them accept the inevitability of the laws of arithmetic and logic and the facts of the real world.

The 1979 Budget, in which VAT was increased (as promised), but to a surprising and unexpected 15 per cent rate, was received more poorly than the 1980 Budget, which, though also very unpleasant, did not catch people by surprise. The 1981 Budget was, like that of 1979, a shock to many observers, who once again were confronted by an unpleasant surprise.[25] This was in line with normal Treasury practice. Until recently the Chancellor has held all budgetary cards extremely close to his chest and not disclosed much of significance even to Cabinet colleagues until very shortly before the announcement – by which time decisions are, of course, in large measure irrevocable. The doctrine of budget secrecy reinforces this practice.[26]

In 1981 the reaction to the Budget, both internally and externally, was, in the main, very critical. The notable exception was the financial markets, which appeared slightly amazed that ministers had been so courageous, and took great heart from what they saw. Indeed, it was clear at the time that for *them* the toughness and initial unpopularity of the Budget of itself succeeded in creating much additional market credibility.

Faced with this widespread hostility outside the City, the Chancellor and his colleagues launched a major exercise in 1981 to explain and win

---

[25] See Appendix on opinion poll research on the 1981 Budget.

[26] In contrast, the unprecedentedly wide publicity about the ministerial arguments in Cabinet in the autumn of 1976 about whether to agree to the terms the IMF sought greatly helped Callaghan and Healey. High-profile newspaper articles and media coverage week by week of the Cabinet's furious arguments paved the way to both internal and general public acceptance of the 1976 economic proposals, which many had initially feared would be impossibly brutal and savage.

support for the Budget, particularly within the Conservative Party, involving:

- occasional dinners with senior ministerial colleagues;
- agreeing to the institution of a periodic Cabinet discussion of economic strategy *before* the Budget, as well as before the annual spending review;
- weekly meetings between the Chancellor and small groups of back-bench Conservative MPs;
- devoting special efforts to preparing full and persuasive replies to important letters from Members of Parliament and the Lords, industrialists, and others of importance and influence;
- a series of major public speeches by Nigel Lawson explaining the case for the Budget;
- careful responses to the work of the Treasury and Civil Service Select Committee (set up in 1979), which was already building an important position; and
- the continuation of vigorous briefing of, and discussion at, the National Economic Development Council, of which unionists, employers and other experts were still active members.

Reactions to the Budget

While most subjective reactions to the Budget were distressed and often critical, objective enquiry quickly disclosed some very interesting patterns. The most objective point by far was that the critics did not have a serious, comprehensive alternative strategy to offer, save for a small minority who advocated some combination of reflation and a retreat into a state-led and planned economy with elaborate controls, including over foreign exchange and trade and many other markets. Prominent in this minority were Peter Shore, then shadow Chancellor, Tony Benn and the Cambridge Economic Policy Group, led by Wynne Godley and Francis Cripps. Within the Conservative Party, several senior ministers were, as is well known, shocked enough to consider resigning, but none did so.[27] Most Conservative parliamentary critics of the Budget tended to pick on specific measures with great emotion, particularly the increases in hydrocarbon taxation (i.e. petrol and diesel prices to the normal voter), but had no coherent broad-brush suggestions to make about a radical change of course. During the course of the Finance Bill debates in the summer of 1981, Treasury ministers therefore proposed lower duty on diesel and higher tobacco duty to compensate, which met much of the

[27] See I. H. J. L Gilmour, *Dancing with dogma: Britain under Thatcherism* (London, 1992), 44–5; J. M. L. Prior, *Balance of power* (London, 1986), 140–1.

concern about fuel prices expressed by the most critical backbenchers. As the economy began to perform better in the latter part of 1981, the government's credibility increased very substantially. By the time of the general election in June 1983, the political battle was largely won, following eight successive quarters of GDP growth at a time when most remaining OECD countries were still in recession. It remained only for the Labour Party to mortally wound its economic policy credentials in an election manifesto famously described by one shadow Cabinet member as the 'longest suicide note in history'.

The wider intellectual and policy debate

There was much more at issue than the political issue of who captured the electors' support after this Budget. In particular, there were several critical economic questions.
(1) Where did the 'anti-deflationists'' criticism of the Budget stand?
(2) Was the MTFS a success?
(3) What about the monetary targets?

In the 1981 context, the anti-deflationists' critique amounted essentially to the claim and the prediction that, by 'deflating', specifically by cutting the PSBR (it was often unclear whether they referred to the actual or cyclically adjusted measure), demand would be reduced – and sufficiently reduced to cause chronic stagnation, recession or, worse still, depression, in the circumstances at the time. It is important to recall that the American National Bureau of Economic Research (NBER) has long defined a recession as two consecutive quarters of falling output. The term 'depression' has never been defined with comparable precision in the United States or United Kingdom, but normally it denotes a very long period of recession or stagnation, accompanied by major financial and industrial failure. What actually happened?

The figures in Table 4.1 show clearly that the second quarter of 1981 constituted the end of the recession as well as the setting for the 1981 Budget. Indeed, anyone with a keen eye on the domestic economy at that time should have spotted the upturn 'coming' by the end of 1980 from the *Financial Times'* monthly service of business opinion and the CSO's cyclical indicators. The CSO's shorter monthly leading indicator, which had a mean lead of five months, moved as shown in Table 4.2 over the relevant period.[28]

---

[28] The longer leading indicator, whose mean lead was thirteen months, had already turned up over the year end of 1979–80, signalling a turning point at much the same time.

Table 4.1 *Quarterly index of real GDP at factor cost (average estimate),*
1978–83

	1978	1979	1980	1981	1982	1983
Q1	97.9	99.7	101.8	98.4	100.3	103.1
Q2	100.5	103.6	100.6	98.1	100.7	103.0
Q3	100.4	103.1	99.1	98.6	100.6	104.4
Q4	100.8	103.1	98.4	99.9	101.7	105.9

Source: Central Statistical Office (CSO), *Economic trends annual supplement* (London, 1985).
Note: 1980 = 100.

Table 4.2 *Shorter leading cyclical indicator*

	Jun	Jul	Aug	Sep	Oct	Nov	Dec
1980	104.6	103.0	101.9	101.3	101.1	101.0	101.3

	Jan	Feb	Mar	Apr
1981	102.1	102.6	103.3	104.3

Source: CSO, *Economic trends (July 1981)* (London, 1981), 88.
Note: 1975 = 100.

Table 4.3 *Trends in the PSBR as a percentage of GDP*

	1978/ 79	1979/ 80	1980/ 81	1981/ 82	1982/ 83	1983/ 84	Average 1978/79– 1980/81	Average 1981/82– 1983/84
Cyclically adjusted	4.8	4.0	3.4	−1.5	−1.4	0.0	4.1	−1.0
Recorded	5.3	4.8	5.4	3.3	3.1	3.2	5.2	3.1

What was the course of the budget balance, whose reduction was
alleged to be so damaging?[29] Robert Neild helpfully quotes the six-year
trend in the CSO's cyclically adjusted PSBR, as shown in Table 4.3.

[29] See Robert Neild, 'The 1981 statement by 364 economists', in this volume, first published in the *Newsletter of the Royal Economic Society* in October 2012.

This six-year period saw a very substantial and sustained reduction by any measure. The marked fall in the cyclically adjusted PSBR until 1983/84 should, on the critics' analysis, have reduced the output trend sharply, particularly the very large fall from 3.4 per cent of GDP in 1980/81 – the depth of the recession – to 0 per cent in 1983/84. Yet the year-on-year GDP growth was 2.2 per cent (1982), 3.8 per cent (1983) and 2.9 per cent (1984). That is at or above the long-term trend in each of these years. Since the same thing happened in two preceding periods of major cuts in the deficit, we should not be surprised.[30]

It has also been argued that the recovery after the second quarter of 1981 was the product of an (almost) devious strategy born of the discomfort encountered by Walters when facing falling dollar/sterling exchange rates as he flew to and fro between London and Washington in the middle of the 1970s.[31] The suggestion was that the MTFS and the associated PSBR cut were devised and promoted by Walters and his associates, almost as a smokescreen for cuts in interest rates and, hence, as a move to reverse sterling's painful appreciation in the previous years. The Walters team's concern about the strength of sterling was in reality shared widely, however. So was the team's concern to cut interest rates in order to help it downwards at last. His was no one-man battle to confound the heretics.

More important was the impact on net exports after the Budget of this sustained weakening in sterling that that Budget had provoked. Though it

[30] The preceding episode of deflation and PSBR reduction was the Healey/IMF measures of 1976, whose broad outline was as follows:

	PSBR/GDP (%)	PSBR at 1980/81 prices (£ billion)
1974/75	9.00	18.6
1975/76	9.75	20.1
1976/77	6.75	14.3
1977/78	3.75	8.4

Thus there was a six percentage point cut in the PSBR as a percentage of GDP between 1975/76 and 1977/8; but GDP grew at some 2.5 per cent per year. One should recall that Wynne Godley wrote to *The Times* on 25 November 1976, as the package was concluded, to state that Healey's 'new measures to reduce the budget deficit by a large amount would gravely accentuate the present recession and that there were no grounds for supposing the resulting further increase in unemployment would be temporary'. Roy Jenkins' post-devaluation and austerity programme of 1968–70 saw the PSBR cut by 4.7 percentage points as a percentage of GDP between 1967 and 1969 and reach a surplus in 1970. During that three-year period GDP grew by nearly 2 per cent per year. W. A. H. Godley, 'Public spending cuts', *The Times*, 25 November 1976; Central Statistical Office.
[31] W. J. G. Keegan, *Mr Lawson's gamble* (London, 1989), 84.

was of great value in restoring competitiveness in the long run, net exports did not increase for a long time and therefore contributed nothing, in the event, to the early years of the post-Budget recovery; indeed, they shrank for several years. So they were not the secret engine of early recovery that Walters is alleged to have cunningly engineered.

The success of the MTFS?

There are two very distinct issues to examine here. First, did the government succeed in meeting the numerical, intermediate objectives embodied in the MTFS in 1980, 1981 and subsequently? Second, did these intermediate objectives and the plan itself embodying them help in achieving the wider ultimate objectives of lower inflation and the re-establishment of sound economic growth?

The answer to the first question is clearly 'No'. While the fiscal targets were narrowly missed, the monetary targets were repeatedly exceeded and revised upwards, and before long the nature of monetary targeting itself changed fairly radically. Thus the 1987 Red Book stated:

[M]onetary conditions are assessed in the light of movements in narrow and broad money, and the behaviour of other financial indicators, in particular the exchange rate. There is no mechanical formula for taking these factors into account; a balance must be struck between the exchange rate and domestic monetary growth consistent with the Government's aims for money and GDP and inflation.[32]

This was a very far cry from the crisp original 1980 MTFS language. It cannot, therefore, be said that the MTFS successfully met one of its most central and innovatory objectives, namely to create an unyielding framework within which to confine the growth of the money supply and other aggregates.

The answer to the second question is clearly 'Yes', however; it *succeeded*, together with other policies, as an exercise in political economy. GDP growth was re-established within a year of the plan's promulgation, as is shown above. Inflation fell sharply before long, reaching an annual rate of some 4 per cent by 1986/87 – a figure unknown since the 1960s. And there was initiated a dramatic and lasting change in labour market conditions and attitudes, reflected among many other things in the great reduction in the number of days lost in industrial disputes. It is important to note what lay behind the success, since the reasons for it extend more widely than is appreciated by the many observers who interpret the MTFS narrowly, *au pied de la lettre*, merely as an exercise in monetary discipline.

---

[32] *FSBR 1987–88* (London, 1987), 9.

The MTFS, in its language and method of operation, was part of a family of policies involving the systematic application of hard budget constraints, for the first time in living memory in the United Kingdom. It was intimately complemented by the imposition, extension and tightening of cash limits in the public sector, when possible by firm limits on the external financing of the nationalised industries, combined with commercialisation and moves towards privatisation, and with a systematic reluctance to extend subsidy indefinitely to 'lame duck' firms and industries in the private sector, particularly in response to non-commercial pressures.

Second, the MTFS was a ringing declaration of commitment to setting out and holding to a set of coherent, interlocking long-term policies, both fiscal and monetary. It called for credibility, ideally from the outset – and, of course, did not generate much for a year or two. But the longer the government persevered with its philosophy in all its aspects, the more its credibility increased, and a virtuous circle necessarily followed. In this context, the union reform legislation of 1980, 1982 and 1984 and the generally tough line taken with the strikes were also of course cumulatively of great importance. The 1981 Budget probably brought about a major step change in credibility once it became clear that growth had resumed and there would be no U-turn, or change in the party of government or its leadership.

Third, the launch of the MTFS institutionalised the importance of money, banking, credit and the financial markets. In the United Kingdom these had long been (and to some extent still are) the Cinderella of the academic world, the civil service and politicians. The MTFS and the surrounding debate forced people to recognise that 'money matters', a lesson that has been of great and lasting importance and interest to many beyond the monetarists and their limited political circle.

Fourth, the MTFS was part of a wider challenge to some of the most pathological tendencies that had bedevilled all governments in the preceding twenty years. It did *not* make maintenance of full employment an overt objective, but pushed much of the onus for its achievement back onto employers, unions, entrepreneurs and the supply conditions prevailing in the economy.[33] The expectation of employees to be treated as if they had a God-given right to a yearly real wage increase and to enjoy their job indefinitely throughout their lives was at last being realistically

---

[33] A critical change of emphasis, which Healey first adumbrated in an often neglected speech as early as 10 January 1975: see S. D. Hoggart, 'Jobs come first, not pay rises', *The Times*, 11 January 1975.

questioned, at a time when to do so was still heresy almost everywhere in the OECD.

What might have been?

Looking back, it is interesting to consider whether an MTFS with workable and stable money supply targets could ever have been devised and put into effect after 1979. On the one hand, had the Conservative Party and government kept exchange controls in place, more or less, and released the 'corset' very slowly, then it might have been easier to formulate and achieve a robust and realistic target for monetary growth for a significant period. The moment of truth, which would probably have arisen when some important exchange controls began to be liberalised, could well have been postponed for some time.

On the other hand, had the opposition planners and the Conservative government and its advisers fully foreseen what the effect of removing exchange controls and the 'corset' was to be, they might have chosen on objective grounds to build the monetary dimensions of the MTFS on one of several very different foundations from the start. All these would have been a long way away from targeting growth in £M3. One approach might have been to target a responsible, steady expansion path for nominal GDP. This was (and is) an intellectually attractive proposal; but it called for more reliable GDP statistics than could be mustered then (or now?). A second possibility was to take the sterling exchange rate and peg it to a target currency (perhaps the deutschmark), or for it to enter a fixed rate currency system such as the European currency 'snake' or the European Union's Exchange Rate Mechanism, if either had become robust enough. A third possibility was to change style more radically still, and to adopt some form of inflation targeting, and face the challenges of determining output gaps and of estimating the 'natural rate of unemployment'.

It is very hard to see how such policies could have been identified or agreed in the circumstances of the last two years of opposition or the early years of government. There were too few players, too little consensus and too much prejudice on all sides; and far too little undisturbed time for a systematic policy exercise, as is noted above in the section on Conservative monetary policy making in opposition.

On the other hand, unbeknown to nearly everyone, as is noted in the earlier section on monetary policy in opposition, there was original work being undertaken at that time by officials in the Treasury and the Bank of England and by economists in other centres, such as the London Business School and the University of Liverpool. It is only now with the opening of archives that the scale and potential value of this work can properly be appreciated. It might have been a very different world had this research work been available to the world outside, had its importance permitted a good-natured technical exchange between the parties over the years and had it also been appreciated by the economic commentariat and other interested parties. Indeed, such a debate should, ideally, have begun at the time of Competition and Credit Control in the early 1970s. But this was not, of course, to be!

One obstacle to such a transparent and civilised exchange was the insistence of officialdom on keeping so much of its research agenda and results so very secret. The motives for this were various: to avoid embarrassing and tying the hands of senior officials and ministers; to prevent officials and civil service 'professionals' from awkward involvement in policy controversy; and to protect the secrecy and, thus, the integrity of the budget process itself and the power of the Treasury that was vested in it. Happily, there has been considerable progress to openness in these areas since the 1970s, with the publication of the Treasury model and Treasury forecasts and the creation of the Institute for Fiscal Studies and, most recently, the Office for Budget Responsibility.

Another obstacle at that time was the emotion-charged nature of the economic policy debate. One cannot but be struck by the frequent ferocity and dogmatism of the criticisms directed at Margaret Thatcher's administration, at her economic team and, above all, at herself. Unusually for a critic of the government, Robert Neild – the leader of the 364 economists – is candid about his own emotions in his 2012 Royal Economic Society article, reproduced in this volume.[34] In it he describes at one point how he 'felt morally indignant that the great achievement of modern economics – the creation of full employment – was being betrayed'.[35] At another point he candidly introduces grudging praise for Thatcher's policies with the words '[m]uch as I abhor the social philosophy of Mrs Thatcher'.[36] Such candour is admirable; but it is also very suggestive. It illustrates how, both then and now, it has been so hard for large parts of the *bien pensant* British political establishment to acknowledge any objective virtue in Thatcher or her government's policies because they loathed her so much. It should of itself make us treat their criticism with special caution!

Making matters worse still, there was – and still is – a casual attitude in the United Kingdom to policy making, particularly by parties in

---

[34] R. R. Neild, 'The "1981 statement by 364 economists" revisited', *Royal Economic Society Newsletter*, 159 (October 2012), 11–14.
[35] Ibid.   [36] Ibid.

opposition. The resources and organisation devoted to it are exiguous, and the policies based on this inadequate foundation are often woefully badly prepared. Despite the useful openings created by the Freedom of Information Act, the present conventions forbidding civil service contacts at working level with opposition parties are still a particularly dismal obstacle to rational objective discussions. To cap it all, authoritative outsiders rarely subject policy making to much serious analysis – understandably, in a sense, because they have so low an opinion of much of it.

In the case of monetary policy – and the possible MTFS – the Conservative Party could have come up with more considered and better policies in 1975–79 *if given the chance*. In particular, we would have benefited greatly from at least knowing in outline what the economists in the Bank of England and Treasury were exploring, discussing and concluding. Sadly, that was not to be. As it was, we used our very restricted time and resources as best we could.

Appendix Opinion poll research on the 1981 Budget[37]

This survey, undertaken within a fortnight of the Budget, recorded many interesting results, such as the following.

(1) Only 15 per cent of the electorate described the Budget as good, as against 33 per cent in 1979 and 42 per cent in 1980.
(2) A large majority found the Budget 'worse than people had expected'.
(3) Only 25 per cent thought the government's total policy was successful, and half thought it should do a U-turn.
(4) Only 20 per cent thought the Budget was fair.
(5) The most memorable increases in the Budget were in duty on petrol, tobacco and alcohol. The increased petrol tax was remembered spontaneously by 90 per cent, more than has been found to remember any change in previous budget surveys.
(6) Given a straightforward choice, the majority of electors would have preferred the basic rate of income tax to have gone up rather than the duty on petrol.

---

[37] This research was carried out by the Louis Harris Group on behalf of the Conservative Party, with the fieldwork taking place between 20 and 23 March 1981.

5   The Bank of England and the 1981 Budget

Charles Goodhart

The main role of a central bank is to maintain the value of its country's currency. So the Bank of England was constitutionally and institutionally bound to support the Conservative government's policy of bringing down inflation. The previous Labour government had tried to do so primarily by means of incomes policies, and these had comprehensively failed, and were discredited.

The alternative policy, which the incoming government would apply, was to restrict monetary growth via the Medium-Term Financial Strategy, relying on a reasonably stable relationship between nominal incomes and the money stock. In this respect, the more credible the policy (to private sector agents), the more that the adjustment could occur, quite quickly, via wage/price adjustments, and the less via reductions in output and increases in unemployment. This caused a problem in relationships between Her Majesty's Government/the Treasury and the Bank. True believers (in monetarism) did, and non-believers felt they had to, express faith in public in the ability of the MTFS to bring down inflation. But this put non-believers in a difficult position; and we in the Bank were non-believers.

The Bank felt that control of £M3 (broad money) was extremely problematical, and, even if such control could be achieved (which was doubtful), it was neither necessary, nor even perhaps sufficient, to control inflation. If incomes policies were ruled out of court, either as politically unacceptable or practically ineffective, then in our view the only alternative route lay in weakening the power of labour (trades unions) via rising unemployment. But there was an appreciation of the argument that, the greater the credibility of the counter-inflation policy (whether via the MTFS or otherwise), the less its damaging effects on output and unemployment might be.

There were, perhaps, two camps in the Bank on economic strategy. The first, represented by the Deputy Governor, Kit McMahon, and the Executive Director (Economics Division), Christopher Dow, was so appalled by the likely loss of output/unemployment from the government's policy that this camp felt that at some point supplementary reliance on some form of incomes policy would need to be reintroduced. McMahon's note of 30 May 1980, reproduced in Appendix 5.1, is a good example.[1] Later, on 14 July 1981 (i.e. after the 1981 Budget), Dow presented a note to the Governors entitled 'An alternative policy', involving sufficient fiscal easing to stabilise output and unemployment.[2] On the front of this, the Executive Director (Home Finance), John Fforde, minuted (in longhand) to Dow (emphasis in original):

I've always thought that the fiscal measures that you suggest, *in the present political context*, would in practice precipitate a pay explosion – especially in the public sector – and could not be contemplated except in exchange for a (??) watertight bargain with the unions or else (& better) a statutory 2-year freeze. In the absence of a freeze, or near freeze, I [would] fear HMG being in the very weak position of failed-monetarists who had given way to disaster and disturbance what they had denied to reasoned argument. But I could be wrong.[3]

The other camp in the Bank was mainly represented by Fforde, the Assistant Director (Gilt-Edged Division), Eddie George, and me. We did not believe that a return to incomes policies was feasible, or likely to succeed. We understood the argument about credibility, but we were intensely sceptical, as was virtually everyone else in the Bank, of tying it to the achievement of a target for £M3 (MTFS). The position of this camp is perhaps most nicely put, though in typically flowery terms, by Fforde, on 30 April 1981, in his note entitled 'The dilemma of the liberal central banker in XXth century Britain (a fragment for Easter)', attached as Appendix 5.2.[4]

Had we had the wit to think of it then, we might well have been staunch supporters of an inflation target, or a nominal income target, as espoused by Samuel Brittan of the *Financial Times*. But even that might not have worked in that conjuncture. Governments had been routinely denouncing inflation and promising to stamp it out for a decade or more, and such promises had lost credibility. The more 'doveish' camp in the Bank would have been reluctant to discard having some regard for real variables. In the absence of incomes policy, there seemed no alternative to the hair-shirt route via unemployment. The MTFS was an intensely uncomfortable mechanism (especially for the Bank) for imposing that hair shirt, but it did have the associated advantage of forcing the Treasury to weigh the

---

[1]   C. W. McMahon, 'Policy', 30 May 1980, London, BOE, 6A264/1, MTFW 128836.
[2]   J. C. R. Dow, 'An alternative policy', 13 July 1981, BOE, 10A153/2, MTFW 128835.
[3]   Dow's reply was anodyne.
[4]   J. S. Fforde, 'The dilemma of the liberal central banker in XXth century Britain', 10 April 1981, BOE, 10A153/2, MTFW 128834.

balance between monetary and fiscal policies in the pursuit of the £M3 target.

Meanwhile, in 1979 and 1980 the economic situation worsened in many respects. Inflation rose even further initially, partly as a result of the VAT increase in 1979 and the acceptance of the Clegg proposals on public sector pay. Despite high inflation in the United Kingdom, the exchange rate soared, driven by a combination of expectations of North Sea oil, faith (perhaps more evident outside than in Britain) in Margaret Thatcher's tough stand against inflation, and high (nominal) interest rates. The corporate sector experienced a huge loss of competitiveness, with costs rising sharply while demand was weak, and remained in financial deficit (whereas the personal sector surplus rose). Monetary growth remained somewhat higher than planned, partly because the banks intermediated between lending to the (deficit) corporate sector on the basis of deposits from the (surplus) personal sector; see Figure 5.1 and Table 5.1.

Prior to the 1981 Budget the overriding concern in the Bank was the unduly high level of the exchange rate and the disastrous effect that this was having on the company sector. David Walker (as he then was), the Bank's Chief Adviser, was particularly articulate on this, a viewpoint shared throughout the Bank. Labour unemployment was bad, but potentially reversible. Company closures were more likely to be irreversible. All kinds of schemes to operate directly on the exchange rate were dreamt up, ranging from a combined monetary/exchange rate target (by me) to a

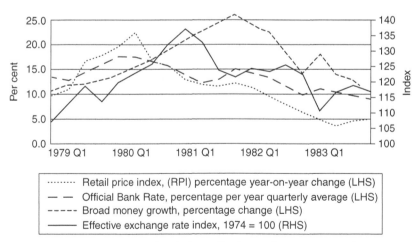

Figure 5.1 Retail prices index, effective exchange rate, nominal interest rate and broad money (£M3), 1979–83
Notes: LHS = left-hand scale; RHS = right-hand scale.
Sources: ONS, Bank of England, IMF.

Table 5.1 *Sectoral surplus or deficit, 1979–83*

	Personal sector	Industrial and commercial companies	Public sector	Overseas sector
1979	7,495	−1,188	−8,566	550
1980	12,207	119	−10,313	−2,820
1981	12,628	1,534	−7,780	−6,628
1982	10,368	3,429	−7,657	−4,587
1983	6,882	5,585	−10,281	−3,758

Source: United Kingdom national accounts (London, 1989).

North Sea Oil Wealth Fund (suggested by the Governor, Gordon Richardson) to direct intervention and/or public statements of preferences for lower rates (suggested by Dow). All were unceremoniously batted away by the government, especially the Financial Secretary, Nigel Lawson. Their view was that high exchange rates were a market-led way of bringing down inflation, and hence to be embraced rather than reversed, especially not by government intervention.

The Bank, as is the standard custom, played no part in the (Budget: secret) discussions on the choice of public sector expenditure cuts and/or tax increases, but it did play a full role in assessing the monetary consequences, especially in the context of the MTFS. In particular, a lower PSBR implied that less pressure would be required on monetary policy, via restraining bank lending or requiring higher gilt sales, in pursuit of a given monetary objective. The implication was that interest rates and, it was hoped, the exchange rate could both be lower, within the context of the monetary(-ist) counter-inflationary policy. The problem, of course, was that no one could foretell in advance how much the lower PSBR in the Budget could allow for some relaxation in the − already intolerable − pressures placed upon (the company sector of) the economy. In practice, no one can predict exchange rates well, and internal (Bank and Treasury) forecasts had (I believe) smaller declines in exchange rates and worse predictions for output/employment than actually then occurred.

Insofar as the 1981 Budget shifted the burden of disinflation from monetary to fiscal policy, and from the company sector to the personal sector, *within a given strategy*, we all welcomed it. The dove-ish camp (McMahon, Dow) disliked the strategy; the hawkish camp (Fforde, George, me) disliked the monetary(-ist) clothes in which the strategy was presented, but (being blind to inflation targeting then) could see no good alternative, and certainly none that the government would have

Table 5.2 *Exchange rate and interest rate movements, May 1979–September 1981*

	Election day (3 May 1979)	Peak	Today (14 Sep. 1981)	Percentage change since	
				Election day	Peak
Effective (1974 = 100)	86.7	105.6 (28 Jan. 1981)	86.6	−0.1	−18.0
£/$	2.08	2.47[5] (24 Oct. 1980)	1.77	−14.6	−28.1
£/Dm	4.0	5.07 (16 Feb. 1981)	4.21	5.3	−17.0

Source: J. O. Kerr, 'Exchange rate and interest rates', 14 September 1981, London, TNA, PREM 19/437.

found acceptable. Being in the Bank, none of us would have been allowed to sign the (in)famous economists' letter. But, had we been allowed, the doves (and most of the economics department then) would have signed. The hawks, and those working on the monetary/financial side, would probably not have done so.

In the event, exchange rates did come down rapidly after the 1981 Budget, but we can, of course, never know how much this was due to the Budget and how much to happenstance. Indeed, so sharply did the exchange rate fall that, by 4 September 1981, the Governor was asking for an increase in interest rates to stem the decline. Table 5.2 sets out the exchange rate movements.

The rest is history. Largely under the influence, in my view, of this fall in the exchange rate, the British economy recovered better in the next few years than anyone had expected at the time. The monetary targets became increasingly wayward and were subsequently discarded. After a number of other experiments with intermediate targets, central banks seized upon inflation targeting in the early 1990s as their touchstone. Had we (the authorities) been following an inflation-targeting strategy, rather than the MTFS, in 1981, should/would the Budget decision have been much the same? In my view, yes, since there was an urgent need to rebalance the

[5] Sterling reached an intraday high of $2.4645 on 24 October 1980 before closing at $2.4495. The figures in Table 5.1 are those reported to the Prime Minister on 14 September 1981.

burden from monetary to fiscal policy. Was the welcome subsequent decline in exchange rates the consequence of that rebalancing, or just an extremely fortunate accompaniment that gave the government and the Bank a 'Get out of jail free' card? Who knows?

Appendix 5.1 McMahon's note of 30 May 1980[6]

SECRET   30. 5. 80
THE GOVERNOR   Copies to   Mr Fforde
                                           Mr Dow
                                           Mr Loehnis
                                           Mr George
                                           Mr Goodhart
                                           Mr Walker
                                           Mr Flemming
                                           Mr Holland
POLICY

Policy is obviously coming under great strain. Some of the criticism comes from those who are sceptical and/or hostile to the whole approach from the start and who want something so radically different (basically protectionism probably) that there is no way of meeting them. Some of the criticism reflects a faint-heartedness of original supporters to a policy who deluded themselves into thinking that inflation could be brought down painlessly and quickly. Obviously it is right to be robust towards such critics. Having been embarked on, the policy must in broad terms be given a reasonable chance to show some success, which we may interpret as continuation until the end of next year.

But there is a strand of criticism which accepts the general thrust of policy as necessary but urges either that it needs supplementing by other measures or that it has become for some reasons 'too severe'. These criticisms need to be taken seriously both on grounds of substance and because we may be faced with such a ground-swell of protest that modifications of policy occur in any case whether well justified or not.

As regards supplementary measures, it is hard to think what anyone could mean beyond some form of more explicit or more severe action on incomes. For example, it is beginning to be urged that we need a freeze. It seems to me that it may come to this and that it would be worth doing some work on what might be involved – when it would be imposed; how it

---

[6] McMahon, 'Policy'.

would be organised and policed; what other ancillary measure might be appropriate with it; what would be likely to be its effects on exchange rate, interest rates etc; and most important of all, how long it would have to last and how one could conceive with coming out of it. But this is perhaps not an immediate question; although a freeze should presumably ideally be imposed at the beginning of a wage round, there is still some time before it is likely that this becomes an urgent policy option.

Short of a freeze there is the question of tackling public pay. Here some of the questions are: should there be a norm for pay or should cash limits continue to be relied on? What should in either case the figure be? When should it be announced? What differential complications arise for local authorities and nationalised industries compared with central government? It may be that it is worth trying to get together some views on these questions. It may be that this is relatively urgent and that one might want to announce something by ? July.

There is further the possibility of somehow backing up the monetary policy for the private sector by more governmental explanation and exhortation. It is not clear what can be said on this other than to urge that ministers talk more firmly to employers (and perhaps the trade unions?). But there is perhaps a question as to whether some degree of quantification should be introduced – despite the government's great reluctance to be seen to be sliding towards a norm. Perhaps general statements about the need for some reduction in real wages?

Outside the field of incomes any other measures are probably best considered not as supplementary to the present strategy but as ameliorations of its arguably excess severity.

There is now a strong chorus against the level of interest rates and the exchange rate. Can or should we do anything about either of these?

The calls for lower interest rates may be muted when the May money figures are known, especially since it seems likely that not only will the total increase be large but that it will be characterised by large government borrowing and relatively modest bank lending. This may help to focus commentators on something they have rather overlooked: i.e. that in terms of any reasonable expectations Government borrowing has been abnormally low for some months and is now bound to move to a much higher level. The trends in bank lending may be seen more clearly as a counterpart of this.

It could still be urged that some limited reduction in interest rates is quite likely compatible with continued adherence to the monetary target and that in any case it would be a risk worth taking to secure a relief on the exchange rate. It would seem to me a dangerous line both because the risks are in fact much greater than commentators suggest (because of the extraordinary difficulty we would have in raising interest rates again later this year if it were necessary) and because there is no guarantee that say a 2% [sic] fall in MLR would do much to bring the exchange rate down. Indeed there is plenty of evidence from the past to suggest it might simply whet appetites for more. More fundamentally, there remains the point that interest rates are almost certainly negative in real terms which would suggest that it would be unwise to reduce them on monetary control grounds.

With the exchange rate, however, it is I think not possible to say that it has to be as high as it is as a necessary part of the overall monetary policy. There are the purely exogenous factors – US interest rates and the effects of oil price rises for example – which must surely have meant a higher sterling exchange rate than could legitimately be expected to follow from the nominal interest rates which the domestic monetary policy required. In addition, there is the structural factor of North Sea oil which, though not new, nevertheless does mean an exchange rate higher for manufacturing industry than policy might otherwise require.

It seems to me that there is a major element of arbitrariness in the level of sterling – as indeed in any exchange rate at any particular time. But at present all factors seem to be conspiring on the upside. It would seem, therefore, quite compatible with full adherence to the general policy stance to wish that the exchange rate were lower. The question then is how to translate the wish into a fact. One method would be to lower interest rates – already dismissed above. The other obvious approach would be to abandon our hands-off policy and intervene heavily in an attempt at least to prevent further increases in the rate. The immediate objection of course is that the intervention would tend to swell the money supply. But it can be argued (see [Goodhart's] note on a mixed monetary target/exchange rate objective strategy) that the potential damage to the money supply objectives would be less certain and less severe from this route than from moving interest rates.

Moreover, it seems to me that though it would represent a major departure from our previous practice, we could take a leaf out of the books of the Swiss and others who have experienced excessively high exchange rates. We could make a public announcement that the exchange rate was too high and that we were going to intervene sufficiently to prevent further rises and (perhaps) to try to bring about some reduction. Such a move might I think produce quite a significant fall in the rate even with unchanged interest rates and without the need for a great deal of intervention. It would need much careful thought. Would there for instance be a risk of beginning another 1976? How would we explain why we were not moving interest rates at the same time? Would we get led into further statements later indicating what we did think was an appropriate exchange rate? But I suggest it is worth thinking about rather seriously, because the problem is so serious.

A possible consequence of perhaps incidental advantage might be that this could be a half-way stage towards entry into EMS [the European Monetary System] which I think may turn out to be a useful option for us in the not-too-distant future.

A final area of 'alleviation' is action to help the company sector. I do not go into it here because much has been written about it already and [Walker] has under consideration everything that would seem likely to help.

Dictated but not seen by
the Deputy Governor

30 May 1980

Appendix 5.2 Fforde's note of 30 April 1981[7]

CONFIDENTIAL

THE GOVERNOR   Copies to   the Deputy Governor
                                             Mr Dow

THE DILEMMA OF THE LIBERAL CENTRAL BANKER IN XXTH CENTURY BRITAIN[*]

(A fragment for Easter)

1 In the autumn of 1976 the British Government adopted a published monetary target. It had for some time been urged by the Bank to do this. Failure to do so in the preceding July was judged to have contributed to the ensuing deepening of the exchange crisis of that year. The move brought us broadly into line with practice in North America and West Germany, and was widely regarded in the financial community as putting into use an effective and overriding brake on British inflation.

2 This adoption of a published target was a response to the manifest defeat of 'orthodox' post-war economic management, marked by the fall of the Heath government in March 1974 and the acceleration of inflation in 1974–75. The new Callaghan government, despite its close links with the Trades Unions, then found that it could not in practice rely upon a combination of cautious demand management and voluntary incomes

---

[*] This title is, with adaptation, stolen from Isaiah Berlin, with humble acknowledgements.

[7] Fforde, 'The dilemma of the liberal central banker'.

policies to re-establish the necessary degree of external confidence in its ability to prevent run-away inflation. So it had to adopt monetary targets, and it had (in its terms) to manage demand downwards in an attempt to hit the targets.

3 This was not in practice a move direct to 'monetarism' though the result was sometimes described as 'practical monetarism' in an endeavour to give it the counter-inflationary kudos without the supposed doctrinal stigma. It would be more correct to say that the move was an exercise in 'practical corporatism' in that it gave or purported to give the Treasury an additional persuasive card in its endless game of pressure against sectional interests. In so far as use of the card required justification in terms of intellectual economics, the result can only be described in retrospect as patently ambiguous.

4 Attention to the money supply was partly justified on arguments that it was the best available indicator of 'thrust', in the context of a continuing if more cautious strategy of demand management and incomes policy, and partly on arguments that a monetary target provided an overriding framework of financial stability within which demand management could subordinately be pursued. As the Mais Lecture saw it: 'Monetary policy is often classed as an *instrument of demand management*: in practice, until we have made more progress with inflation, its services are more likely to be pre-empted by the need to use it as *an instrument against inflation*' (my italics). This was a case of keeping a foot firmly in both camps; as was also strongly suggested by a continued concentration on broad money and its direct links with government finance, bank lending and so forth rather than on the 'black box' characteristics of narrow money.

5 In the end, this experiment in 'practical monetarism' as an adjunct to 'practical corporatism' came to grief in the 'winter of discontent' and the fall of the Callaghan government. There followed the election of the Thatcher administration whose Treasury Ministers, and their private economic advisers, were determined to abandon 'corporatism' and 'practical monetarism' in favour of straight gradualist monetarism, Chicago style. But they were not at first taken altogether seriously. The Budget of July 1979, and retention of a £M3 target, was regarded more as managing demand downwards, in orthodox disinflationary fashion, than as a preliminary exercise in managing the fiscal/monetary balance within an overriding framework of money supply control; while Mr Lawson's argument that the increase in VAT would not put up prices overall was treated as a jeu d'esprit rather than a serious opinion. More importantly, 'rational expectations' failed to respond to the change in political direction and an ominously excessive pay round got under way. As for the Bank, we

remained 'practical monetarists', with feet in both camps, though the monetarist foot was for a time somewhat more in evidence than the demand management foot.

6 It was this reluctance to follow all the way the strategic change in governmental approach to macroeconomic policy that first tended to make communication difficult between the Bank and the government, and set us at odds with it in times of stress. For example, in the discussions on monetary base control that took place in the winter of 1979/80, we were baffled by an appearance of Ministerial indifference to the overriding question of abandoning discretionary control of short-term interest rates and by Ministerial refusal even to consider the domestic monetary implications of full entry into the EMS. For their part, Ministers could not understand why a Bank that seemed to share their monetary objectives did not at the same time show enthusiasm for avant garde methods of monetary control when existing methods did not seem to be effective in controlling £M3.

7 By the spring of 1980, the differences of approach were becoming more apparent. The Bank, as a practical monetarist, objected instinctively to the publication of the medium term financial strategy without perhaps fully appreciating why Treasury Ministers could not possibly do without it. Likewise we were at a loss to understand how the government could insist on a published strategy which in our terms seemed to offer no prospect of sufficient success and every prospect of a dangerous decline in public support. But for Treasury Ministers the MTFS was the Ark of a new Covenant, differentiating their whole approach from that of every other government since the last war; and the gloomy forecasts of Keynesian models were regarded as merely the reflection of the wrongheaded political economy of those who fed in their assumptions. But it was these Ministers, in the conditions of 1980/81, who were about to be forced by the severity of the recession and of the pressures on the corporate sector to behave slightly and very reluctantly in the manner of the 'practical monetarist'.

8 In the spring of 1980 upward pressures on short-term rates were resisted. In July MLR was reduced when the monetary position did not justify it. In November, despite highly excessive growth in £M3, MLR was reduced again – partly in anticipation of lower monetary growth in the future. For Treasury Ministers all of this was somehow accommodated within the philosophy of the MTFS; and an easing of monetary policy was indeed latterly accompanied by a tightening of fiscal policy. At the same time pressure on the Bank to alter the system of monetary control in favour of diminishing discretionary influence on money rates was intensified, with some success.

9 If the stresses of 1980/81 obliged Ministers to temper a little the practical rigour of their strategy, they obliged the Bank to begin re-thinking the ambiguities of its practical monetarism and to contemplate re-establishing its macroeconomic attitudes on firmer ground nearer the 'Keynesian' camp. Examining and assessing the growth of £M3 in terms of sectoral imbalances, judging the pressures on the corporate sector in terms of external competitiveness (including the exchange rate), looking at the PSBR in terms of contracyclical demand management, and judging the Budget's effect on aggregate demand, all came naturally and positively to the Bank. But for the Government most of these seem to have been no more than a check-list of convenient excuses, to be forgotten as soon as possible after use, forgotten notably in the Budget of 1981/82 and its reaffirmation of the MTFS.

10 The basic ambiguity of our 'practical monetarism' was in part the reflection of a compromise on the part of the Bank. On the one side were those who felt that the re-introduction of a declaratory restraint on money, somewhat analogous to the provisions of the 1844 Bank Charter Act, would have a valuable and lasting effect on inflationary behaviour at an acceptable real cost in lost output and jobs. On the other side were those who felt that steering by the monetary aggregates would prove a very hit and miss method of temporarily reducing inflation at very heavy cost indeed. Behind these differences of view about solutions lay differences of view about the ultimate causes of inflation, and their strength; but in the dark days of 1976 it was possible to sink these differences in face of the intractable external crisis and its domestic inflationary implications.

11 These underlying differences of view illustrate the Dilemma of the liberal Central Banker in Twentieth Century Britain. Discerning them has been complicated by the prevailing dominance of econometric models, with their 'forecasts', 'scenarios', 'simulations', 'robust (or unrobust) relationships' and the like. These constructions encourage people to think that 'the economy' is a stable and largely determinist system that will reliably respond in predictable ways to external 'stimuli'. This kind of economy is supposedly rather like a human body that is vulnerable to smallpox but responds predictably to vaccination, and is supposedly quite unlike the body that is vulnerable to the common cold, whose virus mutates so frequently that no vaccination is reliably effective for long. In this way, econometricism encourages lay people to believe that scientific discovery in economics, by white-collar people working with statistics, equations, and computers, can in practice provide *the* solution, or solutions, to obstinate economic problems. It is only when one observes the often remarkable correlation between the

output of models and the political attitude of their operators that one begins to see through the mists of algebra the familiar landscape of economists disagreeing with one another and of laymen using abstract economics to support their own prejudices.

12 This ill-tempered digression about models helps to uncover and illuminate the underlying difference of approach between 'monetarism' on the one hand and (for want of a better word) 'pragmatism' on the other. Monetarists, like marxists and others, are 'system people'. They are possessed of a systemic theory, or Revelation, which provides them with a single normative and overriding solution to economic problems and enables them to regard those who disagree as enemies, to be fought and if possible eliminated. Allegedly determinist theory, on one view logically devoid of ethical content, gets converted into the normative support of a Calvinist crusade. Of course, some degree of expedient softening is allowable: but as Sir Geoffrey Howe aptly remarked at a recent meeting, to the distaste of central bankers present, it is allowable 'only so long as the Ten Commandments remain hanging on the wall'.

13 The dilemma of the liberal central banker, to get back to the point, is that of the pragmatist par excellence who approves of the general direction in which the Crusader wants to go but finds himself dragged too far and then regarded by the Crusader as at best a reluctant fellow-traveller and at worst an enemy within the gates. Central banks in the twentieth century became discretionary managers of money because Calvinist methods, with their Iron Laws, were broken in the West by force of circumstance. Central bankers then became accustomed to saying that theirs was 'an art, not a science'. 'Mechanistic' became one of their terms of abuse. Yet their pragmatism was habitually conservative, and in practice reminiscent of the Calvinism they replaced. Devaluation, inflation, government deficits, industrial democracy, 'living beyond one's means' and the like, were all definitely bad even in quite small doses. Hair shirts were always a good thing. Discretion, in the safe hands of the central bank, was allowed. But in the wrong hands it became 'laxity' and 'permissiveness'. The Bank of England was no exception in these respects; though the eventual agony of its dilemma has been made worse by the lack of independence. Fellow-travelling is bad enough. Being a Crusader's Creature is almost unbearable.

14 The novelist Turgenev, when his like dilemma became unbearable, had a nervous breakdown and fled to Paris from St Petersburg. That course is not open to us. All we can do is either to stop grumbling and fellow-travel without further complaint, or else make quite clear the gulf between us and the system-men. But choosing the latter implies a

willingness to swallow our pride and admit that hair shirts can sometimes be vicious. Perhaps that is the task of the second Mais Lecture.

[Signed by J. S. Fforde]
10 April 1981

Annotation by J. S. Fforde

Mr George, Mr Goodhart – I dare to suggest you might read this. The argument, if there be one, goes unclearly in parts; but the conclusion is not too bad. It is a fragment, out of which quite a lot could be assembled if one had the time.

Annotation by C. A. E. Goodhart

JSFf Thank you. Fascinating. But how do you propose to control inflation without very hairy shirts? By an incomes policy? Can that trick be worked? If not, then what, other than our hair shirts?

6   1981 and all that

William Keegan

The 1981 Budget was a very important event, for several reasons. For one thing, it has gone down in the annals as a turning point, both in the fortunes of the British economy and in the health of the first Thatcher government. For another, it is widely cited as definitive proof that the 364 economists who wrote their critical letter to *The Times* were plain wrong to argue that the Budget was misconceived. Third, what I regard as the mythology surrounding this Budget has influenced recent British economic policy in what, again for me, has been a severely detrimental fashion.

I shall deal with these points in turn. First, however, we must consider the background. The 1981 Budget, and the myths surrounding it, need to be considered in the light of the dramatic impact on the economy occasioned by Sir Geoffrey Howe's first Budget, of June 1979. It suits apologists for the Thatcher governments to argue that they inherited a dangerous inflationary situation and brought it under control. This, for example, was the claim made by Lord Lawson of Blaby at a Treasury/Mile End Group seminar on the 1981 Budget in May 2013.[1] In fact, the annual inflation rate at election time in 1979 was around 10 per cent.[2] Subsequent developments were not helped by the impact on import prices of the second oil crisis, which occurred that year (the first, in 1973–74, having had a direct impact on inflation in the middle of the 1970s). But the development of inflation in the British economy in 1979–80 was far greater than could be attributed to the second oil crisis, with other OECD economies suffering nothing like the experience by which UK inflation rose to a peak of 21.9 per cent in May 1980.[3] Not to put too fine a

---

[1] 'Learning the lessons of past spending reviews: the 1981 Budget', Treasury/Mile End Group seminar held at HMT on 1 May 2013; an abridged transcript is available at www.mileendgroup.com/2013/05/16/learning-lessons-spending-reviews-1981-budget.

[2] The last inflation number published before the May 1979 general election showed the RPI rising by 9.8 per cent in the year to March. The April figure of 10.1 per cent was published a week after the election.

[3] Average OECD inflation in 1980 was 10.2 per cent, versus 18 per cent in the United Kingdom.

point upon it, the inflation crisis the new government was struggling to overcome in 1980–81 was largely of its own making.

A political party whose most memorable campaign poster in the 1979 general election had proclaimed 'Labour isn't working' was presiding over what became the steepest rise in unemployment since World War II. The forecasts presented to ministers such as James Prior, the Secretary of State for Employment, in the run-up to the 1981 Budget were dire. So was the state of much of British industry, which was of increasing concern to ministers, to the official Treasury and to the Bank of England. Yet it need not have been so bad. The incoming government in 1979 was determined to make a splash with its first Budget, and warnings about the implications for the retail prices index of the budgetary measures were cavalierly swept aside. Thus one official recalled warning Margaret Thatcher that the near-doubling of most VAT rates would add a straight four percentage points to the RPI, only to be told 'No it won't, because we will control the money supply'.[4]

The Conservative government's problems with measuring and trying to control the money supply have been well documented. But there remains little understanding of the essential reason for the crisis with which Nos. 10 and 11 Downing Street were faced early in 1981 as the Budget preparations got under way. I include No. 10 as well as No. 11 because the intervention of No. 10 in the Budget strategy was crucial, even if the evidence is not entirely clear from the contemporary documents now available at the National Archives.

It is clear from the recently available archives that the Treasury, the Bank of England and No. 10 were all concerned in 1980 and early 1981 about the state of British industry. As I reported at the time, things had got to the stage that the Chairman of Imperial Chemical Industries – then Britain's 'bellwether' company – went to No. 10 and asked Thatcher whether she wanted his company to remain in Britain. Sir John Hoskyns, then head of the No. 10 Policy Unit, expresses similar worries in his memoirs about the condition of another company, International Computers Ltd, then a beacon of the computer industry. There is abundant evidence that in the Budget preparations the Treasury was anxious, within the constraints imposed by the fashionable obsession with the public sector borrowing requirement, to assist British industry at the expense of the personal sector.[5] The emphasis at the Treasury was on relief for companies to alleviate the impact on their competitiveness and finances of the high exchange rate.

---

[4] Conversation with Treasury official, 1979.

[5] The obsession with the PSBR coincided in January with advice from up-and-coming Treasury official Andrew Turnbull that the Bank was having no problems with sales of gilts.

Britain's real exchange rate (that is, the quoted rate adjusted for inflation) had risen by over 30 per cent between 1978 and 1981. In their obsession with monetary targets, British policy makers thought they were taking a leaf out of West German policy makers' books. But what the Bundesbank was really interested in was the real exchange rate. The then President of the Bundesbank, Dr Otmar Emminger, told the Commons Treasury and Civil Service Committee in 1982 that in 1979–81 the pound had experienced 'by far the most excessive overvaluation which any major currency has experienced in recent monetary history'.[6]

It is true that the Bank, and some in the Treasury, were worried about the high exchange rate. But the fashionable view at the time was that this was the inevitable result of possession of North Sea oil – despite the fact that many other oil producers around the world were not suffering such overvaluations. This is where the influence of Alan Walters, Thatcher's part-time economic adviser, proved vital. Walters was a frequent flyer between London and Washington, and had regular first-hand experience of an overvalued pound, which had risen from a low of $1.56 during the 1976 IMF crisis to a high of $2.46 in 1981.

This brings us to the essence of the 1981 Budget strategy, which the 364 economists could not possibly have known about. Thanks to the crucial intervention of Professor Walters, a study was commissioned from Professor Jürg Niehans, of the University of Berne, which found that no more than 20 per cent of the recent appreciation of the pound could be attributed to sterling's status as a 'petrocurrency', and that the main problem was the very tight monetary squeeze.[7] This was extremely embarrassing to the monetarist evangelicals, who had placed their faith in the broad definition of money supply (£M3) and who were obsessed with the desire to curb its growth. This measure grew by an annualised 19.6 per cent in the fourteen months to April 1981, against a target range of 7 to 11 per cent.[8] Therefore, by the twisted logic of the particular form of monetarism ruling at the time, the monetary squeeze was not tight enough, and the pound was so high because of its petrocurrency status. It was about this period that the Governor of the Bank of England himself, Gordon Richardson, observed to me some time later: 'One had only to look out of the window to realise that monetary policy was too tight.' And I believe it was around this time that I myself coined the term 'sado-monetarism'.

---

[6] Treasury and Civil Service Committee, session 1981–82, international monetary arrangements, minutes of evidence, Monday 25 October, HC 403–viii, 238. Emminger was referring to an earlier paper: O. Emminger, 'Exchange rate policy reconsidered', Group of Thirty Occasional Paper no. 10 (1982).

[7] J. Niehans, *The appreciation of sterling: causes, effects, policies* (Rochester, 1981).

[8] *Bank of England Quarterly Bulletin*, 21, September 1981, tab. 11.1.

Amid the endless disputes, in memoirs and seminars, about this most controversial of Budgets, and despite all the attention devoted to the arcane debates about various forms of monetary control, one thing stands out: the 364 economists did not know that a U-turn was under way in economic policy, and that the strategy was to achieve a devaluation of sterling via an easing of monetary policy. True, the two percentage point cut in interest rates on Budget day might have offered a clue, but it was not an obvious one. Dramatic reductions in the exchange rate in the past (1931, 1949, 1967 and 1972) had boosted output. The intention of the Walters camp was not dissimilar from these historical precedents.

Most of the attention was devoted to the tightening of fiscal policy. The Treasury itself was arguing for a net contraction from the pre-Budget forecast for the growth of the PSBR, but the Walters camp argued for, and achieved, a lower one. And it was, of course, the contraction in PSBR that so distressed the 364 economists.

Within the No. 10 Policy Unit, Walters, Hoskyns and the seconded retailer David Wolfson fought hard in January and February to advocate an even tougher Budget than the one that was being contemplated by the Chancellor and the official Treasury. There was many a difficult moment. For example, Walters and co. contemplated resignation, and Thatcher threatened Sir Geoffrey Howe with the sack should the tougher Budget that No. 10 was advocating lead to political disaster.

One of the ironies of the situation was that the PSBR had risen to acquire such importance because it was a key element in the measurement of £M3. Yet Niehans had demonstrated that £M3 gave a wildly misleading picture and that monetary policy was far too tight. Walters and co. were worried about the reaction of the markets, however, and wanted to ease the passage of the undeclared U-turn on monetary and exchange rate policy with an impressive tightening of fiscal policy. Now, not only did the 364 not know about the strategy, but they were also writing in complete ignorance of subsequent plans to abolish hire purchase controls – a move that gave a hefty contribution to what subsequently became known, from 1983 onwards, as the 'Lawson boom'. Nor did the 364 know at that stage about the enormous Keynesian boost to the world economy that would come from the United States during the 1980s, a contrast in reality to the Reagan administration's rhetoric against 'big government'.

I see no reason to alter the basic judgement I made of the importance of Walters and the unknown (to the 364) strategy in my book *Mrs Thatcher's economic experiment*.[9] In his exhaustive new book *Margaret Thatcher: the*

---

[9] Keegan, *Mrs Thatcher's economic experiment*.

authorized biography, Charles Moore quotes Sir Douglas Wass, who was Treasury Permanent Secretary in 1981, as saying 'The 1981 Budget did enable us to have lower interest rates and therefore did lower exchange rates'.[10] In *Britain's economic renaissance*, Walters writes: 'It seemed to me likely that the exchange rate would fall as a consequence of the monetary easing ... So it did.'[11] The strategy, supplemented by the abolition of credit controls, took time to work, however. With characteristic gusto, Lord Lawson claims that the recovery began with the Budget.[12] This claim does not fit easily with the fact that UK gross domestic product fell by over 1 per cent between 1980 and 1981. As the former senior Treasury official Sir Leo Pliatzky has noted in *The Treasury under Mrs Thatcher*, the second oil crisis caused a general world slowdown after 1979, but 'in 1981 Britain was the only major economy where output was less than in 1979'.[13]

The circumstances surrounding, and the consequences of, the 1981 Budget were such that it seems entirely inappropriate to me that George Osborne should have seen that Budget as an appropriate guide to his Budget strategy of 2010. In 1981 the planned reduction in the PSBR was seen as the necessary counterpart to a plan to ease monetary policy and contrive a devaluation. In 2010 interest rates were already close to rock bottom, 'quantitative easing' was all the rage and there had already been a sensational devaluation of some 25 per cent. In 1981 the level of consumer debt was such a non-problem that it was hardly a subject for discussion. The scope for a rise in consumer spending fuelled by the abolition of credit controls was enormous. By contrast, in 2010 the high level of consumer debt was a matter of huge concern, and has, indeed, proved a major constraint on the revival of consumer demand. The post-1981 recovery was not as rapid as has subsequently been painted, and was certainly not precipitated by the fiscal squeeze.

---

[10] Moore, *Margaret Thatcher*, 632.   [11] Walters, *Britain's economic renaissance*, 145.
[12] Lawson, *The view from No. 11*, 98.
[13] L. Pliatzky, *The Treasury under Mrs Thatcher* (Oxford, 1989), 131.

7   The origins of the Budget in 1980

Christopher Collins

Introduction

Few historians, commentators or politicians are guilty of underestimating the significance of the 1981 Budget. The risk is surely the other way, if one dare write that in a volume dedicated to the event. But it is curious that the literature on the actual framing of the Budget is so much dominated by a relatively narrow (though important) issue, namely the slugging match between No. 10 and the Treasury over the exact size of the planned public sector borrowing requirement, which took place in what was then the eleventh hour in budget-making terms, during the last days of February 1981, over sums well within the Treasury's margin of error in estimating the PSBR.[1] The purpose of this chapter is to gain a longer perspective by examining what one might call the Budget's prehistory, and drawing out some of the implications for the thinking behind it. It looks at the evolution of policy in the last half of 1980, a period of some confusion and fluidity (to put it politely), culminating in the Autumn Statement of 24 November 1980 – a much less well remembered event that came close to entering the historical record under the unhappy, and very unThatcherite, designation of a 'mini-budget'.[2]

The original focus on the final weeks of budget making largely came about because it suited the book, or books, to treat it so. As one of the

---

[1] The margin of error on the annual PSBR forecast at that time was around £3 billion. The cut-off for Budget decisions was supplied by the physical demands of printing and distribution. In 1981 the deadline for indirect tax decisions was lunchtime on Friday 20 February, and for direct taxes the following week (for the Budget on 10 March). By 2009 progress was such that Alistair Darling's Budget that year was safe from further tinkering by No. 10 only when he got into his car en route to the Commons to deliver it: A. M. Darling, *Back from the brink: 1,000 days at Number 11* (London, 2011), 232; R. E. G. Howe, 'Money supply, interest rates, the PSBR and the exchange rate', 7 October 1980, London, TNA, PREM 19/179, MTFW 113260.

[2] Tim Lankester's chapter in this volume addresses the detailed business of budget making, greatly clarifying the record on some crucial points. It is an exemplary reconstruction of economic policy making by a well-placed official observer, with which I have made no attempt to compete, ending my piece more or less where his begins.

small team involved in the writing of Margaret Thatcher's *The Downing Street years*, completed in the summer of 1993, I recall the uncomfortable pressure placed on us by the knowledge that her principal colleagues were racing to bring their recollections to market, with Lawson publishing his brilliant memoir *The view from No. 11* just ahead of her, and Howe serving up a *Conflict of loyalty* not long afterwards.[3] Alan Walters quietly advised us by fax, phone and visit how best to parry and return attack, with Lawson his bête noire. For many years these accounts were the only ones drawing on original documents, and, naturally enough, they shaped the literature. In this battle of the books, the making of the Budget was presented as a conflict between No. 10 and the Treasury, each claiming credit for what they took to be a turning point in economic policy and performance while denying it to the others, or at least restricting their share. But, in playing up the argument over paternity, the fallings-out during Thatcher's last government – still painfully recent when the memoirs were written – were being allowed to condition the reading of earlier times.

One should not underplay tensions within the Conservative leadership, including those between Treasury ministers themselves, but the following account places less emphasis on that aspect. The story looks a little different on a longer focus. One discovers some surprising positions on fiscal policy within government, even settled critics of the monetarist experiment, such as the Bank of England's Deputy Governor, Kit McMahon, and Permanent Secretary Sir Douglas Wass, sometimes favouring a tighter fiscal stance. On the monetary side, the situation was rather different, but, again, there is more to say than the paternity framework allowed.

Overshooting monetary targets in the summer of 1980

Over the summer of 1980 it became ever harder to fit economic and monetary developments within the framework of policy. The Medium-Term Financial Strategy had been announced as recently as March, targeting £M3 growth at 7 to 11 per cent for 1980/81. Following the removal of 'the corset', Minimum Lending Rate was cut by one percentage point on 3 July on the premise that £M3 figures were improving, but when the numbers appeared in early August they showed a 5 per cent increase *over the month*. Meeting Howe on 4 August, the Bank's Governor, Gordon Richardson, admitted '£M3 had grown grotesquely', attributing

---

[3] Thatcher, *The Downing Street years*; Lawson, *The view from No. 11*, republished in abridged form as N. Lawson, *Memoirs of a Tory radical* (London, 2010), edited by me; Howe, *Conflict of loyalty*.

only one-third of the increase to the unwinding of corset distortions.[4] Nigel Lawson 'thought the rate of monetary growth too high but saw no reason to believe that a sudden upturn was at hand'.[5] In fact, the increase in August itself was 3 per cent, with the annualised growth rate over the previous six months reaching 26 per cent, making the £M3 target practically unachievable less than halfway through the financial year.

On a monthly basis the PSBR was also overshooting the MTFS projection of £8.5 billion by a very significant amount. There were hopes that later months would undershoot, but in the event they did not. The outturn was a painful £13 billion. Meanwhile, untargeted and unprojected, but far from unwatched, sterling reached the $2.40s in early September, finally peaking at $2.4495 on Friday 24 October.[6]

Holidaying in Switzerland in late August, the Prime Minister lunched with Professor Karl Brunner, who told her that her monetary policy was right but implementation woeful, casting the Bank as chief villain. Thatcher returned to No. 10 in hanging mood. Apprised of the August money figures, she summoned Richardson and castigated the Bank for becoming a 'lender of first resort' (Brunner's exact phrase) and being 'simply unwilling to implement Government strategy'.[7] In her eyes the clearers were just as guilty, if not more so, because she saw them as natural allies who were letting her down: 'The clearing banks did not seem to be deeply attached to the Government strategy. Indeed they were shovelling money out... She felt that the centre-piece of Government strategy was being undermined by her own supporters.'[8] There were a series of such

---

[4] Richardson will have been quoting here an early estimate by Charles Goodhart. Goodhart now thinks two-thirds would be more accurate (personal communication with C. A. E. Goodhart). Like Lawson, the Bank's Eddie George was hopeful about the horrible July figure, calling it 'not in itself unhelpful, since it gets it out of the way', and adding: 'We have no grounds for complaining to the clearing banks about it since they did provide us with the opening to ask them to stagger reintermediation, which we chose not to do.' E. A. J. George, 'Sir Jeremy Morse's call on the Governor', 22 July 1980, London, BOE, G1/552, MTFW 128603; R. I. Tolkien, 'Note of a meeting held at 11 Downing Street on Monday 4 August 1980 at 5.30 pm', 7 August 1980, BOE, 7A133/2, MTFW 113132.

[5] Tolkien, 'Note of a meeting...4 August 1980 at 5.30 pm'.

[6] Sterling in fact went as high as $2.4645 during the day, so that the peak is sometimes quoted as $2.47; the rate at *closure* was $2.4495. For a definitive account, see Bank of England, 'Foreign exchange and gold market report', 24 October 1980, BOE, C8/52, MTFW 129305.

[7] [? M. A. Pattison], 'Summary record of a meeting held at 10 Downing Street at 1800 hours on 3 September 1980', 3 September 1980, TNA, PREM 19/178, MTFW 115636. A much briefer version of this record was circulated around Whitehall: 'M. A. Pattison to A. J. Wiggins', 3 September 1980, BOE, 7A133/2, MTFW 113137.

[8] [? Pattison], 'Summary record of a meeting...3 September 1980', MTFW 115636.

meetings, long remembered by bruised senior staff at the Bank.[9] Following the one on 18 September, Richardson was sufficiently aggrieved at his treatment to raise it with No. 10 on the phone, and he planned to discuss it with the Cabinet Secretary too.[10] Only with difficulty did Howe dissuade the Prime Minister from summoning the clearers.

The Bank of England's response

The records show that, alongside the monetary overrun, the focus of Thatcher's angst was the high level of sterling. This was a topic on which she and the Bank found some agreement. Scouting a way ahead for the Governor after the 18 September meeting, McMahon rejected the notion that the affronted Bank should offer an *apologia* for its conduct of monetary policy (as Charles Goodhart and Christopher Dow had suggested), and instead proposed building on the common ground:

> Here we now have a good starting point in that in response to your explicit question the Prime Minister has told us that she would like to have the exchange rate lower than it is so long as (a) it was consonant with continuance of the existing monetary policy and (b) it did not involve a plunge. Specifically, she indicated that she felt $2.20 would be low enough. She did not want this achieved through intervention. I also noted, though it is perhaps not immediately relevant, that she did not join Lawson's strong rebuttal of the idea of joining the EMS.[11]

At the meeting the Prime Minister had pressed strongly for inflow controls, in the form of differential interest rates, for which she believed there to be a Swiss precedent. McMahon firmly rejected these, as subject to 'enormous loopholes', perverse effects arising from resulting expectations that high interest rates would persist, and the fact that they had not

---

[9] Thatcher was greatly displeased by John Fforde and Eddie George standing in for Richardson and McMahon, who were both abroad when the August £M3 figures were discussed on 8 September, 'T. P. Lankester to A. J. Wiggins', 9 September 1980, BOE, 7A133/2, MTFW 113138.

[10] Richardson had taken it all much more lightly when others were on the receiving end, using an off-colour phrase to characterise Thatcher's famously confrontational dinner with Permanent Secretaries earlier in the year ('the reverse of a gang bang'): G. Hacche and C. Taylor (eds.), *Inside the Bank of England: memoirs of Christopher Dow, chief economist 1973–84* (Basingstoke, 2013), 153; 'T. P. Lankester to A. J. Wiggins', 18 September 1980, BOE, 7A133/2, MTFW 113143; R. C. W. Mayes, 'Note for the record', 19 September 1980, BOE, 7A133/2, MTFW 114080.

[11] Goodhart believes that McMahon was right in this judgement (personal communication with C. A. E. Goodhart); C. W. McMahon, 'The Bank's position on monetary policy', 18 September 1980, BOE, G3/380, MTFW 128593. No. 10's record of the meeting has the Prime Minister saying that 'a rate of between $2.20 and $2.30 would be desirable; anything below $2.20 would jeopardise the fight against inflation': 'T. P. Lankester to A. J. Wiggins', 18 September 1980, BOE, 7A 133/2, MTFW 113143.

been successfully operated 'except to defend or achieve an explicit exchange rate target and then only as an ancillary to massive intervention':

> This leads then to fundamentals. What is really preventing the achievement of the [£M3] target is the development of the PSBR; and what is really wanted by industry both for its own sake and because of its effect on the exchange rate is lower interest rates. There may not in the end prove to be a need to reduce the PSBR: it *may* not be much above target and come right down in the last months of the financial year. But no-one can predict this with confidence and the risks are severe. Thus, there is a case for cutting it significantly on its own merits. If a significant cut were made it then might be possible to lower interest rates by enough to make a dint [sic] on the exchange rate.[12]

The Treasury's response

There were strong echoes of this thinking in parts of the Treasury. Inflow controls were generally rejected, with the head of the Overseas Finance Division, Sir Kenneth Couzens, describing them as 'a leap in the dark', using arguments similar to McMahon's, and Howe concluding that 'the balance of advantage was decisively against'.[13] As papers were prepared for a Downing Street meeting on the topic, an approach not so different from that sketched by McMahon began to take flesh among officials. On Monday 22 September Sir Douglas Wass, Second Permanent Secretary Bill Ryrie and the Chief Economic Adviser, Terry Burns, met with ministers on the basis of a submission by Wass designed (as he put it) 'to pave the way for contingency work if the money and PSBR figures did not come right in the coming weeks and months. We could not now rely on things going right; and if they did not, the credibility of the Government's policy – which was fundamental to the success of that policy – would be at risk.'[14]

Ministers may well have felt officials were trying to bounce them; the record certainly suggests tension between the two. From the ministerial side, Lawson rebutted Wass lengthily and with force:

> *The Financial Secretary* saw no immediate problem of credibility. Financial markets were strong, and the PSBR would undoubtedly turn round (although a question

---

[12] McMahon, 'The Bank's position on monetary policy', MTFW 128593 [emphasis in original].

[13] A. J. Wiggins, 'Note of a meeting held in the Chancellor of the Exchequer's room, HM Treasury, at 4.45 pm on Tuesday, 16 September 1980', BOE, 7A/133/2, MTFW 113141. Lawson was absent from this meeting.

[14] A. J. Wiggins, 'Note of a meeting held in the Chancellor of the Exchequer's room, HM Treasury at 9.30 am on Monday, 22 September 1980', TNA, T386/544, MTFW 128330. Wass had prepared the ground for this meeting in a minute to Howe ten days earlier: D. W. G. Wass, 'Monetary and fiscal policy', 12 September 1980, TNA, T386/544, MTFW 133715.

remained how small it would be in the first quarter of 1981). Difficulties remained over public expenditure, but although the policy might appear to be in poor condition, the Government's determination to stick to that policy despite the difficulties faced by industry was not in doubt; and the longer the Government persisted in this stance, the more credible the policy would be. The Financial Secretary saw no prospect of achieving significant changes in public expenditure or tax receipts during the current financial year, other than through public services pay; and he saw no reason for tax increases now to reduce the 1980–81 PSBR. There was undoubtedly an imbalance between the personal and corporate sectors, and for this reason he favoured attracting more funds into national savings, even at the cost of a higher mortgage rate, together with restraints on consumer credit. He noted that it might be necessary to increase taxes in the 1981 Budget; but at that stage more options would be open, and it would be undesirable for the Government to take hasty and perhaps inappropriate action now.[15]

Officials struck back:

Mr Ryrie emphasised the strong political and industrial pressures for lower interest rates; but could interest rates be reduced consistently with the Government's strategy without some other action as well? He therefore suggested the possibility of a package of measures as a cover for a reduction in interest rates, and accepted that the measures would have to be primarily aimed at 1981–82. . . Nevertheless an early announcement could give a substantial boost to confidence.[16]

Summing up, Howe withheld explicit authority to plan for a package, although Burns was to prepare a paper on the 'medium-term fiscal stance', in connection with which Howe noted: 'The 1981 Budget was fundamental to the Government's success.'[17]

Meeting without officials a few days beforehand, at Treasury prayers, ministers and advisers had spoken more frankly and in some contrast.[18] In 'extended discussion', there was hope that the 1980/81 PSBR might yet come right, but realisation that it might not, and that significant public expenditure reductions would not be achieved within the current financial

[15] Wiggins, 'Note of a meeting held . . . 22 September 1980', MTFW 128330 [emphasis in original].

[16] Ibid.

[17] Ibid. The Bank received orders that day from the Treasury 'to prepare as quickly as possible contingency plans to restrict non-resident acquisition of BGS [gilts]'. The commissioning of such a scheme was no small thing, given the possibility of a leak. That gilts were initially the focus suggests the Treasury was aiming for the minimum it could get away with. By 14 November 1980 much more extensive controls had been prepared, covering the ability of non-residents to bring new funds into the United Kingdom 'for the purpose of interest-bearing investment'. Bank of England notices were printed in proof: D. A. C. Nendick, 'Contingency plans for inflows controls', 14 November 1980, BOE, 11A56/11, MTFW 128445 (proofs included); D. A. Dawkins, 'Inflow controls', 22 September 1980, BOE, 11A56/11, MTFW 128444.

[18] G. S. Cardona, 'Chancellor's meeting, 17 September 1980', Churchill, Adam Ridley MSS, 'Prayers' file 4, MTFW 113274.

year. It was concluded that, while there was 'a reasonable chance that fiscal measures would not be required before the budget', they *might* be necessary and contingency planning *should* take place.[19] Equally, it is obvious that there was great political discomfort about a step so reminiscent of Healey – the kind of makeshift many of those present had damned and double-damned in recent memory. A large political element entered into the thinking, the meeting agreeing in principle that if a package was required it had best take place before the party conference, then barely a fortnight away, although it was pointed out that such a timetable was 'operationally out of the question'.[20] It was noted also: 'If there were a fiscal package, it would probably be sensible to include some action on consumer credit.'[21] Contingency plans for such action had been drawn up earlier in the year at the bidding of No. 10, Lawson pushing hard to devise a scheme against Treasury resistance. And, on the subject of inflow controls Lawson broke ranks with the general Treasury view, openly colliding with Howe:

> The Chancellor found the argument that, once imposed, such controls would be difficult to remove a persuasive one. The Financial Secretary was less persuaded of the difficulty of removing controls: other countries (e.g. the Swiss) had abolished them. However he was uncertain of the monetary consequences of inflow controls. The Chancellor concluded that the underlying monetary and fiscal situation was what mattered.[22]

One almost has the sense of entering a looking-glass world, transported by MTFS magic. The monetarists ponder direct controls, the Keynesians hanker for emergency action to cut the PSBR. The Keynesians would have preferred to scrap the MTFS outright, naturally enough, and those monetarists who had placed faith in £M3 as the target aggregate (by no means all, of course) were thinking again.[23] Yet few doubted that the government had at least to pretend to live within the strategy for the time being. In this sense, if not in others, MTFS was working as intended.[24]

---

[19] Ibid.   [20] Ibid.   [21] Ibid.   [22] Ibid.

[23] A pregnant footnote to the MTFS table setting out the £M3 targets stated that 'the way in which the money supply is defined for target purposes may need to be adjusted from time to time as circumstances change'. But, of course, that was more easily said than done. Much political capital had been sunk in £M3, not least by the Prime Minister. *FSBR 1980–81*, 16.

[24] McMahon is an exception, his position evolving as sterling rose. Three days before it peaked against the dollar he suggested abandoning MTFS targets in favour of an explicit focus on the exchange rate, backed by 'a substantial visible intervention onslaught'. But even he felt the need to add: 'There can be no question of reversing the broad thrust of the strategy: that would give us the worst of all worlds.' C. W. McMahon, 'The roll-over and policy generally: tomorrow's meeting with the Chancellor', 21 October 1980, BOE, G3/380, MTFW 128440. He included no such proviso in C. W. McMahon, 'Policy and the exchange rate', 27 October 1980, BOE, G3/380, MTFW 128441 (a document handled with the tightest security within the Bank).

It is surprising at first sight that Lawson should have shown any interest in inflow controls. He had been the Treasury minister most ready to defend the counter-inflationary merits of a high pound. He had been the strongest advocate of the early abolition of exchange control and the most eloquent exponent of Thatcherism as a free market creed. But one should examine the context, which supplied many unpalatable options and not much else. At the end of the month Lawson sent Howe his views of a draft Treasury paper entitled 'Inflow controls and other options for reducing the exchange rate'.[25] The paper had been triggered by pressure on the topic from No. 10; its very existence was significant and probably unwelcome to him. Lawson paid it the closest attention. He detected in the paper, and warned against, a weakening of previous Treasury opposition to intervention in the foreign exchange markets and rejected also various suggested approaches to 'talking down' the currency. His objection to talking down was partly that it 'seems to me to miss the point: it is hardly likely to provide the political cover which is inherent in the notion of inflow controls'.[26] He expressed disappointment that 'officials have been able to come up with so little' on the latter and suggested they be looked at again, as a revenue measure:

The advantage of this approach is that we could pronounce ourselves satisfied so long as additional tax revenue was produced: this should greatly reduce the administrative paraphernalia needed to make thoroughgoing inflow controls effective, would not require any justification in terms of an actual flaw in the exchange rate, would be easier presentationally, and would provide greater political cover (and fewer risks) than the 'talking down' option.[27]

Lawson makes no mention of inflow controls in *The view from No. 11* (nor do Thatcher or Howe in their books), but he does concede that sterling offered 'a clear example of overshooting' at the end of 1980 and the beginning of 1981.[28] And surely he was registering the strength of the political wind blowing from No. 10, which had reached storm force by this point. Options within the existing policy were diminishing to the degree that radical departures were rendered thinkable, however unattractive. By late November the Bank had prepared a scheme on forty-eight-hour readiness, and a wide circle knew of it, with all the risks involved.

[25] N. Lawson, 'Reducing the exchange rate: inflow controls and other options', 29 September 1980, BOE, 7A134/16, MTFW 113083; R. Lavelle, 'Inflow controls and other options for reducing the exchange rate', 23 September 1980, BOE, 11A56/11, MTFW 128443. Dow understandably drew attention to the paper, but, as the citation shows, he is wrong to think that the Bank 'was not consulted and did not hear about [it] till later': Hacche and Taylor, *Inside the Bank of England*, 172.
[26] Lawson, 'Reducing the exchange rate', MTFW 113083.   [27] Ibid.
[28] Lawson, *The view from No. 11*, 63.

October–November 1980: planning the Autumn Statement

Tension and uncertainty as to the next steps in policy only deepened as autumn ran on. There was a long and unhappy Downing Street 'monetary policy seminar' on Monday 13 October showing a general movement towards fiscal tightening on all sides – No. 10, Treasury and Bank – albeit with action in the spending round and the next budget in view, rather than an announcement of new taxes in the Autumn Statement.[29] There was significantly less agreement on monetary policy – indeed, signs that it was difficult even to discuss. And there was almost a despairing tone to some of Howe's interventions, for example on inflow controls, when he commented that Treasury analysis had convinced him they would not work, 'though he would not rule out altogether some inflow control measure if only for presentational reasons'.[30] He used a similar formula on interest rates, almost as if inviting people – perhaps one person in particular – to force his hand:

> The Chancellor said that he doubted whether an MLR reduction could be justified on monetary grounds. But it might be necessary – on political grounds and in order to persuade colleagues to further cut public expenditure – to take the risk.[31]

The record suggests that the Prime Minister did not directly respond. In fact, she seems deliberately to have avoided opening up the question of interest rates and sterling at this meeting: having demanded work on inflow controls, she showed no inclination to discuss currency matters in any depth, quite possibly fearing leaks from a group as large, and as miserable, as this one. Instead she closed discussion with the words 'it would be necessary to think further about the possibility of pushing the exchange rate down'.[32] The pound was eleven days short of its peak against the dollar.

A week later, on 20 October, the Chairman of ICI visited the Prime Minister to warn her that the company was about to declare its first ever quarterly loss. Howe was in Luxembourg, and Thatcher summoned Wass

---

[29] Dow felt that the Treasury had arranged for the Bank to carry the can, again, at this meeting: 'The Chancellor's aim must have been, by confessing error and declaring repentance himself, and expecting us to stand up for ourselves, to deflect the wrath of his Goddess onto the Bank.' At the end of the meeting cake was served, which the Prime Minister pressed on everyone; it was a birthday gift to her from a school in Finchley. Goodhart recalls Eddie George whispering that he was not sure he would be able to choke it down (personal communication with C. A. E. Goodhart); Hacche and Taylor, *Inside the Bank of England*, 169; 'T. P. Lankester to A. J. Wiggins', 14 October 1980, TNA, PREM 19/179, MTFW 113264.

[30] Ibid.   [31] Ibid.   [32] Ibid.

for comment. They met for a little over an hour at the end of the working day.[33] Wass later took pains to remind Howe:

The Prime Minister expressed a very strong wish that I should explore ways of mitigating the adverse conditions in which British industry is operating, so that good and viable companies like ICI should not be driven to the wall. You yourself endorsed this wish and authorised me to submit some options to you.[34]

It is impossible to know quite what Thatcher asked or expected Wass to do, but he surely made the most of whatever authority she gave him.[35] He consulted with Ryrie and others 'on a strict "need to know" basis', a group resembling that which had approached ministers in late September, and produced a paper blandly entitled 'Policy options', which Howe forwarded to No. 10. The Governor was told about it 'in general terms'.

This was an unusual initiative, and the document matches it. Wass based his case for a change of policy on the unexpectedly high level of sterling, much as McMahon had pegged that territory as the most hopeful one for the Bank to occupy after its roasting in September. He laid out six options, 'listed in descending order of compatibility with the Government's present strategy of gearing down inflation through strict control of the money supply', namely:

---

[33] 'MT engagement diary', 20 October 1980 ('1845–2000 Sir Douglas Wass'), MTFW 113609. See also D. W. G. Wass, 'The exchange rate', 21 October 1980, TNA, T386/545, MTFW 133716, which recounts part of the discussion. On Wass's initiative officials met separately on 24 October 'to consider the possibilities for action if the exchange rate continued to move upward': J. M. G. Taylor, 'Note of a meeting', 24 October 1980, TNA, T386/545, MTFW 133719.

[34] D. W. G. Wass, 'Policy options', 5 November 1980, TNA, PREM 19/174, MTFW 113271.

[35] An intriguing contemporary document suggests that senior officials felt Wass was sometimes inclined to push ministers harder than was wise. At a regular meeting of Permanent Secretaries in economic departments, plus Sir Robert Armstrong, Terry Burns and Christopher Dow, Wass asked: 'Should they seek to make Ministers take stock of the political dangers facing them – not just a ½ hr discussion in Cabinet, but a ½ day at Chequers? Robert Armstrong took up someone's remark that there would be a clear "kickback" if civil servants started to try to tell Ministers about politics – "Kickback is just the word". No political taking stock would take place unless the PM desired it, which she did not.'
But this response to Wass did not imply confidence in the policy on the part of those present. Dow also noted: 'The to and fro of discussion after some time produced recognition that action to ameliorate the recession – whether via reduction of the exchange rate or by significant aid to industry – could not be done within the present economic strategy. Douglas Wass allowed this conclusion to emerge, while himself maintaining a white mantle of orthodoxy. . . But the general feeling was quite clearly despairing worry at the developing recession and the growing unemployment. The mood seemed to me very clear and unanimous with no difference between Terry Burns and the rest. . . [Armstrong] evidently thinks quite strongly of lowering the exchange rate by any means possible, and of joining EMS.' J. C. R. Dow, 'Short term economic policy group (STEP)', 15 January 1981, BOE, 7A173/8, MTFW 128043.

(1) inflow controls and some minor measures intended to reduce the exchange rate;

(2) a modest cut in interest rates;

(3) a large reduction in interest rates;

(4) an explicit exchange rate policy;

(5) a significant tax switch to the benefit of companies; or

(6) a pay freeze.[36]

That inflow controls were considered the most compatible policy is startling. Wass, like Howe, made a sceptic's case for them, on presentational grounds, offering perhaps 'short-term gains'.[37] Having initially rejected controls, the Treasury and the Bank seem to have reconciled themselves to the possibility that they might be forced to live with them, and were aiming now to minimise the damage. If the Prime Minister wanted them, she could have them, fully informed of the risks, embarrassments and complications. McMahon had similarly switched to advising the governor to take the line that the Bank was not 'doctrinaire' on the question, that such controls might be worth going for 'on a strictly temporary rough and ready basis', although 'very much against the spirit of present policies'.[38]

By a modest cut in interest rates Wass meant two points off MLR 'at most'. He went on, in words that echo Ryrie's remarks, in the 22 September meeting:

There would be some presentational difficulties with a modest interest rate cut, particularly following the October monetary figures. These could be mitigated if the move were linked to some apparent strengthening of fiscal policy – e.g. an announcement of the outcome of the public expenditure review (though this does not now look a promising piece of cover), or of the new taxes that have been under discussion, or the outcome of our consideration of monetary base control.[39]

Cover again. Thatcher annotated the document: 'Preliminary view: options (iii), (iv), (v) and (vi) are <u>NOT ON</u>. The long-term damage would be too great.'[40] Her reaction was immediately relayed to the Treasury.

Thatcher, Howe and Wass met at No. 10 for ninety minutes on 12 November to discuss the paper, Howe arriving fifteen minutes ahead for a preliminary chat. The Bank was not represented at the meeting, and,

---

[36] Wass, 'Policy options', MTFW 113271.   [37] Ibid.

[38] Lukewarm official embrace was probably better calculated to kill off prime ministerial interest in inflow controls than outright opposition, but it might be over-subtle to suggest that was the intention: C.W. McMahon, 'Inflow controls: possible line to take', 16 September 1980, BOE, G3/380, MTFW 128594.

[39] Wass, 'Policy options', MTFW 113271.

[40] Wass, 'Policy options' (annotation by M.H. Thatcher), MTFW 113271 [emphasis in original].

although a full retinue from No. 10 was there, Thatcher asked them not to speak.[41] Discussion focused entirely on Wass's options (1) and (2). Howe now sought, and was given, the authority to cut MLR by two percentage points and 'to demonstrate that the Government was not abandoning the monetary strategy' by announcing 'a credible package of measures', which would require the preannouncement of some of his intentions on tax for 1981/82.[42] He firmly rejected inflow controls, an option that Thatcher seems to have relinquished only with reluctance, looking to bargain them away: 'The Prime Minister said that she hoped that, even if option 1 were not adopted, the Treasury would consider switching Bank "customers"' transactions off market again.'[43]

Howe entered a caveat: it would all involve 'a considerable element of risk; questions would be raised as to whether the Government was doing enough to get the fiscal balance right, and this might mean that the next budget would have to be even more restrictive; alternatively, it might conceivably be necessary to put MLR up again'.[44]

Significance of these events for the Budget

Thus the Thatcher government decided to introduce something that looked very much like a 'mini-Budget' and adopted the stratagem of tightening fiscal policy to give cover for loosening the monetary side. The measures were seen and presented as pointing the way for the 1981 Budget. The initiative largely originated with officials unsympathetic to the fundamentals of policy, who overcame understandable political reluctance because the government was acting *faute de mieux*, the policy climate having become sufficiently hostile to tempt even the Prime Minister to reverse a totemic reform by reintroducing an element of exchange control. The result was that, only six weeks after Thatcher had declared herself 'not for turning', the government was making an MLR cut impossible to fit within the framework of the MTFS – a departure publicly unstated, of course, but privately acknowledged, and all but impossible

[41] 'MT engagement diary', 12 November 1980 ('1445 Chancellor of the Exchequer', '1500–1630 Chancellor of the Exchequer and Sir Douglas Wass'), Churchill, THCR 6/1/2/2, MTFW 113632; Hoskyns, *Just in time*, 244, MTFW 113374.
[42] 'T. P. Lankester to A. J. Wiggins', 13 November 1980, TNA, PREM 19/180, MTFW 113270.
[43] Ibid. The Treasury went through the motions of examining Thatcher's suggestion, then turned it down after a diplomatic delay.
[44] Ibid. It is likely that Lawson also had reservations about the November package: see N. Lawson, 'Bank lending', 1 December 1980, BOE, 7A133/3, MTFW 127435.

to disguise from those who understood the policy.[45] If indeed the November measures pointed the way to the 1981 Budget, from a Thatcherite point of view it had a far from promising origin.

Should one accept, then, that the origin of the Budget strategy lay in the Autumn Statement? Did the idea of tightening fiscal policy in order to ease monetary policy carry through into budget making? Certainly, there was no irresistible progress from one to the other. Perhaps there might have been if the outcome of the Autumn Statement had been triumphant, but it was far from that. One finds instead a variety of strong and weak connections.

Among the most straightforward and significant was that the measures passed muster in the markets. An MLR cut of some kind had already been discounted, the timing and the amount being the main issues. The associated fiscal measures did indeed provide cover, doctrine counting for little. Sterling had peaked against the dollar the month beforehand and continued to fall without trace of a rout.[46] Howe's fear that the two percentage point cut might prove too much of a stretch did not come to pass.[47]

Politically, however, the Autumn Statement proved costly – the government was badly battered in the Commons and the press – and it is more likely to have supplied lessons, or warnings, for the Budget. Howe experienced one of the worst periods of his Chancellorship, being sharply attacked by Conservatives as well as political opponents, who successfully maximised the damage by fastening on the failure of the Statement to spell out the fact that employers' National Insurance contributions were increasing.[48]

---

[45] 'It was noted that the authorities had not sought to determine interest rates by reference to movements in £M3, despite what had been seen as a commitment to do this': A. J. Wiggins, 'Note of a meeting held in the Chancellor of the Exchequer's room, HM Treasury on Friday, 6 February, 1981 at 2.45 pm', 10 February 1981, TNA, T386/550, MTFW 114048.

[46] J. G. Hill, 'Foreign exchange and gold markets: Monday, 24 November 1980', BOE, C8/52, MTFW 128446; J. G. Hill, 'Foreign exchange and gold markets: Tuesday, 25 November 1980', BOE, C8/52, MTFW 128446.

[47] On the gilt side, perhaps more attention was paid to the MTFS: '[T]he discount market welcomed the drop and for the moment is optimistic about the course of events.' The cut had bred an expectation that the November £M3 figures 'must be very good indeed'. They were not, and the caveat grew stronger until, six weeks before the Budget, it was recalled that the reduction 'was not well received by the gilts market': M. T. R. Smith, 'Money markets during the week ended 26 November', 27 November 1980, BOE, C39/2, MTFW 128448; N. J. Monck, 'MLR reduction', 30 January 1981, TNA, T386/549, MTFW 114067.

[48] Notable among the critics was the *Daily Mail*, which published a front-page editorial on 26 November 1980 demanding 'Maggie must do a U-turn' and take charge of the economy herself for six months. Howe was among the 'carriers of self-deception' who should be sacked. In addition, the *Evening Standard* wrote: 'Many MPs think that the next full budget in the spring will be introduced by someone else.' 'Question mark over Howe's future', *Evening Standard*, 26 November 1980. Whether Thatcher retained confidence in her Chancellor was openly questioned: H. J. S Young, 'Chancellor Howe's fatal flaw', *Sunday Times*, 30 November 1980, MTFW 128453.

As the architect of the MTFS and chief apologist for sterling's stratospheric rate, Lawson was scarcely less vulnerable. Under such pressure public divisions emerged within the government, even between ministers counted as Thatcherite. The Chief Secretary to the Treasury, John Biffen, publicly expressed sympathy for the critics' point on NICs, as well as sharply distancing himself from the MTFS in a chat with Conservative backbenchers, while Howe was left for the best part of a week without public support from Thatcher, noticeably and ominously so.[49] Support, when it came, was of a lukewarm variety: a No. 10 briefing to the Sunday lobby stating that a reshuffle was planned shortly and that Howe would not be moved.[50] When Sir Keith Joseph spoke publicly at this time of the government having had a 'lost year', Mrs Thatcher's Press Secretary, Bernard Ingham, told Joseph's anxious press officer that Thatcher was 'quite relaxed about it': 'I believe she agrees with Sir Keith but for the sake of the Government and confidence in it does not say so.'[51]

The political climate for the Treasury remained acutely uncomfortable throughout the run-up to the Budget, and improved only as the first signs of recovery appeared – a fact not reflected as much as one might expect in accounts of the Budget.[52] One consequence was that Howe, who was always inclined to discuss and consult, at length, and – in Thatcher's

---

[49] Ian Gow warned Thatcher that 'Geoffrey and others are concerned about John Biffen's reply to Waldegrave', saying: 'I have never found the MTFS an easy concept to market. I understand people who nail their flag to the MTFS, but it is all a foreign tongue to me. It is liable to excite enthusiasm, too, and that is a very unConservative emotion. For the time being M3 [sic] has lost its credibility.' P. J. Cropper, 'Conservative Finance Committee – 9 December 1980', 10 December 1980, Churchill, THCR 2/6/2/15, part 2, MTFW 112647, and cover note by Ian Gow. Biffen's diary of 16 December 1980 records: 'I was given an oblique dressing down by MT for my Finance Committee speech. "Do we have any more Biffenism to come?".' See W. J. Biffen, *Semi-detached* (London, 2013), 321. In the January reshuffle Biffen was replaced as Chief Secretary by Leon Brittan, an old friend of the Howes. The appointment deeply frustrated Lawson; he tactfully attributes it more to the influence of Willie Whitelaw, the Deputy Prime Minister, than to Howe: Lawson, *The view from No. 11*, 73.

[50] See Adam Raphael, 'Maggie goes to Howe's aid', *Observer*, 7 December 1980. The information proved accurate as to outcome. Hacche and Taylor, *Inside the Bank of England*, 172: 'Maggie left him a week without coming to his aid.' Privately, Thatcher discussed removing Howe, but without seeing her way. Almost her first remarks to Walters when he became her economic adviser in January 1981 were along the lines of: 'What should she do about Geoffrey? Who could she promote? No one.' A. A. Walters, 'Diary entry', 6 January 1981, Churchill, WTRS 3/1/1, MTFW 114203.

[51] 'B. Ingham to J. Woodrow', 1 December 1980, Churchill, THCR 5/2/42, MTFW 113207.

[52] On 15 April 1981 John Hoskyns registered a turning point: 'Before going out to lunch GH asked me to see him at No 11 (Ian [Gow] was there). He discerns signs of upturn and looked more relaxed than I've seen him in weeks, affable and jokey. He said it was also easing relations with the colleagues too.' 'Hoskyns diary', 15 April 1981, Hoskyns MSS (privately held), MTFW 113018; Hoskyns, *Just in time*, 294.

view – to a fault, took particular pains to keep important colleagues in touch with his thinking.[53] He had one notable success. The Environment Secretary, Michael Heseltine, was won around in advance of the Budget to the view that cutting PSBR was essential to the reduction of MLR, which he favoured over particular reliefs as the measure best designed to aid industry. He even urged the freezing of personal allowances to help achieve it.[54] As Secretary of State for Industry, Joseph was involved in these discussions, taking a line that gave some comfort to the wets, perhaps by design.[55] It is revealing that Howe successfully deployed the trade-off argument in this context, and perhaps not altogether surprising that an idea that had commended itself to Wass and Ryrie made appeal to some of his Cabinet critics – as long as they felt constrained to live within the MTFS (which, as events established, finally they did).

Where did the Autumn Statement leave the MTFS? Certainly, the MLR cut on 24 November 1980 decisively established within the government that short-term interest rates were not being set solely, or even primarily, with reference to £M3. The archives are unambiguous on this point. At the very least, then, the November measures opened up the possibility of a further MLR cut at the time of the Budget, regardless of the monetary aggregates. This was a point grasped and reinforced by the markets, forging a relatively strong connection between the two events. But it would be a mistake to suppose that the MTFS was hollowed out by the Autumn Statement and that a reign of 'pragmatism' had begun, as some critics suggested.[56] If anything, the Statement made it more pressing to reassert commitment to the MTFS, so that when Treasury ministers drew up their 'sighting shots' for the Budget two weeks before Christmas a general impulse to tighten fiscal policy was evident, well before any decisions were taken about further MLR cuts or the monetary stance in general. This carried solidly through into the phase of budget making proper. Ministers met to consider their stance on 16 January and

---

[53] The Treasury also seems to have had its doubts on this point. Howe asked Sir Kenneth Couzens whether he should circulate a paper explaining sterling policy to his E Committee colleagues. Couzens pointedly replied that 'you would wish to avoid putting policy on the exchange rate into commission': K. E. Couzens, 'The exchange rate: ministerial briefing', 13 February 1981, TNA, T386/551, MTFW 114073.

[54] 'M. R. D. Heseltine to R. E. G. Howe', 16 February 1981, TNA, PREM 19/438, MTFW 114004.

[55] On measures to help industry, the Employment Secretary, Jim Prior, also noted: 'I am glad to add my voice to Keith's.' 'J. M. L. Prior to R. E. G. Howe', 9 February 1981, TNA, PREM 19/438, MTFW 113995.

[56] Former Cabinet minister Geoffrey Rippon ironically praised the November Statement as a move from 'dogma to something near pragmatism': M. Hatfield, 'I am hemmed in by our election promises, Sir Geoffrey Howe tells Conservative backbenchers', *The Times*, 26 November 1980.

registered 'the need for fiscal tightening in the Budget to demonstrate that the PSBR would be reduced and to help re-establish the credibility of the medium-term financial strategy'.[57]

By this time ministerial hints of one kind or another had reinforced expectations that a further downward move in MLR was coming – expectations that were helping the Bank to sell gilts and that, unsurprisingly, it sought to reinforce ('opportunism', commented the Treasury Deputy Secretary, Peter Middleton).[58] The files suggest that the only debates about MLR within the Treasury and the Bank in January and February 1981 were between cutting before the Budget or at the despatch box, and 1 versus 2 per cent. There was more than market sentiment involved: it was common ground in these internal debates that monetary conditions were tight, whatever £M3 was saying – indeed, that it had perverse characteristics as an indicator.[59]

In the light of these discussions it is hard to share the commonly held view that the 'Niehans report' of January 1981 played an important part in shifting policy by alerting ministers and officials to the tightness of monetary policy and the waywardness of £M3, the Budget adjusting course accordingly. At most, Niehans provided helpful theoretical underpinning for the Treasury and the Bank's existing judgement of market conditions from a source monetarists could not ignore – a kind of imprimatur. The report's influence at No. 10 is also overstated. Walters needed no teaching, while Thatcher herself remained unwilling to relinquish £M3 (of which more below). She also disliked the very idea of such a report – ultimately, a private initiative of Alfred Sherman (one of Thatcher's advisers), Brunner and Walters recommending Niehans – fearing it would leak and undermine credibility. And Niehans' advocacy of intervention to bring sterling down found no takers, the most recent battle on that topic having been fought in the autumn. Ultimately, his report made little or no impact on the Budget, the course for which had already been set.[60]

---

[57] F. A. Cockfield, '1981 Budget', 16 December 1980, private office files of Geoffrey Howe, MTFW 127438. See also A. J. Wiggins, 'Chancellor – 1981 Budget', 18 December 1980, Chancellor's private office files, MTFW 127445 (also 127436–127447); N. J. Monck, 'Meeting with the Governor on Thursday 22 January', 21 January 1981, TNA, T386/549, MTFW 114058.

[58] P. E. Middleton, 'Minimum lending rate', 2 February 1981, TNA, T386/549, MTFW 114066.

[59] P. E. Middleton, 'Minimum lending rate', 10 February 1981, TNA, T386/550, MTFW 114052.

[60] Walters wrote in his diary, 'Told MT about JN's seminar and his findings. MT very defensive: NO ONE must know about it – especially Bank of England. Why? Frightened of calls for relaxation or sops to the wets. Am rapidly learning the political game – never admit to an error.' A. A. Walters, 'Diary entry', 8 January 1981, Churchill, WTRS 3/1/1,

A fortiori, the November measures could not have mattered if the key decisions in the Budget were taken in the last weeks of February 1981. But we have already noted that the eleventh-hour stress in the ministerial memoirs bears the influence of later quarrels, and the detailed account by John Hoskyns in his memoir *Just in time*, which, like them, focuses on the final PSBR decisions, also looks suspect, for all its fascination and richness. Based closely on his diary, Hoskyns frames the Budget as a make-or-break crisis requiring a 'Hayekian' response; Charles Moore's biography of Thatcher was evidently influenced by it.[61] The picture is of No. 10 advisers manoeuvring the Prime Minister into bullying the Treasury to draw up a tough budget. There is something inherently improbable about this version of events, both as to character and the realities of life in Whitehall, and Sir Tim Lankester's chapter in this volume convincingly shows that the process of budget making in January and February 1981 does not bear out the Hoskyns interpretation. Examination of where the Treasury actually stood in the last part of 1980 reinforces this impression. In truth, Hoskyns was a figure on the margin of macroeconomic policy making, despite his location at the centre of power.

Potentially, Walters was in a stronger position to influence the Budget, but at the very beginning of his tenure (he arrived at No. 10 on 6 January 1981) he was not the figure he later became. The Treasury was constrained to be more open with him than Hoskyns, but candour certainly had its limits. And, initially, trust was lacking between Walters and Thatcher herself. She excluded him from some crucial final meetings in the budget-making process; and, at the time, he chose to distance himself from the result, writing to Wass the day after the Budget deadline closed to record his view that not enough had been done to justify a cut in MLR, but that, if one had to happen, in view of strong market expectations, one percentage point was the maximum. He anticipated 'crisis measures after a few months'.[62]

MTFW 114203 [emphasis in original]. Niehans' report was published later in the year 'as originally submitted', but in the United States and with a low profile, as Niehans, *The appreciation of sterling: causes, effects, policies*, and it is available at Churchill, WTRS 1/4, MTFW 128452. On Sherman's role in conjuring up Niehans, see 'A. Sherman to R. G. Puttick (chairman, Taylor Woodrow)', 14 November 1980, Churchill, THCR 2/11/3/1, part 1, MTFW 121407. Sherman also played a crucial role in the appointment of Walters.

[61] Moore, *Margaret Thatcher*, 623 onwards.

[62] Thatcher certainly never forgot the funding crisis of November 1979, which forced a three percentage point increase in MLR, but it is hard to agree with Moore's suggestion that the 'threat of a crisis in the gilt markets dominated everything' in the making of the Budget. If nothing else her determination to see a significant cut in MLR makes little sense in those terms. Clearly she also had in mind ending the recession and rendering the Budget

One is brought then, finally, to the monetary side of the Budget. The November 1980 measures were powerfully influenced by a desire to reduce the value of sterling. How far did this motivation still operate by the time of the Budget? The currency had weakened significantly and steadily against the dollar after its late October peak, falling to $2.2150 on Budget day, only a cent and a half about the level Thatcher had wished for at her meeting of 18 September 1980. On 17 February 1981, when it stood at $2.2635, Howe and Richardson had discussed the rate and felt that 'substantial depreciation would have serious adverse implications for inflation'.[63] The underlying condition was a strengthening dollar, as the tightening introduced by the Federal Reserve Chairman, Paul Volcker, took hold, while the pound was rising markedly against European currencies, so that sterling might now have been constraining a cut in MLR as well as motivating one. And in fact there is no sign that a desire to influence sterling played any part in Treasury thinking on interest rates at the time of the Budget.[64] The case for a reduction in MLR was made in relation to its impact on the finances of the company sector, action on the National Insurance surcharge having been ruled out.

It has been argued that the Treasury did not seek an MLR cut at all. Lawson's memoirs handle this question bluntly, drawing a sharp distinction in the paternity tradition. For the Treasury, he asserts that '[t]he 1981 Budget was essentially a response to the fiscal difficulties which had emerged in the financial year 1980–81', a salutary demonstration of resolve, whereas, for Thatcher and 'in particular Walters', the cutting of MLR was 'its *raison d'être*'.[65] The MLR cut on Budget day he presents as a misguided and ultimately unsuccessful initiative from No. 10, needing to be reversed in the autumn in two successive two percentage point increases.[66]

In fact, the records do not support as sharp a line on the narrow question of MLR. Walters did not consistently press for a cut; as already noted, by the end of the budget-making process his position was quite the reverse. The Treasury and the Bank did, on the other hand, despite their concerns for sterling. The *size* of the cut, and to a lesser degree its timing,

---

politically saleable, reasoning evident in her (and Lawson's) subsequent defence of the Budget. Moore, *Margaret Thatcher*, 627; 'A. A. Walters to D. W. G. Wass', 26 February 1981, MTFW 114026.

[63] A. J. Wiggins, 'Monetary affairs', 17 February 1981, TNA, T386/551.

[64] Advising Howe on 5 March, Couzens thought a two percentage point cut had been discounted by the markets, so that it would not weaken sterling, 'and might cause some rise', there having been expectations earlier of a three percentage point cut: K. E. Couzens, 'MLR in the Budget: the exchange rate', 5 March 1981, TNA, T386/552, MTFW 133731.

[65] Lawson, *The view from No. 11*, 88, 98.   [66] Ibid., 98.

were at issue for them, but not its *desirability*. By this stage monetary conditions were seen as too tight, although there was no agreement as to how to present this insight.

Even as to the size of the MLR cut there was only limited debate within the Treasury. Middleton took the lead in urging two percentage points rather than one, arguing that such a cut would be seen as consistent with the Budget's target for £M3, so that 'the deciding factor might be the general reaction to the Budget and particularly the reaction of industry', for which a one percentage point cut 'just does not seem enough'. (The Budget announced a new target of 6 to 10 per cent annual growth in £M3 over the period from February 1981 to April 1982, helpfully removing the post-'corset' bulge from the figures, the manoeuvre being dubbed a 'roll-forward' or 'rollover' of the previous target in preference to blunter descriptions.)[67] Wass told Howe that he would have plumped for a one percentage point cut '[i]f the Budget were not as tough as it now is and if we were doing a little more for industry', describing the case for a two percentage point cut now as 'in my view largely political'. For good measure, he even circulated Walters' letter warning against a larger cut – a little provocatively, perhaps. Finally, though, Wass concluded: 'On balance, despite the lack of convincing intellectual reasoning, I am inclined to be on the side of those who want a 2 per cent [sic] reduction.'[68] Ryrie trod a similar path. Among ministers, Biffen was adamant on two percentage points, with Lawson also in fact supportive, briefly minuting his agreement with Middleton.

---

[67] The sensitive decision to delay the 'roll-forward' till the Budget was taken prior to the Autumn Statement: A. J. Wiggins, 'Note of a meeting held in the Chancellor of the Exchequer's room, HM Treasury on Thursday, 6 November, 1980 at 4.30 pm', BOE, 7A 133/2, MTFW 113151; R. E. G. Howe, 'Rolling over the monetary target', TNA, PREM 19/180, MTFW 113302.

[68] P. E. Middleton, 'MLR in the Budget', 27 February 1981, TNA, T386/552, MTFW 133722. N. Lawson, 'MLR in the Budget', 2 March 1981, TNA, T386/552, MTFW 133725 (saying a two percentage point cut was needed 'to give a proper balance to the budget'); D. W. G. Wass, 'MLR in the Budget', 2 March 1981, TNA, T386/552, MTFW 133727. Biffen reacted angrily to sight of the Walters letter: J. W. Biffen, 'MLR in the Budget', 3 March 1981, TNA, T386/552, MTFW 133728. See also A. J. Wiggins, 'Note of a meeting held in the Chancellor of the Exchequer's room, House of Commons, at 4.45 pm on Thursday, 19 February 1981', TNA, T386/551, MTFW 114079, in which Ryrie made the case for a two percentage point cut. The most persistent argument for a one percentage point cut was made from a technical point of view: C. J. Riley, 'MLR cuts in the budget', 27 February 1981, TNA, T386/552, MTFW 133723, suggesting a one percentage point cut in the Budget and another later, to achieve 'smoother monetary growth through the year'. See also C. J. Riley, 'MLR in the Budget', 3 March 1981, TNA, T386/552, MTFW 133729; and P. E. Middleton, 'MLR in the Budget', TNA, T386/552, MTFW 133729.

As to the timing, the Bank urged a one percentage point cut before Budget day, and tried to nudge Thatcher and Howe towards openly acknowledging that it was taking place outside the framework of the MTFS, to reflect the behaviour of monetary aggregates other than £M3 and 'to reduce the upward pressure on the exchange rate'.[69] But the Bank was asking for too much, too soon, contributing to the decision to announce the MLR cut from the despatch box in the Budget itself; this was a further politicising of interest rates, disliked by Howe and many other Conservatives, but one that would permit an extensive restatement of the framework, if desired – and give longer to think about it. In the run-up to the Budget Howe was deeply uncertain where monetary policy should go. He wanted the exchange rate to be taken into account, although he rejected an explicit target (and, for the moment, the European Monetary System); he was attracted to monetary base control and saw a valuable role for monetary targets, but 'thought £M3 would have to remain a central feature'.[70]

Lawson's position, as ever, was more crisp. In the last weeks of budget making he twice gave Howe his thinking on this topic, the first via his Private Secretary on 2 February 1981:

[W]e should perhaps learn to have increased respect for our forefathers, who plumped for separate and simultaneous monetary targets (the note issue, the then equivalent of the monetary base M0) and fiscal targets (the balanced budget). He [Lawson] does not think the attempt to conflate these two into a single hybrid target, £M3, has proved an unqualified improvement.[71]

---

[69] Peter Middleton agreed that a cut in these circumstances would be a struggle to present as anything but a departure from the policy framework. He made an ad hoc case for relaxing outside the framework in an unimpressed analysis of the Niehans report: 'If it is accepted – which it usually is – that there is no very clear explanation for the exchange rate in terms of conventional indicators, but that the high exchange rate does exert a strong downward influence in inflation, then so long as the exchange rate remains high there is a case for relaxing domestic monetary policy – something has done the job for you and you do not need to do it twice.' Lawson also noted 'serious shortcomings' in Niehans, thought Middleton's minute 'wholly valid' and later made a similar argument in his memoirs. N. Lawson, 'Niehans', 17 February 1981, MTFW 128602; P. E. Middleton, 'Niehans', 16 February 1981, private office files of Geoffrey Howe, MTFW 128601; 'T. P. Lankester to A. J. Wiggins', 29 January 1981, BOE, 7A133/5, MTFW 127453.

[70] Wiggins, 'Note of a meeting held...6 February, 1981, at 2.45 pm', MTFW 114048.

[71] S. A. J. Locke, 'The money supply target', 2 February 1981, TNA, T386/549, MTFW 114065. Lawson's own turn towards the EMS came in the summer of 1981, towards the end of his time in Howe's Treasury: N. Lawson, 'EMS', 15 June 1981, Oxford, Christ Church College (hereafter 'Christ Church'), Lawson MSS 1/2, MTFW 128449; N. Lawson, 'EMS', 14 September 1981, Christ Church, Lawson MSS, MTFW 128450. During his tenure as Chancellor Howe chose not to press the EMS as an issue, while remaining fundamentally positive towards it: 'HMT wants to push EMS well into the future. FCO does not', 'J. S. Fforde to the Governor', 16 January 1980, BOE, 7A133/2, MTFW 113114.

Then, on 13 February, came a firm prescription:

[N]ominal short-term interest rates should be basically determined by the growth of M0, with some regard however to the other aggregates (*including* £M3) and the level of real interest rates. There should be *no* explicit link with the exchange rate, although inasmuch as exchange rate rises reduce inflation and thus increase the real interest rate, there will be an implicit link.[72]

But one person remained who was far from ready to relinquish £M3. Although Thatcher was attracted to MBC and was more than willing to achieve greater discretion by paying attention to other variables, she saw a high political cost in changing the target, so many painful things having been done in its name. She had a strong suspicion that £M3 meant *something*; after all, hadn't Walters predicted where the 'Barber boom' would end by reference to the broad money supply? And she had no desire either, then or later, to abandon the idea of trading off tighter fiscal policy for looser monetary policy, particularly if tightening could be achieved by public expenditure control rather than tax increases. As Chancellor, Lawson later had many fights with the Prime Minister to refute the notion that she had hit upon a timeless formula to this effect. Unsurprisingly, then, the Budget did not offer a full-scale reformulation of monetary policy; as in November 1980, it was politically impossible to construct a wholly adequate doctrinal basis for the MLR cut.

---

[72] N. Lawson, 'Changes in the banks' money market operations and policy for short-term interest rates', 13 February 1981, TNA, T386/551, MTFW 114074 [emphasis in original].

8   The 1981 Budget and its impact on the conduct of economic policy: was it a monetarist revolution?

Anthony Hotson

Introduction

The 1981 Budget is commonly presented as an important staging post in the Thatcher government's neoliberal programme. Since World War II governments of both parties had accepted that public spending and taxes should adjust counter-cyclically to stabilise aggregate demand.[1] During the 1981 recession the Thatcher government did the reverse, raising taxes with a view to reducing the public sector borrowing requirement. It argued that Keynesian demand management had been found wanting and should be discarded in favour of monetarist policies.[2] Many economists were dumbfounded, and 364 of them signed a letter to *The Times* criticising the Budget.[3] Public officials were not at liberty to sign the letter, but many of them stood aghast as a 'horde of...people...of a dogmatic and superficial turn of mind...stormed the citadels of economic power... under the banner of monetarism'.[4]

Following its election, the Thatcher government's economic policies had not run to plan; in particular, the rate of inflation continued to rise, reaching a peak of 22 per cent in May 1980. This was the result of the second OPEC oil price hike, a build-up of domestic inflationary pressures following the collapse of the previous government's incomes policy, and the new government's VAT increases.[5] In November 1979 Bank Rate, then known as Minimum Lending Rate, was raised to a record level of 17 per cent. To many people's surprise, the sterling exchange rate continued to strengthen, possibly reflecting North Sea oil prospects and

---

[1] S. Brittan, *The Treasury under the Tories, 1951–1964* (Harmondsworth, 1964), 249–59.

[2] Young, *One of us*, 192–222.

[3] D. W. J. Blake, 'Monetarism attacked by top economists', *The Times*, 30 March 1981.

[4] C. W. McMahon, 'Obituary: Christopher Dow', *Independent*, 4 December 1998.

[5] N. H. Dimsdale, 'British monetary policy since 1945', in N. F. R. Crafts and N. W. C. Woodward (eds.), *The British economy since 1945* (Oxford, 1991), 129.

tighter monetary policy.[6] The combination of a strong pound and high domestic inflation meant that the United Kingdom's competitiveness deteriorated by an unprecedented 40 per cent, with dire consequences for industrial output and employment.[7]

Pre-Budget discussions between ministers and senior advisers focused on the need to reduce MLR without a loss of confidence in the foreign exchange and gilt-edged (government bond) markets. It was hoped that a reduction in interest rates would allow sterling to depreciate in an orderly manner, thereby alleviating pressure on industry. However, the government believed that a sustainable cut in interest rates could be achieved only in conjunction with a meaningful cut in the public sector borrowing requirement. A reduction in MLR without sufficient fiscal restraint risked a loss of market confidence and the possibility of being 'blown off course' by a financial crisis, akin to the problems faced by the Wilson government in 1966–67, the Heath government in 1972–73 and the Callaghan government in 1976.[8] The Thatcher government argued that fiscal deficits had not led to the hoped-for sustained expansion but, instead, to stop-go cycles, which had had the effect of inhibiting long-term growth (see Figure 8.1). The 1981 Budget was supposed to be a monetarist revolution, turning Keynesianism on its head by offering long-term growth consequent upon fiscal contraction (Figure 8.2).[9]

The debate about expansionary fiscal contraction has been confusing, to say the least. At the time, ministers argued that an excessive public sector deficit crowded out private investment by keeping interest rates high. A reduced deficit would allow interest rates to fall and the crowding in of private investment. Nigel (now Lord) Lawson, an exponent of EFC at the time, has subsequently suggested that crowding in and crowding out may be a fallacy in a world of international capital flows.[10] There is certainly little evidence of a straightforward set of linkages from short-term policy rates to longer-term real interest rates and investment. The government also hoped that lower interest rates would help to lower the exchange rate and improve competitiveness, but did not want to be drawn into an expression of public intent on what constituted an appropriate level for sterling. In the circumstances, the 'crowding in'

---

[6] C. A. E Goodhart and P. V. Temperton, 'The UK exchange rate, 1979–81: a test of the overshooting hypothesis', paper presented to the Oxford Money Study Group, 6 November 1982.

[7] *BEQB*, 11, 1981, 16.

[8] K. O. Morgan, *Britain since 1945: the people's peace* (Oxford, 1991), 262.

[9] N. Lawson, 'Thatcherism in practice: a progress report', speech to Zurich Society of Economics, 14 January 1981, MTFW 109506.

[10] Lawson, *The view from No. 11*, 89–90.

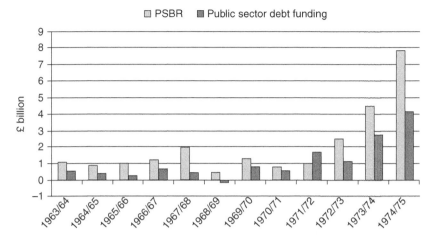

Figure 8.1 The end of Bretton Woods: the dash for growth and fiscal deficits
Source: Bank of England, *Statistical abstract*, Part 2, 1975, tab. 12/3.

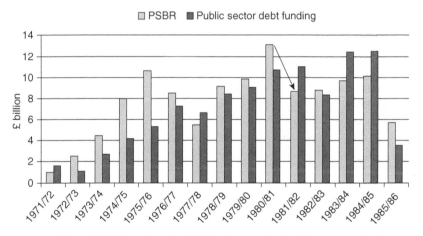

Figure 8.2 Financing the PSBR: from underfunding to overfunding
Source: Bank of England Quarterly Bulletin, tab. 11.3.

mantra provided a convenient shorthand for suggesting that fiscal pain led to other benefits without having to be too specific about the desired exchange rate level. Lower interest rates also had a highly visible effect on mortgage borrowing costs, with important implications for homeowners – a key Thatcherite constituency.

The other set of arguments impinging on the debate over PSBR reductions related to monetary policy and monetarism. After the election victory of 1979 the new Conservative Chancellor, Sir Geoffrey Howe, retained the Labour government's monetary targeting framework. The target range of 8 to 12 per cent for £M3 was reduced by one percentage point to 7 to 11 per cent, starting in June 1979. It was argued that allowance should be made for overshooting in the previous year.[11] Howe did not seem to envisage any changes to the conduct of monetary policy; the government simply aimed to implement it in a more disciplined way than its immediate predecessor. The government made great play of its willingness to use the interest rate weapon more vigorously than the previous Labour government – and, for that matter, the Heath government of the early 1970s.[12]

In February 1979 there had been an exchange of correspondence between key members of the shadow finance team about resetting the 1979/80 growth target for £M3 after the election. One member of the team, John Nott, had expressed concern about the potential squeeze on business profitability and suggested that a higher rate of monetary growth might be appropriate until public borrowing had been brought under control. Sir Keith Joseph and Nigel Lawson argued that this would damage the new government's credibility. Lawson argued that inflation was likely to be around 12 per cent and that a 'no higher than before' target would result in a firm exchange rate, less inflation, lower interest rates and less of a squeeze on the corporate sector.[13] In the event, the inflation outturn was almost double Lawson's forecast, and the loss of competitiveness unprecedented.[14] The newly elected Thatcher government nevertheless felt compelled to stick to heroically low monetary targets, which became enshrined in its Medium-Term Financial Strategy.

The MTFS had been announced by Howe with great fanfare in his Budget of March 1980.[15] This respray of the Labour government's monetary regime was said to have been the brainchild of Lawson, then a junior Treasury minister, and Peter Middleton, a Treasury official.[16] Middleton had been an effective press officer for the Treasury, and he argued that the government could escape from its monetary problems by better presentation of its policies. The centrepiece of the MTFS was multi-year targets for the PSBR and £M3, and these were expected to

[11] Lawson, 'Thatcherism in practice', 4–6.
[12] P. J. R. Riddell, *The Thatcher government* (Oxford, 1983), 57–65.
[13] 'Sir Keith Joseph to Sir Geoffrey Howe', 20 February 1979, Churchill, THCR 2/1/1/10A; Nigel Lawson to Sir Geoffrey Howe, 'Current monetary policy', 21 February 1979, Churchill, THCR 21/1/3/12A.
[14] *BEQB*, 21, 1981, 16.   [15] Riddell, *The Thatcher government*, 2, 58–9.
[16] N. Lawson, 'Thatcherism in practice', 3; Howe, *Conflict of loyalty*, 155.

influence the expectations of wage bargainers and market practitioners. The £M3 target of 7 to 11 per cent for 1979/80 had been overshot by a considerable margin, and it was decided to set the same target range for 1980/81. Emphasis was placed on the n–1 reduction in successive targets announced for the following three years, to 4 to 8 per cent in 1983/84.[17] The government downplayed its failure to keep to monetary targets in the recent past and offered the prospect of virtue in the years ahead.[18]

To get to grips with the various motivations for the 1981 Budget and its longer-term impact on the conduct of policy, the following sections examine three areas of policy development. First, the formulation of Conservative Party policy from Mrs Thatcher's election as party leader in 1975 until the election of 1979, and the problems faced by the first Thatcher government implementing the policy from 1979 to 1983. Second, the role played by publicly announced monetary targets in the Labour government from 1976 to 1979 and their adaptation by the first two Thatcher governments from 1979 to 1987. Third, an assessment is made of the impact of financial deregulation on the conduct of monetary policy.

The following sections consider each of these policy areas in turn. A concluding section makes a number of judgements about the impact of the 1981 Budget on the long-term conduct of economic policy in the light of the foregoing analysis.

Conservative policy formulation from 1975 to 1979 and problems of implementation from 1979 to 1983

After her election as party leader in February 1975, Margaret Thatcher asked her policy mentor, Keith Joseph, to initiate a review. Joseph had a vision of dismantling Britain's corporatist economy and establishing a social market – a theme that coincided well with Thatcher's convictions. He canvassed a range of opinions and wrote a series of discussion papers that set out the tenets of Thatcherism, including fiscal rectitude, monetary discipline, a limited state, lower taxes, markets rather than controls, and homeownership.[19] He wrote a speech, 'Against incomes policy', criticising national pay bargaining and government involvement in it. At the time, it was commonplace to argue that governments should have an

---

[17] Dimsdale, 'British monetary policy since 1945', 131–3.

[18] N. H. Dimsdale, 'The Treasury and Civil Service Committee and the British monetarist experiment', in M. L. Baranzini (ed.), *Advances in economic theory* (Oxford, 1982), 184–5.

[19] K. S. Joseph and A. E. U. Maude, 'Notes towards the definition of policy', 4 April 1975, Churchill, THCR 2/6/1/156.

incomes policy, and Joseph conceded that his antithetical view was probably a minority one among the political and economic establishment.[20] Professor Alan Walters, then at the London School of Economics and a critic of Ted Heath's U-turns, is reputed to have been a key influence behind Joseph's strong stance against incomes policies and in favour of monetary policy as an anchor for controlling inflation.[21]

Despite the support of his leader, Joseph's views were not well received by many in Thatcher's shadow Cabinet, as was made plain in a meeting held in April 1975 to discuss one of his early papers.[22] Dissenters from Joseph's vision of dismantling the corporatist economy ranged from those who saw some virtue in corporatism, including incomes policy, to those who agreed with many of his conclusions but believed that such a wide-ranging attack on the status quo might unnerve the voters and financial markets. There was also a need to develop tactical positions on topical issues, with which to attack the Labour government. In the light of the shadow Cabinet discussions, Thatcher decided that a review of economic policy should be developed under the aegis of the Economic Reconstruction Group, which held its first meeting in June 1975. It was chaired by Howe with Joseph's involvement and half a dozen other MPs, including Nott, Sally Oppenheim, Ian Gilmour, Jim Prior, David Howell and John Biffen.[23] Brian Griffiths, a colleague of Alan Walters, was the sole non-parliamentary member of the ERG.[24]

Much of the ERG's time was spent on current issues of debate with the Labour government, and its chairman encouraged a cautious approach on future policy. In July 1975 Howe reported on the direction of the ERG's initial thinking; on monetary policy, he reported that his committee saw a number of problems with a 'gradualist' monetary approach:

As proposed by Professors Friedman, Parkin, Laidler and others, one would follow for four or five years a programme of steady reduction in the rate of growth of the money supply. The target for monetary growth would be consistently set at a lower rate of increase than that of prices. The policy would thus bear down on rather than accommodate wage and price increases. The Group tended to the view that there would be several serious problems involved in this course of action. A very high level of unemployment would probably be required for four or five years. In the private sector capital expenditure, confidence and growth would be

---

[20] K. S. Joseph, 'Incomes policy' (draft 5 May 1976), Churchill, THCR 2/1/1/37.
[21] 'Sir Alan Walters' (obituary), *Daily Telegraph*, 5 January 2009; Howe, *Conflict of loyalty*, 86.
[22] 'Leader's Consultative Committee: minutes of the 57th meeting', 11 April 1975, Churchill, THCR 2/6/1/156.
[23] Howe, *Conflict of loyalty*, 99.
[24] 'Economic Reconstruction Group: minutes of meeting', 20 June 1975, Churchill, RDLY 2/1/2/1.

damaged. The need to sustain the policy throughout the life of a parliament would raise obvious political difficulties.[25]

Howe's paper went on to rule out dramatic monetary tightening (instantaneous monetarism) and indexation (living with inflation). The paper alighted on an 'ideal' programme that combined three elements: firm monetary policy, fiscal discipline and national pay policy.

In December 1975 the ERG considered a paper prepared by Griffiths and discussed various options for monetary control, including:

(1) continuing with the existing system of direct controls on the banks;
(2) reverting to the Competition and Credit Control regime and relying on interest rates; or
(3) moving to monetary base control by introducing a cash reserve system for the banks.

The ERG did not conclude on this issue and asked for more research.[26] As we shall see, the elected Conservative government moved towards option (2), reverting to CCC, despite the difficult experience of Heath's government in the early 1970s.

In May 1976 there was a discussion of methods of implementing monetary policies, including the first recorded discussion of monetary targets. The minutes recorded rather airily: 'It was thought that monetary targets could be useful. The mechanics for controlling money supply already existed.'[27]

A month later the monetary policy subgroup, which included Griffiths, reported to the ERG and recommended that 'there should be monetary guidelines', 'monetary indicators should be reformed' and outsiders should be inserted into the Treasury and Bank who 'were not dogmatically antagonistic to monetary objectives to enable the switch in emphasis to monetary policy to take place efficiently'.[28] Joseph harboured fears about the Bank's unreconstructed Keynesianism and took exception to the non-monetary explanation of price inflation in the 'Assessment' of the June 1978 edition of the *Bank of England Quarterly Bulletin*.[29] In this context, it is perhaps not surprising that those most interested in reform

---

[25] 'Economic Reconstruction Group: note by the chairman', 24 July 1975, Churchill, RDLY 2/1/2/2.

[26] 'Economic Reconstruction Group: minutes of meeting', 22 December 1976, Churchill, RDLY 2/1/2/1.

[27] 'Economic Reconstruction Group: minutes of meeting', 20 May 1976, Churchill, RDLY 2/1/2/1.

[28] 'Economic Reconstruction Group: minutes of meeting', 24 June 1976, Churchill, RDLY 2/1/2/1.

[29] A. N. Ridley to Sir Keith Joseph, 'Bank of England Quarterly on inflation', 26 June 1978, Churchill, THCR 2/6/1/97.

placed greater emphasis on ministerial intervention in Bank affairs, rather than contemplating the benefits of a more independent central bank modelled on the United States or West Germany. The emphasis seems to have been on ministerial actions rather than on institutional development, and it was taken as read by both political parties that ministerial involvement in interest rate setting should remain. There had been a major sterling crisis in 1976, and Peter Jay, a columnist, had floated the idea of a Currency Commission, but this did not gain traction with the ERG.[30]

It should also be noted that the ERG and Conservative shadow Cabinet were hardly hotbeds of monetarist radicalism: Howe devoted much of the ERG's time in 1977 to 'concerted action', a Conservative variant of the social contract based on West German experience.[31] Thatcher was not impressed, but a majority of the shadow Cabinet appeared unwilling to repudiate incomes policy completely.[32] There seemed to be very little difference between the position of Howe's majority group in the shadow Cabinet and the pragmatic views of the Bank Governor, Gordon Richardson, on the duality of incomes policy and monetary targets: 'Monetary policy should therefore aim to act in concert with other branches of policy, including incomes policy, in slowing down inflation.'[33] Viewed from the spring and summer of 1977, one might have discerned an emerging cross-party consensus based on the West German model in which a national pay norm was run in parallel with monetary targets.[34] During this period the markets concurred with this consensus and tended to assume that a Labour government would make a better fist of incomes policy. When opinion polls showed Tory gains, longer-dated gilt prices often fell, reflecting a deteriorating view of inflation expectations. However, national pay policies in Britain were to suffer a catastrophic loss of confidence.

In July 1977 Denis Healey, the Labour Chancellor of the Exchequer, had announced that the pay norm for Phase II would continue in the 1977/78 pay round (Phase III), and that this would foreshadow a phased return to free collective bargaining. In July 1978, however, Healey set a '5 per cent limit' for 1978/79 (Phase IV). The 5 per cent limit was not statutory

---

[30] P. Jay, 'A solution of last resort', *The Times*, 15 April 1976.

[31] R. E. G. Howe, 'Our attitude towards pay policy: a paper by Geoffrey Howe', 4 March 1977, Churchill, THCR 2/6/1/233.

[32] 'R. E. G. Howe to M. H. Thatcher' 26 May 1977 (and Thatcher's annotation), Churchill, THCR 2/1/3/9.

[33] 'Speeches by the Governor of the Bank of England' (17 January 1977), *BEQB*, 17, 1977, 49

[34] Howe, *Conflict of loyalty*, 101.

but the government sought to impose it on public sector workers and threatened sanctions on government contractors who broke it. The limit was breached by the Ford workers and others in a series of increasingly disruptive strikes by oil tanker drivers, train drivers, health service staff and local authority workers – a period that became known as the 'winter of discontent'.[35] Voter confidence in Labour and its incomes policies dropped significantly between November 1978 and January 1979, and the Conservatives won an absolute majority in the May 1979 general election. In his memoirs, Healey argued that a less aggressive pay limit in 'single figures' might have saved the day.[36] Others have argued that the 1978/79 pay round might have been saved by tighter monetary restraint during 1977/78 and continued fiscal restraint in 1978.[37]

Whatever might have happened, the 'winter of discontent' fatally damaged the economic credibility of James Callaghan's government and assisted in the election of the Thatcher government. However, it left the new government reliant on monetary policy and fiscal discipline as the remaining counter-inflationary instruments. Any thought of 'concerted action' was dead in the water. This turn of events seemed to vindicate Joseph's scepticism of incomes policy, but clarity on the role of monetary policy proved to be woefully lacking.

Labour and Conservative monetary targeting, 1976 to 1983

By the late 1970s Milton Friedman's proselytising about the virtues of controlling the money supply as a means of controlling inflation had entered mainstream political debate in the United Kingdom.[38] In September 1979 Paul Volcker unveiled the Federal Reserve Bank's counter-inflation policy, which involved a form of monetary base control: targeting non-borrowed reserves.[39] This policy initiative led to a sharp hike in US interest rates and recognition that the Fed was serious about squeezing inflation out of the system, notwithstanding an impending presidential election (which was lost by Jimmy Carter, the first-term incumbent).[40] There had been some discussion of MBC at Howe's ERG before the election, and the Fed's initiative rekindled political interest in MBC in Britain. Bank officials argued vehemently that MBC was no

[35] Ibid., 107.   [36] Healey, *The time of my life*, 462–4.   [37] *BEQB*, 20, 1980, 121.

[38] A. Davies, 'The evolution of British monetary targets, 1968–79', University of Oxford Discussion Paper in Economic and Social History no. 104 (2012).

[39] C. A. E. Goodhart, 'The conduct of monetary policy', *Economic Journal*, 99 (June 1989), 324–5.

[40] Greider, *Secrets of the temple*.

magic bullet that could achieve disinflation with less pain.[41] The net result of all this chatter was a government that trundled on with its predecessor's £M3 targeting regime *sans* any national pay policy, but with the addition of multi-year monetary targets in the form of the MTFS. Other government decisions regarding the deregulation of the financial sector were about to initiate an explosion in the domestic balance sheets of the banks and thence the broad money supply. The decision making that led to the deregulation of the financial sector is considered in more detail in the next section, but before tackling that subject it is worthwhile elucidating the various strands in the monetarist/MBC debates that led to so much recrimination at the time.

Friedman famously argued that inflation was, and remains, a monetary phenomenon, and that the price level was related to the money stock. More precisely, he argued that there was a stable demand for money and that inflation could be curbed by controlling monetary growth.[42] In the late 1960s academic work on the demand for money in the United Kingdom appeared to find a reasonably stable relationship. This work was summarised in an article entitled 'The importance of money', published in the *BEQB* in 1970.[43] The subsequent story of the stability of the UK demand for money can be summarised fairly simply. Initial optimism using data from the 1960s was followed by doubts as more data from the early 1970s was added.[44] It was suggested that the breakdown of the broad money equations, particularly the M3/£M3 equation, might have resulted from disruption caused by the introduction of CCC in 1971.[45] It was hoped that this instability would be temporary, but the equations for £M3 continued to misbehave in the late 1970s.[46] Narrow monetary aggregates fared slightly better: M1 was reasonably stable until the introduction of interest-bearing deposits on sight deposits (current accounts) in the late 1970s.[47] Ironically, the most robust equation related the demand for

---

[41] M. D. K. W. Foot, C. A. E. Goodhart and A. C Hotson, 'Monetary base control', *BEQB*, 19, 1979, 149–59.

[42] M. Friedman, 'The role of monetary policy', *American Economic Review*, 58, 1 (March 1968), 1–17.

[43] C. A. E. Goodhart and A. D. Crockett, 'The importance of money', *BEQB*, 10, 1970, 159–98.

[44] L. D. D. Price, 'The demand for money in the United Kingdom: a further investigation', *BEQB*, 12, 1972, 43–55; Goodhart, 'The conduct of monetary policy', 314.

[45] G. Hacche, 'The demand for money in the United Kingdom: experience since 1971', *BEQB*, 14, 1974, 284–305.

[46] R. T. Coghlan and L. M. Smith, 'A preliminary note on the demand for M3', 15 September 1977 (HMT Freedom of Information disclosure, 'Monetary policy in the late 1970s and in the 1981 budget', 9 November 2006).

[47] R. T. Coghlan, 'A transactions demand for money', *BEQB*, 18, 1978, 48–60; J. M. Trundle, 'The demand for M1 in the UK', Bank of England (1982), mimeo.

banknotes (the main component of broad M0) to consumer expenditure. The equation was used to forecast note demand for the Bank's printing works in Debden, Essex.[48]

It was a source of great puzzlement to econometrically orientated economists that British officialdom remained wedded to broad money, in particular £M3, when the evidence suggested – for a time – that M1 was more stably related to prices, and that M0 was consistently the most stable.[49] However, the preference for £M3 was not based on 'demand for money' arguments, but on a 'flow of funds' identity that related changes in £M3 to the PSBR, less funding by way of debt sales to the non-bank private sector, plus bank lending and external flows.[50] A £M3 target provided an indirect way of pressing governments to control the PSBR and raise interest rates promptly to fund deficits and contain bank lending. Narrow aggregates, such as M1 (mostly bank sight deposits) and various definitions of M0 (mostly notes and coin), encompassed only a fraction of banks' sterling balance sheets, and did not provide the same set of constraints.[51]

During the late 1970s the published £M3 target was really a device for putting the Labour government on its mettle to control the PSBR and to raise interest rates to fund the PSBR.[52] The lineage of the published £M3 target can be traced back to the IMF's ceilings on domestic credit expansion in the late 1960s and unpublished M3 guidelines in the early 1970s (Figure 8.3).[53] It was known that short-term interest rate variations had a limited and slow impact on bank lending.[54] Instead, a system of direct controls, known as the 'corset' (the supplementary special deposits scheme), was used to control bank lending, even though it was recognised that some disintermediation took place. The bill leak was an example of disintermediation in which banks accepted commercial bills from corporate borrowers, instead of providing conventional loans, and resold the

[48] 'Bank of England notes', *BEQB*, 18, 1978, 359–64, esp. appendix, 363–4.

[49] J. M. Trundle and P. V. Temperton, 'Recent changes in the use of cash', *BEQB*, 22, 1982, 519–29.

[50] C. A. E. Goodhart, *Money, information and uncertainty* (London, 1975), 165–9; M. V. Hewitt, 'Financial forecasts in the United Kingdom', *BEQB*, 17, 1977, 188–95; T. G. Congdon, *Monetary control in Britain* (London, 1982), 27–58.

[51] A. C. Hotson, 'British monetary targets, 1976 to 1987: a view from the fourth floor of the Bank of England', London School of Economics and Political Science Financial Markets Group Special Paper no. 190 (2010), 13–14.

[52] J. S. Fforde, 'Setting monetary objectives', *BEQB*, 13, 1983, 200.

[53] Needham, *UK monetary policy*.

[54] C. A. E. Goodhart and A. C. Hotson, 'The forecasting and control of bank lending', in C. A. E. Goodhart (ed.), *Monetary theory and practice: the UK experience* (London, 1984), 139–45 (first published as C. A. E. Goodhart, 'Problems of monetary management: the UK experience', Reserve Bank of Australia Paper in Monetary Economics no. 1 (1975)).

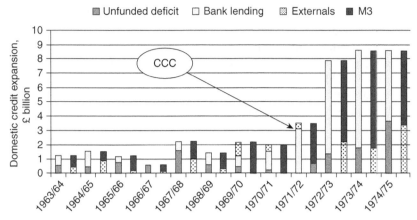

Figure 8.3 The credit counterparts: DCE and M3
Note: Format introduced in table 48, 'Financial statistics', June 1966.
Source: Bank of England, *Statistical abstract*, Part 2, 1975, tab. 12/3.

bills with the bank's guarantee outside the banking system. The system delivered reasonably accurate control – some would say cosmetic control – of reported £M3, with a safety value allowing faster underlying (bill-adjusted) broad monetary growth.[55]

It was surprising, therefore, that the Thatcher government professed to take Friedman's monetarism seriously but stuck with the previous government's leaky £M3 framework, using a monetary aggregate that palpably failed to exhibit a stable demand for money function. The government sought to control £M3 by reining in the PSBR – the essence of the 1981 Budget. Moreover, it was successful at funding and then overfunding the PSBR going forward as a means of controlling £M3.[56] The public sector's contributions to £M3 growth – the unfunded PSBR and public sector external influences – were small or negative during the first Thatcher government. It was excessive growth of bank lending that proved to be the undoing of the MTFS targets, and the decisions that led to this problem are set out in the next section (see Figure 8.4).

One might wonder why the newly elected Conservative government did not give serious consideration to switching from £M3 to a target for M1 (or non-interest-bearing M1: nib M1). The government was serious about its PSBR target and did not need a target for £M3 as a proxy for fiscal discipline. Growth in nib M1 deposits tended to be more responsive

[55] 'The role of the Bank of England in the money market', *BEQB*, 22, 1982, 86–94.
[56] Goodhart, 'The conduct of monetary policy', 327–8.

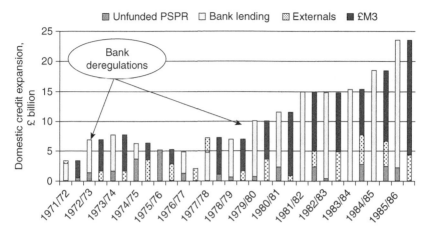

Figure 8.4 The credit counterparts of £M3: bank lending growth following 1971 and 1979 deregulations
Source: Bank of England Quarterly Bulletin, tab. 11.3.

to interest rate changes, and therefore more controllable, than broader aggregates on which deposit interest was paid. Narrow money targeting was popular in some other countries; it fitted with the notion of a transaction demand for money, and it could have been served up as being part and parcel of a monetarist disinflation programme.[57] Indeed, Friedman argued that monetary policy should operate independently of fiscal policy – as it did in the United States – and was perplexed by the British desire to connect the two.[58]

As it happens, the Bank had argued for the targeting of M1, as well as £M3, in November 1977.[59] The Bank's paper had accepted that the two aggregates could give conflicting signals, but suggested that dual targeting could assist the cause of an interpretational, medium-term approach. It is noteworthy that the Bank's chart on monetary objectives in the *BEQB* traditionally included M1 as a secondary indicator alongside M3/£M3. Moreover, the discussion of monetary targets in the June 1977 edition of the *BEQB* included a reference to the possibility of targeting more than

---

[57] S. H. Axilrod, 'Monetary policy, money supply, and the Federal Reserve's operating procedures', in P. Meek (ed.), *Central bank views on monetary targeting* (New York, 1982), 32–41.

[58] M. Friedman, 'Memoranda on monetary policy', Treasury and Civil Service Committee, House of Commons Paper no. 720–11 (1980); Dimsdale, 'The Treasury and Civil Service Committee', 186.

[59] 'Monetary targets, 1978–79' (Bank of England paper), 16 November 1977, London, BOE, 6A50/24.

one aggregate.[60] At this stage, the Bank's forecasting equations for M1 were working well, in stark contrast to the wayward £M3 equations. The Treasury's response to the Bank's internal paper of November 1977 was, however, strongly critical, Michael Bridgeman noting that 'one of the main attractions to the Governor of having M1 as a target [is] that it will give the Bank a much stronger say in interest rate policy'.[61]

At the time, the Treasury's willingness to give up control over interest rates seemed to be as unlikely as the fall of the Berlin Wall.[62] Ministers of the Thatcher government were even more adamant that they should retain ultimate control over interest rates. The idea of delegating tactical responsibility for adjusting interest rates to meet a target set by the government was regarded as inconceivable under British constitutional arrangements. The Bank was seen as the problem, rather than a potential solution. This had the curious consequence of ruling out M1 targeting.

The other candidate for targeting was the monetary base, which became known as M0. Before 1979 the monetary base was not recognised as part of the lexicon of UK monetary aggregates.[63] A statistical exercise had to be undertaken in 1980 to consider some detailed questions about its definition and compute a consistent back series. Broad M0 came to be defined as cash (notes and coin) in circulation with the public, cash held by banks (till money and vault cash) and bankers' balances on deposit with the Bank.[64] The Bank's routine money market operations meant that the banks' holdings of cash and bankers' balances were tiny. Broad M0 was therefore dominated by cash held by the (non-bank) public. The public's cash holdings were reasonably predictable and grew slowly because of advances in money transmission, such as the spread of credit cards, debit cards, cash machines, etc., which allowed the public to economise on cash holdings. Demand for cash was always accommodated by the Bank, and there were peaks at Easter and on bank holidays. The idea that a limit on its growth could limit inflation was regarded as risible, at least by Bank officials. Nonetheless, academic interest in M0 as an indicator remains.[65]

[60] 'Economic commentary', *BEQB*, 17, 1977, 151–2.

[61] J. M. Bridgeman, 'Choice of target variable for 1978–79', 17 November 1977 (HMT Freedom of Information disclosure, 'Monetary policy in the late 1970s and in the 1981 budget', 9 November 2006).

[62] J. M. Bridgeman, 'Monetary targets: rolling targets', 16 November 1977 (HMT Freedom of Information disclosure, 'Monetary policy in the late 1970s and in the 1981 budget', 9 November 2006).

[63] HM Treasury, *Economic trends* (August 1970).

[64] 'The monetary base: a statistical note', *BEQB*, 11, 1981, 59–65.

[65] See M. J. Oliver, 'The long road to 1981: British money supply targets from DCE to the MTFS' in this volume, and N. Batini and E. Nelson, 'The UK's rocky road to stability', Federal Reserve Bank of St Louis Working Paper no. 2005–020A (2005).

For some in the Thatcher government, an M0 target had political appeal because it purported to place an obligation on the Bank to control its balance sheet. As we have seen, the ERG had discussed the possibility of greater ministerial control over the Bank and some sort of MBC as an option. When he arrived at Downing Street in 1980, Walters recognised that monetary policy was extremely tight despite the rapid growth of £M3. Searching for an aggregate that reflected the stance of policy, he commissioned Jürg Niehans to prepare a paper suggesting that broad M0 was a better indicator than £M3. The slow growth of broad M0 in the recession of 1979–80 was said to be indicative of the tightness of monetary policy.[66] Niehans' paper was not made public at the time, but Lawson did go on to adopt broad M0 as an additional published indicator in 1984.

Notwithstanding the MBC debate and political interest in broad M0, broad money targeting remained in place, subject to various interpretational caveats.[67] As a result, the government had to contend with the effect of bank credit on broad money, and this is where bank deregulation met monetary policy.

Financial sector deregulation and monetary control, 1979–86

Deregulation was part of the Thatcher government's neoliberal programme, and the strength of sterling encouraged it to dismantle exchange controls speedily. Their sudden abolition in October 1979 meant that UK residents could deposit funds with, and borrow from, banks based outside the United Kingdom (including the foreign branches of UK high street banks). Banks' operations outside the United Kingdom were not subject to constraints placed on balance sheet growth imposed by the 'corset'. The Euromarkets were likewise free of the 'corset', but this market was available only to non-residents. Without exchange controls, UK residents (including UK companies) could circumvent controls on UK-based banking operations by going offshore – so-called 'offshore disintermediation'. The 'corset' was therefore abolished, opening the door to an expansion of domestic bank intermediation.[68] Deregulation at home raised the prospect of the high street banks – the London and Scottish clearing banks – growing their domestic balance sheets, notably

---

[66] Niehans, *The appreciation of sterling*.

[67] See the joint Bank and Treasury Green Paper *Monetary control*, Cmnd 7858 (London, 1980).

[68] 'The supplementary special deposits scheme', *BEQB*, 22, 1982, 74–85.

through personal lending. The clearers were beginning to look more favourably at domestic expansion, as many of their excursions overseas were starting to look ill-judged. This became more obvious when the Latin American debt crisis broke in 1982 and Midland Bank's recent acquisition, Crocker Bank of California, ran into difficulties, eventually being sold with substantial losses in 1986.

Hitherto, home finance and personal saving had been the preserve of specialist mutual societies, known as building societies. There was a letter of understanding between the Bank and the clearers to the effect that they would not offer first mortgages, leaving the mainstream mortgage market open to the building societies. Homeowners and prospective homeowners tended to have a current account (possibly with an overdraft) with a clearer, and a savings account and – in due course – a mortgage loan from a building society.[69]

The latter's trade body, the Building Societies Association, operated a cartel whereby the politically sensitive mortgage lending rate was kept low relative to wholesale market rates, and building society saving rates were likewise set at an even lower level relative to wholesale rates. Low savings rates did not undermine the building society sector's dominance of the short-term retail savings market because regular saving with a building society was often a precondition for a mortgage loan. Customers tolerated a derisory rate of interest on the understanding that they should subsequently qualify for a loan. The clearing banks did not encroach on the savings flow of the building societies, and government savings schemes (National Savings) were likewise managed not to take too much market share.

Building societies operated in a looking-glass world when compared with modern retail banking. The BSA cartel limited price competition between societies and sustained a healthy gross margin between retail saving and lending rates. More ambitious societies competed against other societies and the banks by extending their high street coverage through branches and agencies, and by building brand and product awareness through regional TV advertising. Building society balance sheets were driven by their ability to attract retail savings, their wholesale funding being limited by law, and by the fact that wholesale borrowing cost more than the BSA-approved mortgage lending rate, which was less than the London Inter-Bank Offered Rate (LIBOR). There was therefore little scope for societies to undertake profitable mortgage lending by tapping wholesale markets. On the asset side of their balance sheets,

---

[69] A. Offer, 'Narrow banking, real estate, and financial stability in the UK, c. 1870–2010', University of Oxford Discussion Paper in Economic and Social History no. 116 (2013).

societies earned more on their liquid assets (LIBOR-related rates) than on their mortgage lending (sub-LIBOR rates). For this reason, the building societies regulator, the Registrar of Friendly Societies, set a 30 per cent maximum for liquidity holdings as well as a 12 per cent minimum. A few societies maximised their profitability by holding close to the maximum level of liquidity allowed.

Building societies regulated their mortgage lending depending on their inflow of retail savings. From time to time a shortfall of savings meant that societies had to ration their mortgage lending, making creditworthy mortgage borrowers wait some months in a queue until they could be granted a loan. One advantage of the system was that house price rises tended to be kept within certain bounds, because excessive rises were choked off by mortgage rationing. When inflows were plentiful, societies lent more, but they did not start to compete on price (lowering margins) or accept lower-quality borrowers. If societies experienced a surplus of inflows over their lending commitments, they would build up their (more profitable) liquidity and, if necessary, curb inflows by pricing their share accounts less competitively (ending special saving offers). As a result, mortgage lending flows were stabilised and house price inflation was not exacerbated by aggressive lending. Conservative lending criteria and few sustained falls in house prices meant that loan quality remained high and loan losses were minute. From time to time smaller societies would encounter problems, usually resulting from weak management and, occasionally, fraud, and the larger societies would take it in turns to absorb them.[70] It was understood that the building society sector would look after its own.

Margaret Thatcher's government was strongly committed to wider homeownership and took a dim view of the BSA's cartel and mortgage lending queues.[71] In 1980 it was agreed that the clearers should be allowed to offer mainstream mortgages, enabling them to compete head to head with the builders. This was arguably one of the most significant acts of deregulation of the UK financial sector in the post-war period. The BSA manoeuvred to allow societies to lend more and to solve the queuing problem by raising the builders' lending rates relative to wholesale rates. The builders found themselves competing against newly formed specialist mortgage lenders that raised funds in the wholesale market. The BSA accepted *faute de mieux* the participation of others, including the clearing banks, in the mortgage market, but argued that they should not be subject to more restrictions than their competitors – the

---

[70] I. F. Hay Davison and M. Stuart-Smith, *Grays Building Society: investigation under section 110 of the Building Societies Act, 1962*, Cmnd 7557 (London, 1979).

[71] Lawson, *The view from No. 11*, 86–7.

proverbial unlevel playing field.[72] The BSA's lobbying proved to be successful, and the government passed the Building Societies Act 1986, which empowered building societies inter alia to raise up to 40 per cent of their funds from wholesale sources and to convert to banking status. The legislation allowed the larger building societies to move from being deposit-led institutions and become asset-led, like the banks.

The sterling balance sheets of the leading building societies were a sufficient match for the retail businesses of the clearing banks, and, when the herd of major banks and builders decided that the growth of mortgage lending was a strategic priority, the home loan market expanded considerably. Building societies found it relatively easy to expand by tapping wholesale markets, in part because they were perceived to be safe institutions and partly because of a quirk: wholesale lenders to building societies were very senior creditors, ranking ahead of the societies' capital and reserves, and retail savers who held share accounts.

Competition did not lead, at least initially, to a diminution of overall margins. Instead, a greater willingness to lend resulted in easier loan ratios, in particular higher loans relative to the values of underlying properties (LTVs) and higher repayments on loans relative to borrowers' income (income multiples). The building societies became more like banks, many of the larger ones converting to banking status, and the clearers became more like building societies as mortgages became a significant part of their sterling loan books.

An aspect of the larger building societies becoming more like banks was their desire to offer a full range of retail banking products, including current (or chequing) accounts. One of the leading mutual building societies, Nationwide, started to pay interest on sight deposits held in current accounts, challenging a long-standing custom of the clearing banks, which did not pay interest. Other banks and builders followed suit, leading to a significant growth of interest-bearing (ib) sight deposits, a component of M1. This led to the breakdown of the M1 equations in the early 1980s.[73] The absence of a workable forecasting equation had not stopped the setting of targets in the past, but it did not help the candidature of M1 or nib M1.

A consequence of bank deregulation was that the maturity mismatch of their balance sheets increased dramatically as they lent 'long' on mortgages, and continued to borrow 'short' in retail and wholesale markets. Traditional building societies had managed a similar maturity mismatch

---

[72] M. Boleat, *National housing finance systems: a comparative study* (London, 1985), 54.

[73] Trundle and Pemberton, 'Recent changes in the use of cash'; Trundle, 'The demand for M1 in the UK'; Hotson, 'British monetary targets, 1976 to 1987', 18.

and faced the risk that short-term savings could be withdrawn, leaving a liquidity problem. However, the building societies had not relied on wholesale funding, and their pool of retail savings was largely protected from competitors, both inside and outside the sector.

UK building societies and banks managed to avoid the problem of duration mismatching (as distinct from maturity mismatching) – a problem that necessitated bailouts for large numbers of US savings and loan associations (SLAs) in the 1980s. SLAs typically offered mortgages with interest rates fixed for five years (long-duration assets). Their savings rates had been relatively sticky, but a greater volatility in short-term interest rates since 1979 forced SLAs to raise their savings rates in line with market rates so as to maintain their funding (short-duration liabilities). Sharp rises in interest rates exposed a serious mismatch between their long-duration assets and their short-duration liabilities, leading to unprecedented losses.[74] In the United Kingdom, duration mismatching was not a problem, because mortgage loans were normally provided with variable (adjustable) borrowing rates and, when fixed rates were offered, duration matched funding was secured. However, borrowers faced considerable interest rate uncertainty, and UK politicians came under electoral pressure to curb interest rate rises.

Aftermath

There was talk of depoliticising interest rates in Britain by encouraging longer-duration lending rates, but this market was slow to develop. This meant that ministers insisted on keeping political control over rates, and there was always a need to balance what was required for monetary control and the interests of homeowners. The balancing act was particularly sensitive for the Thatcher government because of its espousal of home ownership and its policy of selling council houses (social housing).

Deregulation in the 1980s had the disconcerting effect of making a mockery of the MTFS's monetary targets, not just for one year but for each year, until the system was allowed to lapse in the middle of the 1980s. The unforeseen growth in bank lending, sustained through much of the 1980s, led to high levels of broad money growth and lots of political 'egg on face'. However, it did have the beneficial effect of facilitating growth in the economy. This had not been part of the government's monetarist plan, nor had it been predicted by official (Keynesian) forecasters. What it did mean, though, was that the 1981 Budget did not lead to a

---

[74] L. L. Bryan, *Breaking up the bank: rethinking an industry under siege* (Burr Ridge, IL, 1988), 47.

protracted recession but to a sustained recovery. Inflation did come down, but it was hardly a monetarist victory in terms of monetary control leading to disinflation.

With the benefit of hindsight, one might ask why the government was not able to extricate itself more quickly from the political fallout from its doomed attempts to meet heroically low monetary targets.[75] Sir Ian Gilmour joked that monetary policy had become 'the uncontrollable in pursuit of the indefinable', and the 1982 Budget recast the MTFS in a more flexible format, with a bewildering array of targets for a number of broad and narrow monetary aggregates.[76] In addition, a number of indicators (as distinct from targets) were mentioned, including the course of the exchange rate, apparent real interest rates, the state of certain asset markets and the concurrent course of nominal GDP.[77] The government's policy was played out in two curiously disconnected ways: at a political level it was held up as a totem of the Thatcher government's monetarist revolution, but at a technical level it was a means of allowing a non-monetarist policy to operate in monetarist clothing.[78] Would it have been better to come clean more quickly, and openly accept that deregulation required the adoption of financial targets other than broad money? Nominal GDP and the exchange rate were possibilities touted at the time.[79]

In his Zurich speech of January 1981, before the linchpin Budget of that year, Lawson advanced the argument that broad money tended to grow excessively while interest rates were high and inflation was being squeezed out of the system. He suggested that this would be a temporary phenomenon and that broad money growth would settle down after a period of time.[80] Lawson and the inner circle of economic ministers ploughed on with the MTFS and hoped the edifice could be got to work. This did not happen, and the government's public enthusiasm for monetary targeting was severely tested. In Lawson's first Budget as Chancellor, in April 1984, he dropped the targets for narrow money (M1) and the broadest official definition of money (PSL2, which included building society accounts). These aggregates happened to be overshooting, and he adopted a target

---

[75] Healey, *The time of my life*, 489.

[76] Young, *One of us*, 203; Riddell, *The Thatcher government*, 82; Goodhart, 'The conduct of monetary policy', 306.

[77] Fforde, 'Setting monetary objectives', 200.

[78] G. T. Pepper, *Inside Thatcher's monetarist revolution* (London, 1998); Keegan, *Mrs Thatcher's economic experiment*, 159–82; Keegan, *Mr Lawson's gamble*, 60, 67.

[79] R. Leigh-Pemberton, 'Some aspects of UK monetary policy', *BEQB*, 24, 1984, 475, 477–8.

[80] Lawson, 'Thatcherism in practice', 6.

for broad monetary base (M0) that had a track record for growing at a predictably slow rate.[81]

In practice, Lawson continued the custom, established in Howe's later years, of adjusting interest rates in the light of exchange rate developments. Sterling's weakness in the summer of 1984 and in the first quarter of 1985 led the government to raise base rates to 14 per cent and tighten fiscal policy. In the Budget of April 1985, the Chancellor announced that over-funding would cease and be replaced by a policy of full funding. £M3 started to overshoot its target, but the authorities allowed base rates to decline in view of the strength of sterling, and in October 1985 the target for £M3 was suspended. In the Budget of March 1986, a £M3 target of 11 to 15 per cent was set, but even this was overshot by the banks expanding their mortgage lending. No target was set for broad money in the Budget of March 1987.[82]

Opponents of the Thatcher government argued that the 1981 Budget was no more than a plan to reduce demand and raise unemployment, thereby undermining the trades union movement. As we have seen, Howe's ERG had been concerned that unemployment resulting from disinflation policies could last for more than one Parliament, with damaging consequences for the incumbent government at the next election. Biting the bullet early does appear to have been a factor behind the 1981 Budget, although the memoirs of those involved do not make this abundantly clear. After the event, some of those involved, notably Robin Leigh-Pemberton, Richardson's successor as Governor of the Bank of England, suggested that the economy had indeed needed a shock for the medicine to work.[83]

By the end of the second Thatcher government, in 1987, there was no appetite to extend the MTFS, or formulate policy in terms of monetary targets. Thatcher was resistant to joining the European Exchange Rate Mechanism, but her Chancellor, Lawson, shadowed the deutschmark for much of 1987. In 1988 the Treasury sought to promote a policy rule in which MLR was adjusted in response to changes in nominal income and the exchange rate. A formulaic policy rule proved to be too mechanical, however, and it had to be overridden after a short period. In his resignation speech, Lawson concluded that the Bank should be given greater autonomy for tactical decisions on interest rates, but it was clear that the Prime Minister would not countenance such a change.[84]

---

[81] Dimsdale, 'British monetary policy since 1945', 133–4.   [82] Ibid., 136–7.
[83] Leigh-Pemberton, 'Some aspects of UK monetary policy'.
[84] C. A. E. Goodhart, 'The Bank of England over the last 35 years', in *Bankhistorisches Archiv*, supplement 43, *Welche Aufgaben muß eine Zentralbank wahrnehmen? Historische Erfahrungen und europäische Perspektiven* (Stuttgart, 2004), 44.

In 1989 Lawson's successor, John Major, prevailed upon Thatcher to join the ERM, aligning sterling with the deutschmark. Sterling's ignominious exit from the ERM in 1992 left the Conservative government, by then led by Major, without a policy. His Chancellor, Norman Lamont, was replaced by Kenneth Clarke. Faced with a situation in which the government's credibility in the markets had hit rock bottom, Major and Clarke were willing to consider a more independent role for the Bank and its then Governor, Eddie George. It was agreed that the government would set an inflation target, the Bank would publish an inflation forecast, and the minutes of periodic meetings on interest rates between the Chancellor and the Governor would be published.[85] The process became known as the 'Ken and Eddie show', and proved a considerable success. The Chancellor retained final control over Bank Rate, but greater transparency encouraged prompt policy responses to deviations of prospective inflation from target. This radical change in British procedures was influenced by New Zealand's pioneering use, since 1989, of an inflation target and rate setting by an independent central bank. Other countries were to follow this example, Canada being an early adopter in 1991.[86]

In 1997 the incoming Labour government, led by Tony Blair and with Gordon Brown as Chancellor, retained the inflation-targeting regime and developed the process further by appointing an independent Monetary Policy Committee (MPC) within the Bank, charged with making monthly interest rate decisions. The first Blair government sought to distance itself from 'tax and spend' policies and emphasised financial prudence, adopting a 'golden rule' for public sector deficits over the cycle. Not everyone had become a monetarist, but counter-inflation policy was given pride of place.[87]

Inflation targeting combined with interest rates as an instrument of policy proved to be highly successful, and it has to be asked why the authorities had bothered with an intermediate target for money in the 1970s and 1980s. Money supply might be a useful indicator for forecasting inflation, but it was unlikely to be the only indicator.[88] As it happens, money proved to be a terrible indicator in the 1980s, and targeting inflation directly would have provided a solution. There was no need to

---

[85] Ibid., 42–3.

[86] B. S. Bernanke, T. Laubach, F. S. Mishkin and A. Posen, *Inflation targeting: lessons from the international experience* (Princeton, NJ, 1999).

[87] M. D. Woodford, *Interest and prices: foundations of a theory of monetary policy* (Princeton, NJ, 2003).

[88] M. D. Woodford, 'How important is money in the conduct of monetary policy?', *Journal of Money, Credit and Banking*, 40, 8 (December 2008), 1561–98.

be too dogged about the monetary aggregates.[89] Sceptics of monetary targeting had made this point in the early 1980s – to no avail.[90] So why did the authorities remain wedded to monetary targets for so long? The answer seems to be that DCE ceilings in the late 1960s, the unpublished monetary guidelines of the early 1970s and the published M3/£M3 targets of the late 1970s were indirect means of containing the PSBR via the counterparts identity. The Thatcher government took PSBR targeting seriously and did not need £M3 as a proxy for controlling the PSBR. It nevertheless kept a £M3 target as a self-denying ordinance in recognition of monetarist arguments.

Conclusion

By all accounts, Margaret Thatcher's government did not achieve a monetarist revolution. Inflation was curbed, but not monetary growth. The MTFS was a disaster and eventually dropped, and the Thatcher government did not create an institutional bulwark against inflation. It took the calamity of sterling's exit from the ERM in 1992 to overcome prime ministerial opposition to independent central banking. This is not to suggest that an independent central bank is the only way to control inflation; in certain circumstances, 'concerted action' might have been the answer. The point is that the Thatcher government failed to develop processes – either inside or outside government – that had counter-inflationary credentials.

If the 1981 Budget did not achieve a monetarist revolution, was it an aberration – a one-off response to earlier policy errors? It was motivated in large measure by a desire to save the doomed MTFS. It was viewed as a counter-Keynesian revolution, notably by the 364 economists in their letter to *The Times*. The government's palliative arguments about EFC and crowding in have tended to be discounted, not least by some of those involved at the time. This has been interpreted to imply that the 1981 Budget was no more than a deflationary budget.[91] However, the notion that controlling inflation should be the primary objective of economic policy did take hold. Eddie George's successor as Bank Governor, Mervyn King, argued that keeping inflation within a target range would help to stabilise the real economy, whereas attempts to stabilise real output

---

[89] M. A. King, 'No money, no inflation: the role of money in the economy', *BEQB*, 42, 2002, 162–77; P. M. W. Tucker, 'Managing the central bank's balance sheet: where monetary policy meets financial stability', *BEQB*, 44, 2004, 359–82.

[90] F. T. Blackaby, 'Comments on Michael Foot's paper "Monetary targets"', in B. Griffiths and G. E. Wood (eds.), *Monetary targets* (London, 1981), 54–61.

[91] Dow and Saville, *A critique of monetary policy*, 111–14.

directly – Keynesian counter-cyclical policy – could lead to inflation. High inflation would eventually have to be curbed with disinflationary policies and recession.[92] King's argument was a revival of an earlier critique of activist demand management advanced by Samuel Brittan, among others, in the early 1970s. This argument was accepted, in part, by the Labour government from 1975 onwards, and with more fervour by the Thatcher government.[93]

Brittan's argument was based on experience rather than a well-articulated economic model, and as such it did not gain much traction with economists, particularly those versed in the Keynesian tradition. However, the intellectual case for basing policy on published rules, rather than relying on discretion, was being developed in the late 1970s.[94] The case for policy rules had initially been formulated in terms of money rules, but attention shifted to inflation targets when it became clear (to most people) that monetary targets were impractical. Inflation targets were rationalised as commitment devices that helped to stabilise inflation expectations, and thence output and employment.[95] Confusingly, the models used to articulate this approach were described as 'New Keynesian' (at least by American academics).[96] Not to be outdone, Friedman claimed that inflation targeting followed the spirit of his money rule:

We've all worked on getting rules, my rule and others, [on the ground that] it's such a hard job to keep prices stable. Then along comes the 1980s, and central banks all over the world target price stability; and lo and behold, all of them basically succeed... So it must be that [it] is easier to do than we thought it was... Once [central banks] really understood that avoiding inflation, keeping prices stable, was their real objective, their first order objective, and put that above everything else, they all turned out to be able to do it.[97]

So there you have it. The 1981 Budget did not pan out to be a monetarist revolution in any normal sense of the term. It was motivated, in part,

---

[92] M. A. King, 'Monetary policy: practice ahead of theory', Mais lecture, *BEQB*, 45, 2005, 226–36.

[93] S. Brittan, *Steering the economy: the role of the Treasury* (Harmondsworth, 1971), 463–7, 472–83; cf. Brittan, *The Treasury under the Tories*, 249–59; Leigh-Pemberton, 'Some aspects of monetary policy', 475.

[94] F. E. Kydland and E. C. Prescott, 'Rules rather than discretion: the inconsistency of optimal plans', *Journal of Political Economy*, 85, 3 (June 1977), 473–92; Goodhart, 'The conduct of monetary policy', 296.

[95] Woodford, *Interest and prices*.

[96] R. G. J. Clarida, J. Gali and M. Gertler, 'The science of monetary policy: a New Keynesian perspective', *Journal of Economic Literature*, 37, 4 (December 1999), 1661–707; C. E. Walsh, *Monetary theory and policy* (Cambridge, MA, 2010).

[97] 'Agreeing to disagree: Robert Kuttner speaks with Milton Friedman', *The American Prospect*, 5 January 2006; Woodford, 'How important is money?', 1565.

by political expediency and the need to address past policy mistakes, but that is not the whole story. It was a counter-revolution against traditional Keynesianism and an augury of so-called 'New Keynesianism' – a step towards the re-establishment of a nominal anchor in economic management. While inflation targeting worked, both Keynesians and monetarists claimed that it had been their idea all along.[98] In Britain it took more than a decade to develop institutions with credibility to deliver low inflation. The delay had as much to do with the Thatcher government as any other: a ministerial veto on the depoliticisation of interest rate setting, not helped by a turf war between the Bank and the Treasury.

Thatcher's government also set in train another set of institutional developments with important implications for monetary stability, or the lack of it. Financial sector deregulation led to a banking system that was, and remains, asset-driven, dominated by property-related lending and dependent on wholesale funding. It proved possible to use interest rate policy to keep the economy close to its inflation target, although the exact way this worked remains unclear.[99] What is clear, however, is that the interest rate weapon had little effect on the deregulated banking sector, and therefore on monetary growth. Although the inflation target was met, this did not stop an overexpansion of the banking sector and its implosion in the credit crunch of 2007–8. Monetary growth and its credit counterparts may not have mattered much for the conduct of inflation policy, but they were important for the soundness of the banking system.

---

[98] P. R. Krugman, 'Who was Milton Friedman?', *Journal of Monetary Economics*, 55, 4 (May 2008), 835–56; P. R. Krugman, 'Response to Nelson and Schwartz', *Journal of Monetary Economics*, 55, 4 (May 2008), 857–60.

[99] Goodhart, 'The conduct of monetary policy', 328–30.

9   The 1981 Budget: 'a Dunkirk, not an Alamein'

Duncan Needham

Introduction

The 1981 Budget is principally remembered for the decision to raise taxes in the depths of the worst UK recession for a generation. By tightening fiscal policy in a slump, Margaret Thatcher's government flew in the face of the post-war Keynesian orthodoxy, famously incurring the wrath of the economics establishment. But, while the major public debates were over fiscal policy, an often neglected driver of the 1981 Budget was the need to restore monetary policy credibility. Like its Labour predecessor, the Conservative government had placed the fight against inflation at the heart of economic policy. Unlike its predecessor, it hoped to win the battle without resorting to an incomes policy.[1] In March 1980, in line with Milton Friedman's dictum that 'inflation is always and everywhere a monetary phenomenon', Sir Geoffrey Howe launched the Medium-Term Financial Strategy, laying out a four-year series of declining target ranges for the broad money supply (£M3), and explaining that 'control of the money supply will over a period of years reduce the rate of inflation'.[2]

In March 1981, with £M3 growth significantly above target and inflation still higher than when they had taken office, ministers recognised that the monetary leg of the MTFS was flawed.[3] This chapter explains why it

---

This chapter draws upon D. J. Needham, *UK monetary policy from devaluation to Thatcher, 1967–82* (Basingstoke, 2014), and I acknowledge the kind permission of Palgrave Macmillan in consenting to its inclusion here.

[1] There was, of course, no escaping the government's obligations towards determining incomes in the public sector.

[2] £M3 comprised currency in circulation with the public and the sterling deposits of UK residents. There was also a declining four-year 'projection' for the PSBR, intended to be 'consistent with achieving the planned reduction in the growth of money supply over the medium term with lower interest rates': *FSBR 1980–81*, 16, 19.

[3] The final RPI release before the 1979 election showed prices rising by 9.8 per cent in the year to March 1979. In March 1981 inflation stood at 12.6 per cent, having peaked at 21.9 per cent in May 1980.

was flawed. Sir Adam Ridley suggests elsewhere in this volume that budget making is like organising a naval convoy. Here I extend the analogy to policy making in general. Successful monetary policy implementation requires that all three members of the 'macroeconomic executive' – the government, the Treasury and the Bank of England – be travelling in the same direction, if not always at precisely the same speed.[4] In 1980–81 the government, the Treasury and the Bank were heading in broadly the same direction on fiscal policy. The same could not be said of monetary policy. With a brief history of monetary targeting in the United Kingdom, this chapter shows why the Bank and sections of the Treasury were sceptical about the monetary leg of the MTFS from the outset.

As Table 9.1 shows, monetary targets in various guises had been in place since the late 1960s. Some were published, others were known only to a handful of politicians and officials. Few conformed to any narrow monetarist definition of a 'target'. As Christopher Allsopp points out, 'Monetary targets may have many justifications other than those that arise conventionally from monetarist theories.'[5] Monetarists do *not* have a monopoly on monetary targets.[6] What matters is the level of commitment. What the authorities did as a consequence of monetary targets, unpublished or published, usually proved to be more important than what they said.

Experience of operating monetary targets in the 1970s had persuaded many senior Bank and Treasury officials that tight control over the broad money supply was impracticable in an open economy such as the United Kingdom. That is not to suggest that they were against monetary targets per se. The M3 target announced by Denis Healey in July 1976 was pressed upon him by the Bank of England's Governor, Gordon Richardson, with the support of his Keynesian Chief Economist, Christopher Dow. It was blessed by a sceptical Permanent Secretary to the Treasury, Sir Douglas Wass, for the beneficial impact it might have on market sentiment. Healey's money supply targets were designed for a specific set of circumstances in the 1970s. They were conceived partly to replace the financial discipline lost after the collapse of the Bretton Woods system of fixed exchange rates and partly as an adjunct to incomes

---

[4] The term 'macroeconomic executive' is from J. S. Fforde, 'Setting monetary objectives', in Bank of England, *The development and operation of monetary policy 1960–1983: a selection of material from the Quarterly Bulletin of the Bank of England* (Oxford, 1984), 65.

[5] C. J. Allsopp, 'Macroeconomic policy: design and performance', in M. J. Artis and D. P. Cobham (eds.), *Labour's economic policies, 1974–1979* (Manchester, 1991), 30.

[6] For an explanation of how a Keynesian could reconcile himself to monetary targets, see Hacche and Taylor, *Inside the Bank of England*, 61–2.

Table 9.1 *Unpublished and published DCE, M3 and £M3 objectives, 1968–79*

	Period	Objective	Outturn	Source
M3	1968	Below £1.2 billion	£986 million	1967 Letter of Intent
DCE	1969/70	Below £400 million	*minus* £541 million	1969 Letter of Intent
DCE	1970/71	Below £900 million	£1.4 billion	1970 Budget speech
M3	1971/72	3% per quarter	15% in 1971/72	1971 Budget speech
M3	1972/73	20%	27%	Unpublished
M3	1973/74	'Not more than 15%'	25%	Unpublished
M3	1974/75	Below nominal GDP	10% (vs 13% GDP)	November 1974 Budget
M3	1975/76	Below nominal GDP	9% (vs 26% GDP)	1975 Budget speech
M3	1976/77	Below nominal GDP	10% (vs 18% GDP)	1976 Budget speech
M3	1976/77	12%	10%	22 July 1976 Statement
£M3	1976/77	9–13%	8%	December 1976 mini-Budget
DCE	1976/77	£9 billion	£3.8 billion	1976 Letter of Intent
£M3	1977/78	9–13%	16%	1977 Budget speech
DCE	1977/78	£7.7 billion	£4.1 billion	1976 Letter of Intent
£M3	1978/79	8–12%	11%	1978 Budget speech
DCE	1978/79	£6 billion	£6.8 billion	1976 Letter of Intent

Sources: D. P. Cobham, *The making of monetary policy in the UK, 1975–2000* (Chichester, 2002), 50; *Bank of England Quarterly Bulletin*; ONS; Hansard; the National Archives.[7]

policy in the battle against inflation. They grew into a fiscal constraint on the spending ambitions of the Labour government. For reasons that are explained below, this pointed to targets for the broad money supply. But few doubted the fiscal convictions of the Thatcher government after 1979. The Bank's unease with the MTFS stemmed largely from the choice of

[7] There were also ceilings for bank lending and bank deposits (the 'corset') for much of the period. For the 1968 M3 target, see L. J. Callaghan, 'Letter of Intent', 28 November 1967, TNA, T326/730; and I. d. L. Radice, 'Working party no. 3: speaking notes for Sir D. Rickett', 28 November 1967, TNA, T326/730 (which specifies £1.2 billion). For the 1971/72 quarterly target, see HC Deb., 30 March 1971, vol. 814, col. 1374; and C. J. Riley, 'Monetary assumption', 1 October 1971, TNA, T338/68. For the 1972/73 unpublished 20 per cent target, see D. V. A. Allen, 'Monetary policy – post-Budget', 21 March 1972, TNA, T326/1562; A. M. Bailey, 'Monetary policy – post-budget, 23 March 1972, TNA, T326/1562; and F. Cassell, 'Monetary policy', 26 April 1972, TNA, T326/1562. For the 1973/74 unpublished 15 per cent target, see G. S. Downey, 'Monetary policy', 16 February 1973, TNA, T233/2505. For 1974/75, see HC Deb., 12 November 1974, vol. 881, c256; and J. B. Page, 'Monetary policy', 24 October 1974, BOE, 6A50/14. For 1975/76, see HC Deb., 15 April 1975, vol. 890, c279; and P. E. Middleton, 'Possible monetary policy objectives', 31 October 1975, TNA, T386/274. For the 1976/77 'below nominal GDP target', see HC Deb., 6 April 1976, vol. 909, c237. Samuel Brittan interpreted this to mean a 15 per cent M3 target: S. Brittan, 'Another gamble on incomes policy', *Financial Times*, 7 April 1976. The remaining targets are all a matter of public record.

monetary aggregate.[8] The econometric relationship between narrow money (M1) and nominal income had survived the monetary upheavals of the 1970s; the relationship between £M3 and inflation had not.[9] In 1980 Conservative ministers launched a medium-term strategy based not on econometric evidence but on the beneficial impact monetary targets might have on confidence and expectations. A strategy based on managing down inflationary expectations relied on the government actually hitting its targets. For this, they had chosen the wrong aggregate. In doing so, they subjected themselves, and the British economy, to a monetary policy roller-coaster ride.

A brief history of UK monetary targets

In the 1960s British monetary policy was guided by the findings of the 1959 Radcliffe Report. The report dismissed the importance of the monetary aggregates: '"The supply of money" – whatever that may be made to mean – is not by itself a reliable policy measure.'[10] With the demand for money assumed to be unstable, monetary policy was assigned a subordinate role to fiscal policy in managing aggregate demand: '[M]onetary measures can help, but that is all.'[11] Insofar as the UK authorities did look at money, it was within a framework that divided the broad money supply (M3) into its counterparts, principally bank lending to the private sector and the public sector borrowing requirement.[12] In an era of (generally) balanced budgets, this meant ceilings on bank lending to the private sector. The Radcliffe Report had warned that ceilings were inimical to an efficient banking system.[13] They froze lending at an arbitrary date, favoured established bank customers at the expense of newer businesses and inhibited competition between the banks. Nonetheless, ceilings remained in place for most of the 1960s. This is because, with

---

[8] Officials were also nervous about extending targets out over a four-year period.

[9] M1 comprised currency in circulation with the public and UK residents' sterling sight deposits with UK banks. In September 1977, despite 'a touching faith that improved econometric techniques would save the day', Bank officials finally admitted that 'there is no obvious simple, single equation, demand for M3 balances': Hotson, 'British monetary targets, 1976 to 1987', 6.

[10] *Radcliffe Committee*, Cmnd 827, para. 504.   [11] Ibid., para. 514.

[12] The counterparts approach analysed the flow of funds between sectors such that ΔM3 = Δ currency + Δ reserves + bank lending to the private sector + bank holding of government securities – Δ non-bank liabilities: F. H. Capie, *The Bank of England: 1950s to 1979* (New York, 2010), 28. Batini and Nelson trace this approach to M. W. Holtrop's 1958 evidence to the Radcliffe Committee, based on his earlier IMF staff paper: Batini and Nelson, 'The UK's rocky road to stability', 31.

[13] *Radcliffe Committee*, Cmnd 827, para. 527.

sterling fixed under the Bretton Woods regime, attempts to run the economy at full employment led to a succession of balance of payments crises as demand increased imports and diverted exports back to the domestic market. With a chronic shortage of foreign currency reserves in the 1960s, balance of payments crises often meant recourse to the International Monetary Fund.

Britain borrowed more from the IMF than any other country in the 1960s.[14] Initially, loans came with low conditionality.[15] The shift in emphasis came after loans to the new Labour government in November 1964 and May 1965. The Treasury explained:

> The Government's undertakings to the IMF as a result of the extensive use of the Fund's facilities during this period compelled the authorities to modify their approach to monetary policy... [W]hile policy continued to place great emphasis on controlling bank lending to the private sector, greater attention was paid to money supply and to domestic credit expansion.[16]

To secure another IMF loan after devaluation in November 1967, the Chancellor, James Callaghan, acknowledged 'the expectation at present that bank credit expansion will be sufficiently limited to ensure that the growth of the money supply will be less in 1968 than the present estimate for 1967'.[17] Accordingly, the banks were told to freeze aggregate lending at the mid-November 1967 level. This was the first time that a lending ceiling had been publicly linked to IMF assistance, because of the stigma attached to having policy imposed from outside.[18] The link was cemented in May 1969 when Callaghan's successor, Roy Jenkins, agreed to a published £400 million domestic credit expansion ceiling, comprised of an

---

[14] Britain drew upon IMF resources in 1948, 1956, 1961, 1964, 1965, 1968 and 1969 (and again in 1972, 1976 and 1977).

[15] In 1959 a Treasury official suggested that 'it would be repugnant to the dignity of a country of the UK's status' to have *any* conditions applied to IMF loans: 'Note to D. H. F. Rickett', 8 May 1959, TNA, T236/5740 [emphasis in original]. Increasing conditionality was also a result of the United Kingdom borrowing higher 'tranches' of its IMF quota. Borrowing from the first 'gold' tranche came with few strings attached. As members drew on successively higher credit tranches (each 25 per cent thick), however, they could expect increasingly harsh conditionality from the IMF.

[16] 'Control of credit in the private sector', T267/30, 3.

[17] In November 1967 the 'present estimate' for M3 growth in 1967 was £1.2 billion: Radice, 'Working party no. 3: speaking notes', T326/730; Callaghan, 'Letter of Intent', T326/730.

[18] The 1961 loan came after an 'IMF-friendly' statement by Selwyn Lloyd, the then Chancellor: B. M. Clift and J. D. Tomlinson, 'Negotiating credibility: Britain and the International Monetary Fund, 1956–1976', *Contemporary European History*, 17, 4 (November 2008), 552. In 1965 the IMF insisted that bank advances to the private sector over the next year be limited to 105 per cent of the April 1965 total: 'Control of credit in the private sector', T267/30, 5.

unpublished £250 million target and a £150 million margin of error, as a condition for a further loan.[19]

DCE was the IMF's preferred aggregate and adjusted the money supply for financing of the balance of payments from official reserves.[20] It rested on the assumption, shared with the monetarists, that the demand for money was both stable and predictable.[21] In order to test this assumption, the Bank set up the internal Money Supply Group in October 1968. Despite initial hostility towards the 'neo-quantity theorists', members found themselves agreeing with a number of core monetarist principles.[22] Disavowing the Radcliffe Report, they found that the velocity of circulation (and therefore the demand for money), was 'fairly stable' – a conclusion that was 'generally consistent with the quantity theory point of view as expounded by Friedman'.[23] The group's final report was published in 1970. It stated that, 'in the United Kingdom, movements in the money stock have preceded movements in money incomes' and that, 'in the absence of evidence to the contrary, a consistent lead is a prima facie indication of causation'.[24] Combined with the evidence that the demand for money could be controlled with interest rates, this was a powerful rejection of the Radcliffian approach. As the principal author of the Money Supply Group's final report, Charles Goodhart, pointed out:

The main conclusions of this were that the chief intermediate objectives of monetary policy should be the rates of growth of the monetary aggregates, i.e. the money stock, in one or other of its various definitions, or DCE (and not particular components of these, such as bank lending to the private sector).[25]

The Money Supply Group's theoretical work underpinned the introduction of Competition and Credit Control by Ted Heath's government in 1971, recognised by Forrest Capie as 'the biggest change in monetary

---

[19] A. J. C. Edwards, 'Note for the record: domestic credit expansion and the central government borrowing requirement', 12 May 1969, TNA, T326/979; 'Control of credit in the private sector', T267/30, 22.

[20] The IMF's initial focus was on the central bank's balance sheet (i.e. the monetary base). After negotiation, officials persuaded the Fund that, in the United Kingdom's case, DCE should be predicated on the broad money supply.

[21] David Laidler refers to the stability of the demand for money as the sine qua non of monetarism: D. E. W. Laidler, *Monetarist perspectives* (Oxford, 1982), vii.

[22] In January 1969 Goodhart wrote that he 'was not sorry to see evidence unfavourable to the neo-quantity theorists': C. A. E. Goodhart, 'Visit to Mr A. O. Hughes of Nottingham University on 28th January' (covering note), 31 January 1969, London, BOE, 2A128/1.

[23] A. D. Crockett, 'The velocity of circulation of money', 2 April 1969, BOE, 2A128/2.

[24] Goodhart and Crockett, 'The importance of money', 176–7.

[25] Goodhart, *Monetary theory and practice*, 96.

policy since the Second World War'.[26] CCC swept away the panoply of lending controls in use throughout the 1960s and replaced them with the 'interest rate weapon' – more active use of Bank Rate to control the broad money supply. This was recognised at the time by politicians, officials, practitioners and academics alike. Commending the proposal to the Prime Minister, the Chancellor, Anthony Barber, wrote that 'the new system will operate on the money supply as a whole, putting more reliance on changes in interest rates'.[27] In February 1971, opening the first meeting to discuss the Bank's proposal, the Permanent Secretary to the Treasury, Sir Douglas Allen, declared: 'It should be assumed that it was still desired to have a numerical target for the monetary aggregates.'[28] Explaining the policy to his clients four months later, the influential City analyst Gordon Pepper, of W. Greenwell & Co., explained that 'the main emphasis will be placed on attempting to control the domestic money supply'.[29] The monetarist academic Brian Griffiths agreed: 'The intention of the new system is to move away from control of bank lending to control of one of "the broader money aggregates".'[30]

CCC was predicated upon more flexible use of Bank Rate. This produced the first unpublished M3 target, in March 1972.[31] In his 1972 Budget, Barber announced a 5 per cent real GDP growth target. The Bank's demand for money equations estimated that M3 would have to grow by 20 per cent simply to accommodate the fiscal stimulus announced in the Budget.[32] Less than 20 per cent and the government might not finance its 5 per cent GDP growth target; more than 20 per cent

---

[26] Capie, The Bank of England, 427.

[27] A. P. L. Barber, 'New approach to credit control', 6 May 1971, TNA, T338/40.

[28] D. A. Harding, 'Minutes of a meeting held on 18 February 1971 to discuss the Bank of England paper', 22 February 1971, TNA, T326/1261.

[29] G. T. Pepper, 'The gilt-edged market and the Bank of England's proposals', June 1971, 1, Churchill, THCR AS 3/17.

[30] B. Griffiths, 'Resource efficiency, monetary policy and the reform of the UK banking system', Journal of Money, Credit and Banking, 5, 1 (February 1973), 72.

[31] Susan Howson concludes that monetary targets 'could not be seriously adopted until the government had given up the commitment to a fixed exchange rate' in June 1972. An independent monetary policy is compatible with a fixed currency, however, if the foreign exchange reserves are sufficient. As Brian Tew and Peter Browning point out, the return to current account surplus in 1971 was an important factor in the timing of CCC. With less strain on the currency reserves, monetary policy could increasingly be directed towards the domestic economy. S. K. Howson, 'Money and monetary policy since 1945', in R. C. Floud and P. A. Johnson (eds.), The Cambridge economic history of modern Britain, vol. III, Structural change and growth, 1939–2000 (Cambridge, 2004), 157; J. H. B. Tew, 'Monetary policy: part I', in F. T. Blackaby (ed.), British economic policy, 1960–74 (Cambridge, 1978), 239; P. Browning, The Treasury and economic policy, 1964–1985 (London, 1986), 276.

[32] F. Cassell, 'Monetary policy – post-Budget', 20 March 1972, TNA, T326/1562.

and there might be an additional, unwanted, monetary stimulus. This would run the risk of overheating the economy. But 20 per cent M3 growth was unprecedented. Heath had already shown his hostility towards the higher interest rates that would be required to rein in any excessive monetary growth, either by increasing the cost of bank lending, or by raising yields on new gilt-edged securities.[33] In an attempt to secure the interest rate flexibility demanded by CCC, the Bank and the Treasury turned the 20 per cent M3 forecast into a target:

Numerical targets for money supply were not given in the Budget Speech. But the Chancellor has accepted our advice that for the present policy should be directed towards a target rate of growth of money supply of about 20% in the financial year 1972/73 – 20% being the growth which the Bank of England's demand-for-money equations suggest will be required, given the outlook for real output and prices, if there is to be no significant rise in interest rates from their present levels.[34]

What followed was one of the most intense periods of monetary chaos in recent British history. By the time the policy was de facto abandoned, in December 1973, M3 had grown by 72 per cent. Britain's highest ever inflation followed hard on the heels of Competition and Credit Control, apparently vindicating Friedman's assertion that excess monetary growth leads inevitably to higher prices after a lag. There also followed the worst banking crisis since the nineteenth century, and, despite its adroit handling of the 'Lifeboat' operation to rescue the stricken secondary banks after the property boom ended in 1973, the Bank's reputation suffered a serious blow.[35] Failure to control the money supply under Competition and Credit Control would shape the Bank's attitude to monetary policy for years to come.

There were a number of technical problems with the unpublished M3 target agreed in March 1972.[36] But the simple fact was, despite the econometric evidence that had suggested otherwise in 1970, it was just

---

[33] For a fuller explanation of Heath's reluctance to raise Bank Rate, see D. J. Needham, 'Britain's money supply experiment, 1971–73', Cambridge Working Paper in Social and Economic History no. 10 (2012), available online at www.econsoc.hist.cam.ac.uk/working_papers.html.

[34] Capie implies that the Treasury was trying to cap interest rates and M3 at the same time. They were not. They were trying to ensure that M3 growth above 20 per cent would trigger a higher Bank Rate. Capie, *The Bank of England*, 646; F. Cassell, 'Monetary policy', 26 April 1972, TNA, T326/1562.

[35] During the 'Heath–Barber boom' house prices more than doubled and commercial prices nearly trebled. See M. I. Reid, *The secondary banking crisis, 1973–75: its causes and course* (London, 1982); Capie, *The Bank of England*, 524–86; C. Gordon, *The Cedar story: the night the City was saved* (London, 1993).

[36] See Needham, *UK monetary policy*, for a detailed discussion of the technical problems associated with CCC.

not possible to exercise tight control over the broad money supply in the United Kingdom, especially when the power to set interest rates lay in the hands of a politician such as Ted Heath who was more committed to a high-profile GDP growth target than to an unpublished M3 target. Heath was concerned that higher interest rates would be construed as a return to the 'stop-go' policies of the 1960s.[37] He was also worried that higher debt servicing and mortgage costs would derail the delicate negotiations with the employers and unions over incomes policies, then seen as the natural solution to cost-push inflation. As the President of the Confederation of British Industry pointed out in 1972, 'The recently announced further increase in bank base rates to 7% will damage the prospects of agreement on a package to contain inflation.'[38] Clearly, the CBI had not been bitten by the monetarist bug.

After M3 growth of 27 per cent in 1972/73, the Bank was told to find a way of controlling the money supply that did not rely on higher interest rates.[39] The result was the supplementary special deposits scheme (the 'corset'), which penalised banks that grew their interest-bearing liabilities (deposits) above published thresholds, themselves derived from unpublished M3 targets.[40] The Bank explained: 'The prime objective of this device is, quite simply, to contain the growth of M3. A second objective is to avoid producing any perceptible further upthrust to the general level of interest rates.'[41]

Different institutions drew different conclusions from the failure of CCC. In 1975 Goodhart admitted:

The monetarist edifice rests largely on the stability, and predictability, of the demand-for-money function. Econometric study of the data in the 1960s had suggested that in the UK we, too, could build parts of our monetary policy on this basis. Subsequent experience has revealed weakness in this foundation.[42]

That same year he formulated Goodhart's law: 'Any observed statistical regularity will tend to collapse once pressure is placed on it for control purposes.' This was not abstract theorising; it was a reflection on the painful experience of failing to control M3 under Competition and Credit Control.

The Bank concluded that M3 was a 'decidedly defective' measure and began a long campaign to shift the emphasis to M1, which continued to

[37] 'R. T. Armstrong to A. M. Bailey', 16 June 1972, TNA, T326/1563.
[38] G. S. Downey, 'Bank base rates and the CBI', 24 July 1972, TNA, T326/1564.
[39] 'A. P. L. Barber to G. W. H. Richardson', 15 November 1973, TNA, T233/2508.
[40] Capie, The Bank of England, 521.
[41] A. L. Coleby, 'Controlling growth in M3', 29 November 1973, BOE, 6A50/12.
[42] Goodhart, Monetary theory and practice, 113.

enjoy a more robust econometric relationship with nominal GDP.[43] The Treasury had always been sceptical of the Bank's ability to control the money supply, and fell back on its traditional remedy for cost-push inflation: incomes policy. Just as officials were retreating from M3, however, Conservative ministers were becoming increasingly enthusiastic targeters. The Financial Secretary, Terence Higgins, responded to Allen's recommendation of a 15 per cent target ahead of the 1973 Budget by arguing that 'we are aiming too low and should go for 13% rather than 15% as a target growth of money supply (M3)'.[44] The Minister of State, John Nott, was persuaded against publishing the target only because it would look too high compared to the Europeans, who had recently agreed to limit money supply growth to 6 per cent, albeit on a narrower measure than M3.[45]

The Conservatives were out of office by March 1974. The monetary objective of the new Labour Chancellor, Denis Healey, was to keep M3 growth at or below nominal GDP growth.[46] With the economy moribund in the post-oil-shock recession, and inflation high, this was easily achieved. In July 1975, however, with inflation above 25 per cent, Healey launched a new incomes policy. Wage increases would be limited to £6 per week.[47] It was hoped that this would reduce inflation to below 10 per cent by the autumn of 1976. But, perversely, by hitting its inflation target the government would almost certainly breach its monetary objective: 10 per cent inflation implied nominal GDP growth of 13 per cent, versus forecast M3 growth of 15.4 per cent.[48] This created a conundrum: bank lending to the private sector would have to increase for economic recovery to take hold; consistent with the counterparts approach, this would require an offsetting PSBR reduction to ensure compliance with the objective of keeping M3 growth below nominal GDP growth. Healey had endured a torrid time getting less than £1 billion of cuts through Cabinet ahead of his 1975 Budget, so there was little chance of reducing

---

[43] Goodhart had argued as early as February 1971 that the structural changes brought by CCC 'make the case for concentrating on M1': C. A. E. Goodhart, 'A new approach to credit control: some quantitative implications', 25 February 1971, 3A8/11; J. B. Page, 'Monetary policy', April 1973, BOE, 6A50/8.

[44] C. W. Kelly, 'Monetary policy', 19 February 1973, TNA T233/2505.

[45] D. Haig, 'Monetary policy', 22 January 1973, TNA, T233/2505.

[46] J. B. Page, 'Monetary policy', 24 October 1974, BOE, 6A50/13.

[47] £6 equated to about 12 per cent for average wage earners. Incomes were frozen for those earning more than £8,500 per annum: The attack on inflation, Cmnd 6151 (London, 1975).

[48] Home Finance Division, 'Counter-inflation policy: monetary policy', 27 June 1975, TNA, T233/2831; G. E. A. Kentfield, 'Money supply: a look ahead', 7 July 1975, BOE, EID4/200.

the PSBR with further spending cuts.[49] In July 1975 officials were charged with 'restricting the growth of M3 other than by cutting the PSBR'.[50] The eventual solution, despite the traumas of CCC, was another M3 target. Bank Director Kit McMahon explained:

If we can establish internally, with the Treasury, the principle of keeping the growth in money supply down and taking any necessary measures to that end, we will in due course get an extra lever on the Chancellor to attack public expenditure itself. . . [I]f we could get a public statement of a target for the growth of money supply, we should have a tighter rope round the Chancellor's neck.[51]

The M3 target imposed on Healey in July 1976 was born of the need to keep monetary policy consistent with incomes policy in the fight against inflation. Because of the counterparts approach, it grew to become a restraint on the spending ambitions of the Labour government – fiscal policy via the monetary policy back door. There was also the need to calm the gilt market, which was increasingly concerned about money supply growth in the crisis year of 1976. As Wass remarked, 'Notwithstanding the pain a target could inflict on us later on, the confidence-raising value in the package could make all the difference between success and failure. Since we cannot afford failure we must have a target.'[52]

But, unlike the unpublished M3 target agreed with his Conservative predecessor in March 1972, there was no econometric evidence under-pinning Healey's published target in July 1976. As Anthony Hotson points out, 'Britain's monetary regime was not built on the back of a stable equation or model of money, but on a conceit intended to shackle the state's spending bureaucracies.'[53] As Goodhart explained at the time:

The statistical basis for monetarism – a stable relationship between the monetary aggregates and nominal incomes – which has always been weaker in the UK than in the USA for example, has recently largely collapsed. A time when the authorities have moved towards quantitative monetary targets. . .is perhaps not the best time to make a big splash about the breakdown of these relationships.[54]

January 1977 was not the time to 'make a big splash' about the lack of econometric evidence linking the broad money supply to nominal incomes because, alongside a two-year programme of DCE and PSBR ceilings agreed with the IMF in return for yet another loan, the Labour

---

[49] D. W. G. Wass, *Decline to fall: the making of British macro-economic policy and the 1976 IMF crisis* (Oxford, 2008), 100–1.
[50] Kentfield, 'Money supply: a look ahead', EID4/200.
[51] C. W. McMahon, 'Monetary policy', 26 September 1975, BOE, EID4/200.
[52] Wass, *Decline to fall*, 212.   [53] Hotson, 'British monetary targets, 1976 to 1987', 3.
[54] C. A. E. Goodhart, 'Provisional bulletin article on special deposits and supplementary special deposits', 31 January 1977, BOE, 6A50/20.

government had just announced a new 9 to 13 per cent target range for £M3 growth in 1976/77. For the next two years the government would be under the surveillance of both the IMF and the financial markets. Partly because of this, 1977 saw a rapid return of confidence, allowing Healey to boast that he was one of the few post-war Chancellors to preside over a growing economy, falling inflation, falling unemployment and a balance of payments surplus.[55]

Conservative monetary policy in opposition

The principal architect of the Medium-Term Financial Strategy, Nigel Lawson, points out that, in contrast to the detailed consideration of fiscal policy, an 'error, in hindsight, was to do so little work in Opposition on the conduct of monetary policy'.[56] This is a startling admission from a minister in a government that placed monetary policy at the heart of its agenda. After cautiously concluding in favour of published M3 targets in June 1976, a month before Healey revealed his 12 per cent target, the Conservatives announced in their October 1976 policy document, *The right approach to the economy*, that 'it would now be right to announce clear targets for monetary expansion as one of the objectives of economic management'.[57]

By Lawson's account, there was little further consideration of monetary policy while the Conservatives remained in opposition.[58] Detailed work on the MTFS had to wait not only until the Conservatives were back in power but until Howe's first Budget was out of the way, in June 1979.[59] In the meantime, although there were several meetings between Conservatives and senior Bank officials, they rarely touched upon the technicalities of monetary policy.[60] Lawson admits: 'We. . .assumed too readily that the task was essentially one of applying with conviction the approach that a reluctant Labour government had had forced upon it by

[55] Healey, *The time of my life*, 400–1.   [56] Lawson, *The view from No. 11*, 17.

[57] 'Economic Reconstruction Group: minutes of meeting', 24 June 1976, Churchill, RDLY 2/1/2/1; Howe et al., *The right approach to the economy*, 24.

[58] Ridley points out that this also reflected doctrinal differences between the Conservatives' various monetarist advisers. Christopher Johnson compares these to the disputes between Swift's Lilliputian 'Little-Endians' and 'Big-Endians' over which end of a boiled egg should be cracked open. C. Johnson, *The economy under Mrs Thatcher, 1979–1990* (London, 1991), 40; Lawson, *The view from No. 11*, 17–18; conversation with Sir Adam Ridley, 9 July 2013.

[59] Lawson, *The view from No. 11*, 17.

[60] Howe reported to Sir Keith Joseph that 'I sat next to [Bank Director] McMahon at lunch and, to me at least, he took a slightly different line to the effect that the Bank and Treasury did know more than you imply about the technicalities': 'R. E. G. Howe to K. S. Joseph', 2 July 1976, Churchill, THCR 2/1/1/30 [underlining by M. H. Thatcher in original];

the International Monetary Fund.'[61] Nonetheless, glimpses of a medium-term monetary strategy do emerge from the period of opposition. As Sir Alan Budd explains in this volume, much of the intellectual foundation for the MTFS came from the work done at the London Business School after the imposition of the IMF package in December 1976.[62]

Before the 'winter of discontent' most Conservative policy makers assumed, like their Labour counterparts, that incomes policy rather than monetary policy would be the principal weapon against inflation. Therefore, a great deal of attention was paid by both parties to the German system of *Konzertierte Aktion* ('concerted action'), whereby management and the unions combined with a group of 'wise men' to arrive at, inter alia, an acceptable annual wage norm.[63] Howe saw such 'realistic bargaining' as a viable alternative to free collective bargaining and the dirigisme of statutory incomes policies.[64] But 'concerted action' perished alongside Callaghan's wage policy in the winter of 1978–79. Monetary policy would be forced to bear a far greater share of the anti-inflationary burden than had ever been intended.

A respray of Labour's monetary regime[65]

In May 1979 the Conservatives inherited an economy recovering smartly from the 'winter of discontent'. GDP grew by 4.25 per cent in the second quarter, and, while inflation was rising, at just below 10 per cent it was a long way off the 1975 peak.[66] Fiscal policy making in opposition had

---

A. N. Ridley, 'Meeting with the Bank of England 18th October 1977', 20 October 1977, Churchill, TCHR 2/12/2/3; R. K. Middlemas, *Power, competition and the state*, vol. III, *The end of the post-war era: Britain since 1974* (Basingstoke, 1990), 216.

[61] Lawson, *The view from No. 11*, 18.

[62] See also ibid., 69. Howe refers to a March 1978 speech setting out a medium-term strategy that he delivered as a riposte to speeches by the Governor and the Permanent Secretary: Howe, *Conflict of loyalty*, 109. An earlier medium-term plan was laid out in 'Programme for economic stability', *The Times*, 20 September 1976.

[63] Thatcher responded to Howe's proposal by suggesting that successful wage bargaining in Germany had little to do with 'concerted action' and everything to do with 'the German character'. As she explained, '[T]his German talking shop works because it consists of Germans': S. Zweig, 'Die Konzertiete Aktion', 1977, THCR 2/1/1/31 [annotation by M. H. Thatcher]; 'R. E. G. Howe to M. H. Thatcher', 26 May 1977, Churchill, THCR 2/1/1/31 [annotation by M. H. Thatcher].

[64] Despite Thatcher's initial hostility, 'concerted action' made it as far as the 1979 Conservative election manifesto.

[65] Hotson, 'British monetary targets, 1976 to 1987', 19.

[66] Inflation bottomed out at 7.4 per cent in June 1978. Some of the rapid GDP growth in 1979 Q2 was consumer spending brought forward in anticipation of the VAT rise in the Budget. This may not have been obvious to ministers and forecasters in the summer of 1979. The 1979 Q2 GDP figures were not released until September and initially showed a 3 per cent rise over the quarter: 'GDP up after winter', *Guardian*, 22 September 1979; ONS.

focused on identifying public expenditure cuts sufficient to finance the desired income tax cuts.[67] In the buoyant economic conditions of mid-1978, it had appeared that modest cuts, combined with the proceeds of a growing economy, would be sufficient.[68] As declining growth and a rising public sector wage bill increased the PSBR during the winter of 1978–79, however, it became clear that income tax cuts would have to be financed by indirect tax rises. This formed the basis for Howe's first Budget, in June 1979, when he reduced the basic rate of income tax from 33 to 30 per cent, and the highest rate from 83 to 60 per cent, while raising VAT to 15 per cent.[69] Howe regards this as his most popular Budget.[70] Yet this was the Budget that precipitated the deepest recession in Britain since the 1920s. Treasury economists estimated that the 'revenue-neutral' tax switch alone would shrink the economy by 1.7 per cent, wiping out the pre-Budget estimate of 1.5 per cent growth in 1979/80.[71] Chancellors traditionally included a passage in their Budget speeches estimating the net effect of the measures on growth. This was dropped in 1979.[72] Officials were told that ministers doubted the reliability of the forecasts and that, given the apparently critical state of the economy, there was no realistic alternative to benchmark the Budget against.[73] The 1979 *FSBR* did publish a growth forecast for the coming year of minus 1 per cent. The only indication that this might be policy-induced was on page 4: 'In the short term the reduction in public expenditure is likely to reduce economic activity

---

[67] Lawson, *The view from No. 11*, 17.

[68] D. J. Needham, 'Fentiman Road: drawing the Conservative fiscal policy threads together in 1978' (June 2011), available at www.academia.edu/2431227/Fentiman_Road_drawing_the_Conservative_fiscal_policy_threads_together_in_1978, MTFW 114053.

[69] Prior to the 1979 Budget the standard rate of VAT was 8 per cent, with a 12.5 per cent rate applied to petrol and certain luxury goods.

[70] Howe, *Conflict of interest*, 121–36.

[71] Ministers appear to have overlooked the different behavioural consequences of direct and indirect tax changes. In the short term, individuals tend to react to a decrease (increase) in net income (after a direct tax change) by drawing down (adding to) savings to maintain existing levels of consumption. By contrast, an indirect tax rise increases the cost of existing consumption, causing individuals to substitute tax-exempt goods for the (now more expensive) taxed goods, thus narrowing the indirect tax base. The increase in the general price level after an indirect tax rise also discounts the stock of real wealth. Since individuals tend to want to hold their real wealth fairly constant, they react to higher prices with increased saving. This further reduces the overall level of consumption, with additional negative consequences for overall output. J. B. Unwin, 'Preparations for the Budget', 10 May 1979, TNA, T366/456.

[72] Thatcher was advised that 'certain aspects of this forecast, notably unemployment, the exchange rate, interest rates and the economic effects of the Budget, are not being quoted publicly': H. P. Evans, 'Post-Budget forecast: the economic outlook to end 1980', 14 June 1979, TNA, PREM 19/25.

[73] [?], 'Points for brief B4: effects of Budget', June 1979, TNA, T414/37.

slightly. This is probably also true of the net effect of reducing direct and raising indirect taxes.'[74]

The 1979 Budget was also notable for lowering the £M3 target range inherited from Labour to 7 to 11 per cent. Howe had flagged his intention of operating a tighter monetary policy when he first met the Bank Governor on 9 May.[75] This was despite the cautious advice he received on his first day in the job from both the Treasury and the Bank. The initial briefing from his own officials warned that 'no one has succeeded in establishing a relationship between M3 [sic] and money incomes which has proved stable during the 1970s'.[76] The Chancellor was also advised 'to bear in mind that there is no close relationship between £M3 and the PSBR' and that exporters were concerned about the consequences of tighter monetary policy on an already strong pound.[77] The Bank's advice was similarly cautious:

Proper control of the money supply is unlikely to become a simple matter... [W]ith a combination of correct judgement and good fortune, the authorities are able to steer a course that allows the money supply to grow within its permitted range without this being accompanied by unforeseen, unwelcome, or unacceptable behaviour of either the rate of exchange or the rate of interest.[78]

Nonetheless, ministers were keen to provide the markets with 'a declaration of intent' that the new government was more serious about monetary policy than its predecessor.[79] Despite the latest figures showing £M3 accelerating out of Healey's 8 to 12 per cent target range, Howe decided to lower the target to 7 to 11 per cent.[80] Contained within his announcement was an early indication that a more pragmatic form of 'monetarism' would trump 'believing monetarism'.[81] Ministers were not prepared to take responsibility for the rapid growth of the money supply during the two months of the financial year that had fallen under Healey's stewardship. The target would apply only for the ten months from the date of Howe's first Budget. If ministers really believed that the way to reduce inflation was to reduce the

[74] *FSBR 1979–80* (London, 1979), 4.
[75] A. M. W. Battishill, 'Domestic and overseas monetary policy', 10 May 1979, TNA, T386/524.
[76] Home Finance Group, 'Monetary targets and control', May 1979, TNA, T388/93.
[77] Central Unit, 'Budget', 26 April 1979, TNA, T388/92; EFI Division, 'The exchange rate', 25 April 1979, TNA, T388/92.
[78] Bank of England, 'Problems of monetary control', 30 April 1979, TNA, T386/524.
[79] N. Lawson, 'Monetary policy', May 1979, TNA, T386/524.
[80] In the six months to April 1979 £M3 grew by an annualised 12.8 per cent: 'R. E. G. Howe to Prime Minister', 10 May 1979, TNA, T386/524.
[81] For a distinction between the various types of monetarist, see G. T. Pepper and M. J. Oliver, *Monetarism under Thatcher: lessons for the future* (Cheltenham, 2001).

rate of growth of the money supply, then it should not have mattered whether £M3 had grown under a Labour or a Conservative government.[82]

After growing modestly during the first three months of the new target period, the money supply burst out of its new range in October 1979.[83] The gilt market reacted in typical fashion, and called a buyers' strike. At a crisis meeting on 14 November, Richardson told the Prime Minister that the Bank would need to sell £500 million gilts within the week simply to get monetary policy back on track.[84] In order to do this, interest rates were raised three percentage points to the highest nominal level in British history, before or since: 17 per cent. To further placate the markets, Howe extended the £M3 target for another four months to October 1980.[85]

The Medium-Term Financial Strategy

The November 1979 monetary mini-Budget delayed the introduction of the MTFS, which Lawson had been working on since the election. As the Prime Minister's Private Secretary, Tim Lankester, remarked, 'There is no point in having *a medium-term financial plan* when the Markets are dubious about our ability to stay within the existing target.'[86] The prospect of smoothing out the short-term monetary difficulties was integral to the MTFS, however. Lawson reformulated his plan in early 1980. As Howe explained to Mrs Thatcher, there was

---

[82] Thatcher was already exhibiting a Heath-like distaste for higher interest rates, arguing that a two percentage point rise in MLR on Budget day would affect the Conservative vote in the forthcoming European elections. Commenting on this episode, Charles Moore writes: 'Mrs Thatcher was perfecting a technique she was often to deploy – permitting a decision, but distancing herself from it.' Moore, *Margaret Thatcher*, 463; 'T. P. Lankester to A. M. W. Battishill', 11 June 1979, TNA, PREM 19/33.

[83] Bank lending to the private sector hit a new record. Bank lending to the public sector was also higher as VAT payments and telephone bills were delayed by strikes. The Treasury accountant had failed to anticipate either of these, so the Bank had not scheduled significant offsetting gilt sales, which, after redemptions, were negative during the month. J. M. Bridgeman, 'Gilt edged market: tap stock', 6 September 1979, TNA, T386/526.

[84] 'T. P. Lankester to M. Hall', 14 November 1979, TNA, T386/525.

[85] Howe also announced that consultations would commence on moves towards a system of monetary base control. The monetary base (M0) comprises notes, coin and bankers' balances at the Bank of England. As a backward-looking, demand-determined aggregate, M0 has no causative effect on nominal GDP. The Bank privately rejected MBC after extensive analysis in 1977, and then publicly in 1979; see P. E. Stevenson, 'Monetary base, bankers' balances and movements in money: some results', 11 October 1977, BOE, 6A50/23; and Foot, Goodhart and Hotson, 'Monetary base control'.

[86] 'T. P. Lankester to Prime Minister', 9 November 1979, TNA, PREM 19/34 [emphasis in original].

a good deal of force in the argument that by displaying a credible strategy for the medium term we shall be better able in the Budget to ride out the immediate problems of high monetary growth and interest rates, which, whatever course we follow, are still likely to take some time to control.[87]

Despite substantial gilt sales in January 1980, £M3 was still outside the 7 to 11 per cent target range at the time of the Budget.[88] Lawson's proposal offered a way of terming the current monetary difficulties out over a four-year period. It also offered the tantalising prospect of 'jam tomorrow' in the form of tax cuts just ahead of the next election:

Although the situation in the next two years is still likely to be extremely tight, the prospect thereafter – as we feel the full benefit of higher North Sea oil revenue – is a good deal easier and offers the prospect of substantial fiscal relaxation.[89]

The proposal contained no empirical evidence that control of the broad money supply was either a necessary or sufficient condition for lower inflation. As Lawson admitted, it rested on 'the beneficial effects on confidence (and hence expectations)'.[90] But, as his Cabinet colleague Sir Ian Gilmour points out, '[r]egrettably, trade unionists were not well versed in monetarist doctrine and had no such expectations, rational or otherwise'.[91]

The lack of robust econometric evidence had worried Goodhart when he was sent a similar proposal by the newly appointed Treasury Chief Economic Adviser, Terry Burns, and his London Business School colleague, Alan Budd. Drawing on his practical experience with monetary targets, Goodhart drafted a letter to Budd:

What really gets to me is the implicit self-confidence that you, Alan Budd, have now identified a stable demand-for-money function, on which future policy can firmly be based. After all our experience in recent years, can you seriously claim that 'your calculations' – undemonstrated – are a sound basis for official policy. Frankly I feel that the process of picking numbers in this way for serious policy recommendations is breath-taking in its irresponsibility.[92]

Four months later the Governor was equally annoyed to discover that Lawson's proposal had gone to the Prime Minister before being discussed

---

[87] R. E. G. Howe, 'Medium Term Financial Strategy', 20 February 1980, TNA, PREM 19/177.

[88] Annualised £M3 growth during the target period was 12.1 per cent: C. J. Riley, 'Recent developments', 7 February 1980, TNA, T386/527.

[89] Howe, 'Medium Term Financial Strategy', PREM 19/177.

[90] N. Lawson, 'A medium term financial plan', 24 September 1979, TNA, T386/525.

[91] I. H. J. L. Gilmour, *Dancing with dogma: Britain under Thatcherism* (London, 1992), 22.

[92] 'C. A. E. Goodhart to A. P. Budd', 24 October 1979, BOE, 6A50/31. The letter was never sent, and, after a conciliatory lunch, the article was toned down for publication.

with Bank officials. He told Howe that the Bank had 'serious reservations about the credibility of the sort of document produced and the wisdom of publishing it'.[93] He believed that the strategy was 'undesirably dogmatic, mechanical and rigid', and reiterated that there was no clear relationship between changes in the money stock and the price level.[94] Richardson addressed his concerns directly to Thatcher: 'Monetary policy had to be defensible. It was hard enough to set a monetary target for one year ahead: it was much harder for a four year period.'[95] The Prime Minister replied simply that 'she and the Chancellor were convinced that it would be right to publish the medium-term targets on the lines of the draft; she hoped that the Governor would be able to live with this'.[96]

The Bank was not the only part of the official machine with misgivings. The head of the Central Policy Review Staff, Sir Kenneth Berrill, warned that, by 'deliberately hooking itself on a programme for M3 [sic] which it intends to stick to come what may', the government could be in for 'a very bloody battle indeed with interest rates, exchange rate, reduced investment, bankruptcies, at unknown levels'.[97] The Cabinet Secretary, Sir Robert Armstrong, agreed. Publishing the target ranges four years ahead allowed 'nothing for the unforeseen, or for slippage', and would 'make life even more difficult than it is in any case bound to be'.[98] More significant was opposition from within the Treasury ministerial team itself. On 4 March the Chief Secretary, John Biffen, told the Prime Minister that demand for the strategy came from 'journalists, academics and commentators rather than from those in the commercial world'.[99] Belying his own monetarist reputation, Biffen doubted whether there was any mechanistic relationship between the PSBR, the monetary aggregates and inflation. He finished with pointed criticism of his colleague, Nigel Lawson: 'Our monetary policy is still at the stage of apprenticeship. The Financial Secretary, on the other hand, will suggest a certainty about pace and direction that we do not possess, either technically or politically.'[100]

After guiding the proposal through Cabinet, Howe published the MTFS alongside his March 1980 Budget.[101] He also announced that

---

[93] A. J. Wiggins, 'Note of a meeting held in the Chancellor of the Exchequer's room, HM Treasury at 9.30 am on Friday, 22nd February 1980', 25 February 1980, TNA, T386/528.

[94] A. J. Wiggins, 'Note of a meeting in the Chancellor of the Exchequer's room, HM Treasury on Monday, 3 March at 10.15 am', 5 March 1980, TNA, T386/528.

[95] 'T. P. Lankester to A. J. Wiggins', 10 March 1980, TNA, T386/529.　　[96] Ibid.

[97] K. E. Berrill, 'Medium Term Financial Strategy', 25 February 1980, TNA, PREM 19/177.

[98] R. T. Armstrong, 'Medium Term Financial Strategy', 26 February 1980, TNA, PREM 19/177.

[99] W. J. Biffen, 'Medium Term Financial Strategy', 4 March 1980, TNA, PREM 19/177.

[100] Ibid.　　[101] FSBR 1980–81.

the 'corset', back in place since 1978, would be discarded for the final time in June 1980. The 'corset''s designers were fully aware that its application had only a cosmetic effect on the £M3 statistics. Quantitative limits simply pushed lending out to the overseas branches of the clearing banks, the wholesale markets and the commercial bill market. Until Howe abolished exchange controls in October 1979, however, there was a limit to how much lending a UK bank could divert to, for instance, its Paris branch. After October 1979 there was no such constraint.[102] Nonetheless, the Bank estimated that £M3 would rise by about 3 per cent when the 'corset' was finally discarded.[103] Howe left open the question of whether the target for 1980/81 would include this 'reintermediation'.[104] Once again, critics were left asking just how strong ministerial monetarist credentials were when they were prepared to write off another 3 per cent of £M3 growth.

Further questions were asked four months later when, despite the latest figures showing the money supply moving out of the target range, Minimum Lending Rate was cut by one percentage point to 16 per cent.[105] The Governor pressed for the cut because 'pressure on the corporate sector caused by high interest rates and the high exchange rate had become too great and needed to be moderated'.[106] The British economy was enduring its worst recession for sixty years. This was partly because of the high price of oil.[107] It was partly because of the 1979 Budget, which shrank the economy with its switch from direct to indirect tax and public expenditure cuts. But it was mainly because of a misconceived monetary policy that, whatever the £M3 figures indicated, was imposing an unprecedented squeeze on British business. The strong pound would soon make Britain a net importer of manufactured goods for the first time

---

[102] The abolition of exchange controls also effectively ruled out monetary base control. As Goodhart commented in July 1979, any attempt to limit bank lending by squeezing the monetary base in the absence of capital controls would produce offshore disintermediation 'with a vengeance': C. A. E. Goodhart, 'Some notes on Middleton's "negotiable base asset scheme"', 10 July 1979, BOE, C40/1444.

[103] P. E. Middleton, 'The monetary prospect', 7 November 1979, BOE, C40/1448.

[104] HC Deb., 26 March 1980, vol. 981, cc1442–6.

[105] Annualised £M3 growth in the current target period was 11.2 per cent: 'T. P. Lankester to A. J. Wiggins', 3 July 1980, TNA, PREM 19/178. Minimum Lending Rate replaced Bank Rate in October 1972 and tied the Bank's discount rate to Treasury bill rates then prevailing in the market, by taking the rate at the previous weekly tender, adding fifty basis points (one basis point is a hundredth of a percentage point) and then rounding up to the nearest twenty-five basis points.

[106] Ibid.

[107] We cannot simply blame the oil shock. The upper turning point in the United Kingdom's cycle came in May 1979. The US economy (and the rest of the OECD) continued to grow through 1979, briefly contracted in the second quarter of 1980 and entered recession in the final quarter of 1981 as Britain, an oil exporter, was *exiting* its much deeper recession.

since before the Industrial Revolution.[108] Gross domestic product fell by 5.9 per cent in the 1979–80 recession.[109] Manufacturing output shrank by 15 per cent.[110] Manufacturing investment shrank by 26 per cent, and unemployment reached levels not seen since the 1930s.[111]

Despite the risks to the credibility of the MTFS, the Prime Minister and Chancellor agreed to the interest rate cut. As the Governor pointed out, 'The money supply figures on their own would scarcely justify a reduction.'[112] Four months into the MTFS, and the Treasury was engaging in intellectual acrobatics to convince ministers that the strategy was on course: 'The one point reduction in MLR in July was therefore a calculated risk; it was not justified by the monetary situation to date but by the prospects of slower money growth in the future.'[113] But, as Andrew Britton points out, the July 1980 MLR cut meant that 'the retreat from monetarism had begun'.[114]

The authorities narrowly avoided a rout with the publication of the next month's banking figures. £M3 grew by 5 per cent in July. Even adjusting for reintermediation, annualised £M3 growth was 16 per cent, versus the 7 to 11 per cent target range.[115] By focusing media attention on the post-'corset' distortions, the authorities just managed to sail through. But no amount of press briefing could hide the fact that the strategy was off course when £M3 grew by a further 2.9 per cent over the next month. Annualised growth was now 17 per cent, even after adjustments. Lawson concluded that 'our existing techniques of monetary control have failed'.[116] Thatcher reached a similar conclusion after meeting the Swiss economist Karl Brunner while holidaying on Lake Zug. Glossing over the fact that the Swiss had recently suspended their own monetary target, Brunner assured Thatcher that the Bank of England could easily control the UK money supply within a 2 per cent band simply by adopting Swiss techniques.[117] The immediate outcome

---

[108] In January 1981 sterling was 20 per cent higher against a trade-weighted basket of currencies than when the Conservatives took office in May 1979.

[109] G. Chamberlin, 'Output and expenditure in the last three UK recessions', *Economic and Labour Market Review*, 4, 8 (August 2010), 52.

[110] A. J. C. Britton, *Macroeconomic policy in Britain, 1974–87* (Cambridge, 1991), 49. From its 1979 Q2 peak to its 1982 Q4 trough, manufacturing output fell by 17.6 per cent: Chamberlin, 'Output and expenditure', 54.

[111] *Economic trends annual supplement* (London, 1994), 185.

[112] 'T. P. Lankester to A. J. Wiggins', 3 July 1980, TNA, PREM 19/178.

[113] HMT, 'Money supply, interest rates, the PSBR and the exchange rate', 6 October 1980, TNA, T386/545.

[114] Britton, *Macroeconomic policy*, 53.

[115] P. E. Middleton, 'Monetary policy', 29 August 1980, TNA, T386/543.

[116] N. Lawson, 'Monetary policy', 1 September 1980, TNA, T386/544.

[117] 'K. Brunner to M. H. Thatcher', 10 September 1980, TNA, PREM 19/178.

was a series of bad-tempered meetings with senior Bank officials, followed by two MBC seminars at which the participants would re-rehearse the arguments about the merits of monetary base control.[118] The more important outcome was the transformation of the MTFS into what Sir Samuel Brittan calls the 'Medium-Term Fiscal Strategy'.[119]

The 'Medium-Term Fiscal Strategy'

In his 1980 conference speech, the Director General of the CBI, Sir Terence Beckett, launched an outspoken attack on the government:

> You had better face the brutal fact that the Conservative Party is a rather narrow alliance. How many of them in Parliament or the Cabinet have actually run a business? This matters. They don't all understand you. They think they do, but they don't. They are even *suspicious* of you – many of you – what is worse they don't take you *seriously*. I would not advocate what I am going to say were the cause not noble – we have got to take the gloves off and have a bare knuckle fight because we have got to have an effective and prosperous industry.[120]

On 20 October 1980, after the bellwether Imperial Chemical Industries had warned that it was poised to announce its worst trading results since 1930, the Prime Minister (a former chemist) asked Wass to 'explore ways of mitigating the adverse conditions in which British industry is operating, so that good and viable companies like ICI should not be driven to the wall'.[121] Wass offered a range of options, including lower interest rates, capital controls and a pay freeze. The fiscal options were limited because, despite the autumn forecasts showing that the PBSR outturn for 1980/81 was likely to overshoot the implied MTFS objective by nearly £3 billion (equivalent to 1¼ per cent of GDP), the Cabinet had, the day beforehand, reneged on a July commitment to find a further £2 billion of spending cuts.[122]

The government's response to the distress being felt by British business revealed its new ordering of priorities. With the PSBR overshooting

---

[118] 'Summary record of a meeting held at 10 Downing Street at 1800 hours on 3 September 1980', 3 September 1980, Churchill, PREM 19/178; 'T. P. Lankester to A. J. Wiggins', 9 September 1980, TNA, PREM 19/178; 'Monetary control seminar: Church House, 29 September 1980: record of the discussion', TNA, T388/129; T. P. Lankester, 'Note of a meeting between the Prime Minister and foreign participants in a seminar on monetary base control: 1430 hours 30 September at 10 Downing Street', TNA, T388/129.

[119] S. Brittan, *The role and limits of government: essays in political economy* (London, 1983), 248.

[120] T. N. Beckett, 'Director-General's national conference speech 1980', 11 November 1980, TNA, PREM 19/490 [emphasis in original].

[121] D. W. G. Wass, 'Policy options', 5 November 1980, TNA, T386/534.

[122] Howe, *Conflict of loyalty*, 189.

its MTFS ceiling, tax cuts for business were ruled out. But £M3 was also overshooting its target range. Nevertheless, Howe plumped for the second of Wass's options: a 'modest' cut in MLR from 16 to 14 per cent. This would reduce the cost of debt servicing and help exports by weakening the pound, 15 per cent higher on a trade-weighted index since the Conservatives took office. But it would require careful explanation. There was simply no way of justifying a two percentage point cut in MLR within the current MTFS framework. So, in the Governor's words, the monetary target was taken 'out of action' until the Budget.[123]

Fiscally, all the Chancellor could do was target the two sectors that were performing well. The 1979 income tax cuts and continuing high wage settlements had produced a large shift of wealth to the personal sector. Howe partially reversed this with a one percentage point hike in employees' National Insurance contributions. The high oil price in the wake of the Iranian revolution meant that the oil industry was generating large profits, so the Chancellor also announced a supplementary petroleum duty. But, since neither of these measures would take effect until 1981, there would be little impact on the PSBR in the current year, then estimated at £11.5 billion (5¼ per cent of GDP) versus the £8.5 billion (3¾ per cent of GDP) forecast in the Budget.[124] It was now clear, however, that the fiscal leg of the MTFS was taking priority over the monetary leg. The government was relieving itself of what Colin Thain calls its 'naïve monetarist baggage'.[125] A more pragmatic approach was required. The money supply had overshot, the PSBR had overshot, the economy was in a policy-induced recession and unemployment was about to break through 2 million. As Britton points out, 'At this stage "the new beginning" introduced by the Conservative government seemed an almost unmitigated failure.'[126]

The 1981 Budget

The origins of the 1981 Budget lay in attempts to mitigate the difficulties companies such as ICI were experiencing as a result of the deliberate

[123] To retain some credibility, the MLR cut was followed by the announcement of three further monetary measures: the phasing out of the reserve asset ratio, a greater role for the market in determining MLR and a new role for the cash ratio observed by the banks. A. J. Wiggins, 'Note of a meeting held at 11 Downing Street on Thursday, 20 November, 1980 at 9.00 am', 20 November 1980, TNA, T386/547.

[124] HC Deb., 26 March 1980, vol. 981, cc1446–9.

[125] C. Thain, 'The education of the Treasury: the Medium-Term Financial Strategy 1980–84', *Public Administration*, 63, 3 (autumn 1985), 283.

[126] Britton, *Macroeconomic policy*, 54.

squeeze on profits, operated through a misconceived monetary policy. Early budget planning focused on ameliorating the situation by transferring resources from the personal sector to the corporate sector. Given the political difficulties of raising income tax rates so soon after the 1979 Budget, this would likely involve only partial indexation of the personal allowances and higher indirect taxes. As William Keegan points out, given Lawson's close involvement with the Rooker–Wise amendment, which had codified indexation in 1977, this 'might have embarrassed a lesser man'.[127] Lawson himself recalls that he 'had no hesitation in supporting this course of action' since indexation, while a presumption, was not automatic.[128]

Potential measures to help companies included the abolition of the employers' National Insurance surcharge (the CBI's preferred option), reduced corporation tax, a reduction of heavy fuel oil duty and relief from local rates. As the Budget approached, however, successive forecasts showed the PSBR significantly overshooting the MTFS-implied £7.4 billion ceiling for 1981/82. Even allowing for the £2 billion of tax rises announced in the November Statement, the winter forecast generated a PSBR estimate of £10.2 billion (4.1 per cent of GDP) for the year ahead – a figure Howe revealed to a gathering of ministers and advisers at Chequers on 17 January 1981.[129] Thatcher was 'not amused'.[130] Any extra revenue coming from the personal sector would now have to go towards reducing the PSBR rather than alleviating corporate distress if the MTFS were to retain any credibility. As Sir Tim Lankester shows in this volume, barring some horse-trading between No. 10 and the Treasury over the exact size of the tax hike, the fiscal lines of the 1981 Budget were set.

The monetary policy lines had been laid down by the decision to reduce interest rates the previous July, and then again in November, despite above-target monetary growth. The decision to further loosen monetary policy was given traction by a report from the Swiss economist Jürg Niehans into the causes of sterling appreciation.[131] Alfred Sherman of the Centre for Policy Studies had commissioned the report by Alan Walters' former Johns Hopkins University colleague in October 1980. On 7 January 1981 Niehans reported his findings to a group of officials and policy advisers. Flatly contradicting the Treasury view that the pound was strong because of North Sea oil, he concluded that the root cause was monetary. £M3 may have been growing well above target, but M0 had

[127] Keegan, *Mrs Thatcher's economic experiment*, 169.
[128] Lawson, *The view from No. 11*, 95.
[129] H. P. Evans, 'Summary of short-term forecasts', 12 February 1981, TNA, T388/197.
[130] Howe, *Conflict of loyalty*, 202.   [131] Niehans, *The appreciation of sterling*, WTRS 1/4.

been *shrinking* in real terms since the middle of 1979. Claiming a link between M0 and the exchange rate, Niehans recommended that interest rates be cut immediately and M0 allowed to expand by 5 to 6 per cent. This, according to Niehans, would allow sterling to fall from $2.40 to a more comfortable $2.15.

Walters, newly arrived as Mrs Thatcher's economic adviser, wrote in his diary that the No. 10 advisers greeted the news that the government had inflicted unnecessary damage on the economy by following the wrong monetary aggregate as a 'bombshell'.[132] The Prime Minister's reaction fell some way short of her 1979 manifesto pledge for 'more open and informed discussion of the Government's economic objectives': 'Told MT about JN's seminar and his findings. MT very defensive: NO ONE must know about it – especially Bank of England. Why? Frightened of calls for relaxation or sops to the wets. Am rapidly learning the political game – never admit to an error.'[133] Walters' colleague in the No. 10 Policy Unit, John Hoskyns, elaborates: 'Niehans' advice was not politically welcome. Despite the diplomatic language in which it was couched, it advocated actions that could be seen as a public admission that the Government had done the economy a great deal of damage by mistake.'[134]

The report bolstered the Prime Minister's view that the principal aim of the forthcoming Budget was to relieve corporate distress by continuing to lower interest rates, without appearing to execute the U-turn that she had so publicly ruled out at the Conservative Party conference the previous October. She hoped to achieve this by lowering the PSBR. This rested on the belief that the lower the deficit, the lower the interest rate. Lawson now admits that this belief is 'largely a fallacy'.[135] He goes on, however: 'Many of us, I confess, believed in it to some extent at that time, but nobody believed in it more strongly than she did.'[136] The intention had always been to attack wage inflation by using tight monetary policy to bear down on company profits. Confirmation that the additional misery heaped upon British business by the high exchange rate was *not* an inevitable conse-quence of North Sea oil, however, meant that a monetary problem (the strong pound) could now be met with a monetary solution (lower interest rates), albeit via a fiscal route (higher taxes). This would have the added advantage of reducing the corporate debt-servicing burden, since each

---

[132] A. A. Walters, 'Diary entry', 7 January 1981, Churchill, WTRS 3/1/1.
[133] *1979 Conservative Party general election manifesto* (London, 1979); Walters, 'Diary entry', WTRS 3/1/1 [emphasis in original].
[134] Hoskyns, *Just in time*, 279.
[135] Needham, Oliver and Riley, 'The 1981 Budget: facts and fallacies', 33.   [136] Ibid.

percentage point off MLR would reduce the company sector's interest payments by £270 to 300 million.[137]

Niehans may have reinforced the view in No. 10 that monetary policy needed to be further loosened. Lawson claims that, as far as the Treasury was concerned, the report was 'inconsequential'.[138] Certainly, the initial reaction was sceptical, with Middleton branding it 'theology'.[139] Despite Thatcher's prohibition, officials enlisted Bank support to challenge its findings. Goodhart has described the report as 'one of the most important unpublished papers of our times'.[140] This is not to say that he agreed with it. He dismissed its claim to have found causation running from the monetary base to the exchange rate.[141] Similar work by Bank officials had failed to establish any such link, and, given their long campaign against monetary base control, they were reluctant to accept that M0 had much to contribute to exchange rate management.[142] Nonetheless, while they disagreed with Niehans' method, they agreed with his conclusions. Interest rates had to be lowered before more British businesses were unnecessarily bankrupted.

Given its difficult experience with the money supply since the early 1970s, the Bank had been hostile to the monetary leg of the MTFS from the outset. By early 1981 even MTFS cheerleaders within the Treasury were reluctantly coming round to the Bank's long-held views about the limited merits of £M3 targets. In their ongoing search for a stable demand for money function, Treasury economists had recently formulated an equation that showed financial wealth to be the main driver of money balances.[143] Since individuals like to keep their proportion of money to financial assets fairly steady, it was not surprising that, in a year of rapidly rising money incomes (up 18 per cent in 1980/81), the

---

[137] S. J. Davies, 'Effect of interest rate change on ICC's finances', 24 February 1981, TNA, T386/552; J. R. Lomax, 'Effect of cut in MLR on companies', 25 February 1981, TNA, T386/552.

[138] Needham, Oliver and Riley, 'The 1981 Budget: facts and fallacies', 27.

[139] Upon being told that the strong pound was a consequence of monetary policy rather than North Sea oil, Hoskyns reports that 'Peter's face was a study': Hoskyns, *Just in time*, 256; P. E. Middleton, 'Study by Niehans', 3 February 1981, TNA, T388/200.

[140] Ibid. The paper was published as Niehans, *The appreciation of sterling: causes, effects, policies.*

[141] 'C. A. E. Goodhart to J. R. Lomax', 25 February 1981, TNA, T388/189.

[142] G. Hacche, 'The appreciation of sterling in relation to monetary developments: further equations using M1 and base money', 20 February 1981, TNA, T388/189.

[143] Indeed, Treasury economists concluded that income 'has no role to play'. Elsewhere, Britton suggested that the relationship between £M3 and financial assets was 'new and controversial': A. J. C. Britton, 'The money supply target in retrospect', 13 January 1981, TNA, T388/187; Bennett, 'Direct forecast of the money supply', January 1981, TNA, T388/186.

money supply should have grown by a similar amount. Monetarist orthodoxy stated that this large rise in £M3 would inevitably lead to higher
inflation, after the usual time lag. If the personal sector had merely been
restoring its real money balances to an equilibrium level, however, then
the extra money would *not* lead to an inflationary increase in spending
on goods and services. This was the view of the Treasury minister, Lord
Cockfield, who argued that 'the growth in the money supply has no
implications for the future: its potential for future trouble was exhausted
even before it was created'.[144] The extra money was simply an ex post
facto validation of increased personal wealth. This was a sizeable blow to
the monetarist theory underpinning the MTFS.

The monetarist case was further undermined by the findings of a
thoroughgoing Treasury study, which concluded that inflation was *not*
simply a monetary phenomenon.[145] As Andrew Britton, then at the
Treasury, pointed out, 'The simple account of inflation in terms of
monetary growth two years previously, which received a lot of public
attention in the mid-seventies, has not stood up well to closer inspection,
or to the test of time.'[146] World prices, the exchange rate, indirect taxes,
and incomes policies had all made significant contributions to RPI
growth.[147] This is what the Conservative Treasury team had assumed in
1975 before the monetarists' Jacobin revolution.[148]

Even Peter Middleton, the Treasury official most associated with the
MTFS, was losing his faith:

The events of the last year or two have called in question the status of £M3 as 'the'
money supply. It is difficult to control, either by existing methods or by MBC; its

[144] F. A. Cockfield, 'The money supply and inflation', 21 January 1981, TNA, T386/549.
[145] HMT, 'Report of money supply and inflation research group', 9 December 1980, TNA, T388/195.
[146] A. J. C. Britton, 'Conditionality and money supply targets', 16 January 1981, TNA, T388/187. As former Bank Director William Allen points out: 'The events of 1971–75 appear to have been unique: there is no other episode in UK monetary history in the last century in which broad money gives so accurate a prediction of future inflation.' W. A. Allen, 'Recent developments in monetary control in the United Kingdom', in L. H. Meyer (ed.), *Improving money stock control: problems, solutions, and consequences* (Boston, MA, 1983), 104.
[147] Britton, 'Conditionality and money supply targets', T388/187.
[148] In June 1975 Adam Ridley advised Howe's Economic Reconstruction Group: 'Money, like other commodities, is subject to the laws of supply and demand. It follows directly therefore that a Government cannot have exclusive and total control over the money stock and its deployment.' He went on, '[Inflation] is not determined uniquely by any single one of the unions and monopoly power, expectations, excess demand, militancy, wages, the money supply or the Government. To focus on one factor to the exclusion of the others is to indulge in a dispute which is at best semantically confusing and at worst deliberately misleading.' A. N. Ridley, 'Institutional considerations', 26 June 1975, Churchill, RDLY 2/1/2/2 [emphasis in original].

economic significance is not as clear-cut as it once seemed, and it does not provide a clear guide to short term interest rates.[149]

There was nothing in this statement that the Bank could not have told him nearly a decade beforehand. It made a mockery of Lawson's reference to 'those variables – notably the quantity of money – which are and must be within the power of Governments to control'.[150] It also chimed with the findings of a report by the majority-Conservative Treasury and Civil Service Committee, which concluded, a fortnight before the 1981 Budget, that there was no evidence of causality running from £M3 growth to inflation.[151] The report was particularly scathing of the view that monetary targets could reduce inflation by working on expectations, and called for a more pragmatic approach that relied less on any single monetary aggregate. By this stage, even the Conservative Research Department had given up: 'The fact is that the MTFS, as set out in last year's Red Book, is a shambles whether one takes M3 [sic], Government spending, PSBR, or growth rates, and the publication of precise monetary targets has made political life more difficult than would otherwise have been the case.'[152]

The need to retain political credibility militated against abandoning £M3 targets straightaway. But, with the MTFS target set at 6 to 10 per cent for 1981/82, there was simply no way the eight percentage point overshoot in 1980/81 could be clawed back without plunging the economy even further into recession. The Chancellor would have to point to other factors to explain why he was doing nothing about the overshoot. But, as Middleton explained, '[t]he more successfully we justify that overshoot, the more our *unconditional* commitment to future targets and the precise MTFS path is weakened'.[153] Ministers and officials considered making the £M3 target conditional upon an exchange rate objective.[154] They considered giving £M3 and M1 equal billing. They even considered the Bank's long-preferred option of switching to an M1 target. Unable to reach a consensus, and with the imminent arrival of a new M2 aggregate holding out the prospect of a better alternative, the Treasury

---

[149] P. E. Middleton, 'The money supply target', 29 January 1981, TNA, T386/549.

[150] Lawson, *The view from No. 11*, 69.

[151] Third report from the Treasury and Civil Service Committee: *Monetary Policy* (London, 1981).

[152] C. Mockler, 'Monetary policy', 5 February 1981, Oxford, Bodleian Library, Conservative Party Archive, CRD 4/4/11.

[153] Middleton, 'The money supply target', T386/549 [emphasis in original].

[154] A. J. Wiggins, 'Note of a meeting held in the Chancellor of the Exchequer's room, on Tuesday, 3 February, 1981 at 3.00 pm', 4 February 1981, TNA, PREM 19/438.

settled on a fudge.[155] In his 1981 Budget, Howe restated the annualised MTFS target range of 6 to 10 per cent £M3 growth over the fourteen months to April 1982, while admitting that he would also monitor the behaviour of M1 and two wider measures of private sector liquidity, PSL1 and PSL2.[156] In the course of his speech, he also mentioned the exchange rate, inflation and house prices as influences over monetary policy, while skating over the question of the previous year's overshoot by simply stating, without precise commitment, that 'it may be desirable to recover some of the past year's high monetary growth in the form of lower growth over the medium term'.[157]

All this would seem to belie the claims of those involved that monetary policy was of secondary importance in planning the 1981 Budget.[158] This is because, despite a series of complicated tactical decisions, No. 10, the Treasury and the Bank were all agreed that monetary policy had to be loosened. The only question was by how much. Anticipating a cut ahead of the Budget, the markets had taken wholesale rates below MLR, creating the room for a one percentage point cut in early February. The Governor and the Chancellor were keen.[159] So too was the Prime Minister, who expressed her clear wish 'to give industry a boost'.[160] The decision to wait for the Budget was ultimately about salvaging political credibility. As Lawson pointed out to Howe: 'In political terms the announcement of an MLR cut promises to be the one bull point of your Budget speech, when it ought to be possible to present it in an appropriate monetary and fiscal context. To put in your finger and pull out that plum now would leave the Budget cake very unappetising indeed.'[161] Lawson was referring to the 'unappetising' decision, discussed above, to reverse some of the 1979 income tax cuts by (at that stage) only partially indexing personal allowances, and further raising indirect taxes. As Tim Lankester shows, the exchanges between No. 10 and the Treasury over the next fortnight

---

[155] M2 comprised M1 plus UK private sector sterling time deposits with UK deposit banks.
[156] PSL1 comprised M1 plus private sector time deposits with a maturity of up to two years, private sector holdings of sterling certificates of deposit, and private sector holdings of monetary instruments (bank bills, Treasury bills, local authority deposits and certificates of tax deposit). PSL2 comprised PSL1 plus private sector holdings of building society deposits (excluding term shares and SAYE), plus National Savings (excluding saving certificates, SAYE and other long-term deposits), minus building society holdings of money market instruments and bank deposits. Hotson, 'British monetary targets, 1976 to 1987', 30; *FSBR 1981–82*, 16.
[157] HC Deb., 10 March 1981, vol. 1000, c762.
[158] Howe, *Conflict of loyalty*, 205; Lawson, *The view from No. 11*, 88.
[159] A. J. Wiggins, 'Monetary affairs', 12 February 1981, TNA, T386/550.
[160] T. P. Lankester, 'Note for the record', 13 February 1981, TNA, T386/550.
[161] N. Lawson, 'Minimum lending rate', 11 February 1981, TNA, T386/550.

concerning the finer details made only a marginal difference to the final package. And any lingering suggestions that the 1981 Budget was 'Made in Downing Street' at the eleventh hour are dismissed by the text of a collective letter of resignation, drafted by the three No. 10 Policy Unit advisers, Walters, Hoskyns and David Wolfson, when they saw the final package:

We believe the time has now come for your No. 10 advisers to disband and leave Whitehall. The opportunity to turn the UK economy round, presented by the May 1979 mandate has passed... We have had 3 misjudged budgets in a row with no consultation with the colleagues. Even AW has been kept out because he was being 'awkward'. Treasury officials know it's a disaster but, in contrast, they daren't say so.[162]

As Lawson points out, paternity claims over the 1981 Budget arise from the subsequent eight years of economic growth.[163] The mood of the time was very different. It is summed up by the then head of the No. 10 Policy Unit, John Hoskyns: 'For me, and I think for the other Number Ten advisers, the Budget was never some great battle honour to be celebrated in song and legend. We saw it as a Dunkirk, not an Alamein; a narrow escape, the closest we had come to an early end of the Thatcher experiment.'[164]

Conclusions

In the introduction, it was suggested that successful policy implementation requires that all the members of the 'macroeconomic executive' be travelling like ships in a convoy; in the same direction if not always at precisely the same speed. It also requires that each ship's crew have a clear idea of the destination. This was not the case during the two least successful periods of monetary policy in post-war Britain. In 1971 the Bank mis-sold Competition and Credit Control to the Heath government on its supposed competitive merits. In 1980 the Thatcher government bounced the Bank into the Medium-Term Financial Strategy without adequate consultation. The result, in both cases, was above-target money supply growth. In 1972–73 this was followed by higher inflation. In 1980–81 it was not.

Another contrast between these two periods of rapid monetary growth is that, in 1971, the Bank believed it had firm econometric evidence to show that the demand for broad money in the United Kingdom was

---

[162] 'A. A. Walters, D. Wolfson and J. L. A. H. Hoskyns to Prime Minister', 3 March 1981, Churchill, WTRS 1/1.
[163] Lawson, *The view from No. 11*, 88.   [164] Hoskyns, *Just in time*, 283.

stable, predictable and controllable, and that (for the most part) causality ran from M3 to nominal incomes. After CCC, officials knew, once again, that none of this was true. Elsewhere in this volume, Anthony Hotson explains why the Bank's narrow money equations also broke down in the early 1980s. In 1979, though, the Bank believed it had identified a tolerably robust relationship between M1 growth and nominal income. Why, then, was the MTFS not predicated on M1 targets? The answer lies in the institutional structure that prevailed. The credit counterparts approach suggested that the broad money supply could be influenced by fiscal policy (the PSBR), bank lending to the private sector, and the external accounts. By contrast, controlling M1 is principally about more frequent interest rate changes. This would have meant more interest-rate-setting powers for the Bank – something the politicians and the Treasury were not prepared to countenance until after the ERM debacle in 1992. As the Treasury's Michael Bridgeman noted in 1977, the Bank was 'pursuing a dream of being given a monetary target and independent authority to achieve it, and against this background M1 had definite advantages for them'.[165] Conservative ministers' mistrust of the Bank prevented them from choosing monetary targets they might have been able to hit.[166]

Failure to engage with the Bank on the MTFS produced a policy with two fundamental flaws in 1980. First, despite the failures of Competition and Credit Control, more active monetary policy had re-emerged as an adjunct to incomes policy in 1975. After the 'winter of discontent' the broad money supply target had to fill the role it had previously shared with a wage norm between 1975 and 1979. As we have seen, it was not up to the job. A policy based on credibility and managing expectations relied on the government actually hitting its targets, and, as the Bank, the Chief Secretary, the Permanent Secretary, the Cabinet Secretary and the CPRS warned in 1980, this was not likely to happen with £M3.

Second, if minsters had engaged with the Bank, they would have known that the primary purpose of the M3 target imposed on Healey in July 1976 was fiscal rather than monetary. It was 'a tighter rope round the Chancellor's neck' on public expenditure. This also went to the heart of the Bank's objections to monetary base control. As Goodhart pointed out in July 1979, quite apart from the lack of econometric evidence linking M0 growth to nominal incomes,

[165] K. V. Watts, 'Note of a meeting held in Sir Douglas Wass' room at 3.15 pm on Wednesday, 9 November', 10 November 1977, TNA, T386/269.

[166] Thatcher referred to Richardson as 'that fool who runs the Bank of England', while Lawson makes the extraordinary suggestion that the Bank 'had never at that time taken monetary policy very seriously or. . .thought deeply about it'. Moore, *Margaret Thatcher*, 462; Lawson, *The view from No. 11*, 17, 83.

The ability to control the growth of the quota regulated monetary aggregate [M0] would relax the present monetary discipline on the authorities, allowing them to run higher PSBRs and keep MLR down, 'secure' in the knowledge that quota restraint was keeping £M3 on track. It could encourage a considerable degree of comfortable self-deception among the authorities.[167]

Money supply targets in the late 1970s were primarily about restraining the spending ambitions of the Labour government. Before the emergence of the Social Democratic Party and victory in the Falklands, this was an issue that might have re-emerged after the 1983 general election. But few doubted the Thatcher government's desire to reduce the PSBR. There was little need to influence fiscal policy by the monetary policy back door. By failing to engage with the Bank, Conservative ministers selected the wrong target. This had profound consequences for British economic performance in the early 1980s.

We must consider the possibility that minsters were perfectly aware that there was no robust relationship between £M3 growth and inflation, and that money supply targets were simply 'cover' for tough deflationary action.[168] After all, this was the approach taken by Paul Volcker at the Federal Reserve. In 1978 Volcker saw 'no need to accept as complete, or even adequate, a simple causal explanation running from monetary behavior to price behavior'.[169] But he was quite prepared to use monetary targets as cover for a deflationary squeeze. Lawson commented privately in the 1970s that 'the conditions for monetarism in Britain do not exist'. When asked what they were, he replied: 'Water cannon.'[170] Cockfield was certainly under no illusions about the monetary transmission mechanism: 'Control of the money [supply] operates through the simple but brutal means of butchering company profits. Ultimately insolvency and unemployment teach employers and workers alike that they need to behave reasonably and sensibly.'[171]

Nonetheless, subsequent comments by ministers, officials and advisers show that we should take their public statements about monetarism at the time at face value. Looking back on the MTFS, Lawson quotes Robert

---

[167] Goodhart, 'Some notes on Middleton's "negotiable base asset scheme"', C40/1444.

[168] Wass commented in November 1980 that 'nor can it be argued that business conditions as they have evolved this year are very much worse than we expected when we set the current targets and formulated the MTFS': Wass, 'Policy options', T386/534.

[169] P. A. Volcker, 'The role of monetary targets in an age of inflation', *Journal of Monetary Economics*, 4, 2 (April 1978), 330.

[170] Quoted by R. K. Middlemas, 'Margaret Thatcher, 1979–1990', in V. B. Bogdanor (ed.), *From new Jerusalem to new Labour: British prime ministers from Attlee to Blair* (Basingstoke, 2010), 151.

[171] Cockfield, 'The money supply and inflation', T386/549.

Burns: 'The best laid schemes o' mice an' men/Gang aft a-gley.'[172] Middleton has commented that 'having a target and missing it turned out to be quite a good policy. It allowed for flexibility.'[173] And Hoskyns writes that 'the excessive monetary squeeze of 1979–81 [was] an embarrassing error and. . .the Government's most difficult and unpopular action in its first term, the 1981 Budget, [was] designed to correct it'.[174] As Christopher Collins explains in this volume, the fiscal tightening of the 1981 Budget helped to provide 'cover' for the unwinding of the monetarist experiment.

In October 1980 Thatcher declared 'the lady's not for turning'. Five months later, having already taken the money supply target 'out of action', her Chancellor executed a brisk U-turn on monetary policy. By this stage it was clear that monetary policy was being driven at least as much by the exchange rate as by the money supply. In June 1981 Lawson sent Howe a note extolling the virtues of British membership of the European Monetary System, the policy that would reach its full expression with Britain's ill-fated membership of the Exchange Rate Mechanism after 1990.[175] In his March 1982 Budget, Howe formalised the shift away from £M3 targets by introducing targets for M1 and PSL2. He also raised the remaining £M3 target by three percentage points, again with no attempt to claw back the 3.7 percentage point overshoot in 1981/82. This enabled the Conservative government, in 1983, finally to hit one of its (revised) £M3 targets. At Thatcher's suggestion, signed charts were produced to commemorate the event.[176] The Bank's Chief Economist, Christopher Dow, assumed that this was a joke.[177] It was not.

After the 1983 general election, Howe was succeeded as Chancellor by Lawson, who, after briefly suspending his broad money target in October 1985, published his final – 11 to 15 per cent – £M3 target range in March 1986.[178] But, as Christopher Johnson remarks,

In March 1986 £M3 was dragged out of its coffin for a last death-ride. Unlike El Cid, riding dead in the saddle at the head of his troops to his final victory, it impressed nobody.[179]

[172] Lawson, *The view from No. 11*, 72.
[173] Quoted by P. F. C. Stephens, *Politics and the pound: the Tories, the economy and Europe* (London, 1997), 34.
[174] Hoskyns, *Just in time*, 391.   [175] Lawson, *The view from No. 11*, 111.
[176] Howe, *Conflict of loyalty*, 282.
[177] Hacche and Taylor, *Inside the Bank of England*, 216.
[178] The M1 and PSL2 targets were replaced by M0 in 1984.
[179] Johnson, *The economy under Mrs Thatcher*, 55.

Within a year Lawson was shadowing the deutschmark, the policy that presaged Britain's brief and unhappy membership of the ERM.[180] In 1988 Middleton wrote: 'Monetary policy. . .has assumed the role for which it is best suited: the achievement of whatever goals are set for nominal demand.'[181] The authors of the Radcliffe Report would have recognised this twin focus on the exchange rate and demand management. Monetary policy had come full circle. It was almost as if the monetarist 'revolution' had never happened.

---

[180] 'Monitoring ranges' for M0 and M4 remained in place until 1997 but were relatively unimportant to the conduct of monetary policy.

[181] Middleton succeeded Wass as Permanent Secretary in 1983: P. E. Middleton, 'Economic policy formation in the Treasury in the post-war period', *National Institute Economic Review*, 127, 1 (February 1989), 50.

10 Macroeconomic policy and the 1981 Budget: changing the trend

Ray Barrell

Introduction

The debate around the merits of the 1981 Budget has probably been more extensive than over any other single fiscal package in the last fifty years, except, perhaps, the similar debate around the Darling and Osborne Budgets in 2010. In both cases this in part reflects the radical intentions of some Conservative politicians, who desired to change the way the UK economy worked. But it also in part follows from the strong disagreement expressed by a large number of academic economists. Many similar issues entered both Budgets, and I reflect on them in this chapter, in particular on the size of multipliers and the role of the state. Some people considered that these Budgets were designed in such a way that their effects would not be contractionary. I comment on the debate on 'expansionary fiscal contractions' below, but in neither case is there any evidence other than that the Budget reduced the growth of output noticeably. In both cases some economists argued that the effects of the contraction would be large and long-lasting, and, again, the evidence suggests that they were wrong. The impact was negative in both cases, but not enormously damaging. The economy showed clear signs of automatic recovery, with market mechanisms working to return the economy to equilibrium, albeit slowly.

In 2010 I was director of forecasting at the National Institute of Economic and Social Research (NIESR) in London, and expressed criticisms of the 2010 Budgets in the Institute's *Economic Review*.[1] They were excessively contractionary given the situation facing the economy, and the reasons for the tightening, which centred on the potential costs of excess borrowing, were essentially spurious. There was a clear agenda to

---

[1] Initial reaction to the April and June 2010 Budgets is given by R. Barrell and S. Kirby, 'UK fiscal prospects', *National Institute Economic Review*, no. 213 (July 2010), F66–70. A longer-term perspective is provided by R. Barrell, 'Fiscal policy in the longer term', *National Institute Economic Review*, no. 217 (July 2011), F4–10; and R. Barrell, 'Fiscal consolidation and the slimmer state', *National Institute Economic Review*, no. 215 (January 2011), F4–9.

reduce the size of the state as a share of output in the 2010 Budgets, and that agenda was shared by the drafters of the 1981 Budget. There were other, more compelling, reasons for a fiscal contraction in 1981, although, at the time, potential increases in borrowing costs were considered important by Alan Walters.[2] I was a lecturer in economics at Brunel in 1981, but the head of department, Walter Elkan, so strongly disapproved of the views expressed in the letter eventually signed by the 364 economists that he did not mention to other members of staff that he had been asked to circulate it until after it was published. Although I was a member of the Labour Party at the time (and still am), the letter would not have been signed by me, as it was not clear that it showed a real understanding of how the economy operated, or of the economic analysis in macro-economics current at the time. There were good reasons, associated with inflation, for tightening fiscal policy in 1981, and the analysis used to support that view had been standard in textbooks used in macroeconomics for a decade when the Budget was presented.

I left Brunel in 1984 to work as a civil-service-based economic adviser at the Treasury, and at that time worked closely on forecasting and analysis of the UK economy with other people mentioned in this volume. The unjustified optimism about the transformation of the economy, and hence the unsupported assumption that trend GDP growth would be over 3 per cent a year, was a major factor behind both the excessive expansion of demand in the late 1980s and my move to the NIESR to run (world) forecasting in 1988. Brunel beckoned again in 2011, but over the intervening twenty-five years my views have been publically aired, mainly in the *National Institute Economic Review*. In the first section of this chapter I look at the degree of success achieved by the radicals who wished to raise trend growth. In the second I look at the immediate impact of the Budget on the economy. In both cases I also reflect on current debates, as they are very similar to those of the early 1980s.

Trend growth and structural reform

In the post-war period UK growth was strong, but, as has been shown, it lagged behind that of our continental European neighbours.[3] All these countries were catching up with the United States, as was Britain, and it

---

[2] I was taught transport economics and microeconomics by Alan Walters at the London School of Economics at undergraduate and postgraduate levels. Walters was not considered to be a macroeconomist at the time. Brian (later Lord) Griffiths taught me macroeconomics, and, clearly, Walters and Griffith shared views.

[3] N. F. R. Crafts, 'Recent European economic growth: why can't it be like the Golden Age?', *National Institute Economic Review*, no. 199 (January 2007), 69–81.

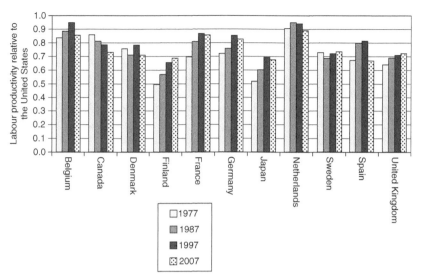

Figure 10.1 Productivity per person-hour relative to the United States

appeared that the Germans and the French were better at doing so. By the late 1970s output per person hour in these countries had passed UK levels by a noticeable margin. Of the nine countries plotted in Figure 10.1, only Finland had lower productivity per person hour than the United Kingdom in 1977, and the comparison with Germany would be more striking if I used only West German data for 1977 and 1987, as productivity there was noticeably higher than in all Germany (data for which I use here). The United Kingdom is the only country (apart from Finland) that continued to 'catch up' with the United States in every decade after 1977, but productivity clearly remained higher in Germany, France and the Low Countries in 2007. Between 1977 and 1987 the United Kingdom performed well in productivity terms but, as we can see, it was neither the best performer nor was the change particularly dramatic. Of course, it could be claimed that, without reform, relative decline might have continued, and this may well have been the case. Evidence of the effects of structural reform on productivity is limited, however.[4]

---

[4] There are a number of academic studies, and also studies by the OECD, that suggest the impacts exist and are significant, but are not particularly large, such as R. Barrell, D. Holland, I. Liadze and O. Pomerantz, 'The impact of EMU on growth in Europe', in M. Buti, S. Deroose, V. Gaspar and J. Nogueira Martins (eds.), *The euro: the first decade* (Cambridge, 2010), 607–37.

The 1970s saw two inflationary episodes in the global economy, partly associated with the collapse of the Bretton Woods fixed exchange rate system and partly because of shifts in the relative price of oil. Over the period 1973 to 1975, when global inflation surged, the UK inflation rate was higher than that of the other major advanced economies, largely because fiscal and monetary policy makers performed worse than those in other major economies. The inflationary surge in the late 1970s and into 1980 also saw poor domestic policy making, with Britain taking on a larger rise in inflation than most other major economies.[5] Output growth was also slow over the decade, and it was common to blame this on the sclerotic effect of the style of the conflictual trades-union-based wage bargaining then operating in the country. In particular, underlying productivity growth was slow, and this was attributed variously to the size of the state, the scale of nationalisation in industry, the effects of the wage bargaining process and the impact of high income taxes on incentives. The 1981 radicals addressed all these presumed faults, and over the first decade of the Conservative administration the state shrank, industries were privatised, trades unions were shackled and the highest rates of income tax were cut

In the 1980s it was too easy to assume that trend growth had been changed, but evidence has accumulated to suggest that it had not. I first look at the longer-term evidence, using growth accounting in a comparative framework. I then look at statistical estimates of trend output over the period. Trend growth depends on a number of factors, with the most important being the growth of the labour supply, the rate of increase in the efficiency of factor use and technical progress in the economy. There can be sustained surges in capital deepening that will also increase productivity, and these may depend on changes in technology as well as on the volatility of output.[6]

Many of the factors affecting output growth are common across countries, and it is useful to look at the United Kingdom in this context.[7]

---

[5] The comparison is particularly damaging as performance was worse even than in Italy in the 1974–75 episode, when UK inflation (as measured by the consumer expenditure deflator) was the highest in the major seven economies, peaking at 23 per cent in 1975, compared to the Italian peak of 22 per cent in 1974. In the 1979–81 episode UK inflation, at 16 per cent in 1980, was the second worst in the major seven economies, with Italian inflation peaking at 21 per cent in 1980.

[6] R. Barrell, D. Holland, I. Liadze and O. Pomerantz, 'Volatility, growth and cycles', *Empirica*, 36, 2 (May 2009), 177–92, discuss capital deepening and the impact of the volatility of output on it.

[7] Economists describe the productive capacity as the interaction between factor inputs, such as labour and capital, the state of technology and any other influences that may affect the quality or efficiency of the production process. Growth may vary across

UK output increased at an average annual rate of 2.4 per cent in the thirty years from 1978 to 2007, with similar growth rates in the first two decades and somewhat stronger rates in the final decade, as we can see from Table 10.1. UK growth has not been as rapid as US growth, but this has been because labour input has been rising rapidly in the United States, driven mainly by the growth of the population. The supply of labour in use in the United States rose by around 1.4 per cent a year throughout the period, while in Britain it fell by 0.2 to 0.4 per cent a year in the first two decades, before rising by 0.7 per cent a year in the decade to 2007. High levels of immigration have been particularly important in increasing overall US growth, and also in the United Kingdom in the last decade, when productivity growth accelerated. The evidence suggests that this increase in immigration has had only a small and temporary impact on productivity growth. While overall UK growth performance compares favourably to the other countries in the table, the improvement did not come immediately after the reforms in the early and mid-1980s, but rather later.

Policy makers in the United Kingdom in the early 1980s wanted to improve the efficiency of use of the factors of production, and also to change the labour market so as to increase the effective supply of labour. Table 10.1 reports growth in output per person-hour, or productivity, and we can see that it grew more rapidly in the first decade around the 1981 Budget than it did subsequently, suggesting that some reforms were having an impact. Labour market reforms reducing employment protection and the power of trades unions are likely to have effects on participation in the labour force and on the equilibrium level of unemployment, and changes in these are likely to increase equilibrium output. It clearly took some time for reforms to impact upon the economy, and it was not until well into the 1990s that unemployment was able to fall without significant inflationary consequences. The reforms may well have contributed to the increase in the efficiency with which factors were being used, but they did little to encourage investment, as capital deepening in Britain over the first decade made a smaller

countries because factor input growth differs over time and space. Labour supply depends on institutions, preferences and demographics, and its equilibrium will change when the structures of these institutions, preferences and demographics change. Capital input growth may also differ over time, either because investment growth changes or because the rate of depreciation of the existing capital stock changes. The productive capacity of factor inputs depends on their innate quality and is driven by, for example, the skill level of the workforce, and on the technology used to combine factor inputs, which may depend on the domestic research base as well as on access to innovations developed abroad.

Table 10.1 *UK growth in comparison*

		Belgium	Denmark	Finland	France	Germany	Netherlands	Sweden	United Kingdom	United States
									Percentage point contribution to average annual GDP growth	
GDP at base prices (% change)	1978–87	1.5	1.9	3.4	2.2	1.9	2.0	2.2	2.2	3.3
	1988–97	2.3	2.3	1.7	2.1	2.7	2.7	1.7	2.3	3.0
	1998–2007	2.2	1.8	3.6	2.3	1.8	2.6	3.3	2.9	3.1
Output per person-hour	1978–87	2.2	1.0	3.1	3.1	2.2	2.1	1.1	2.4	1.6
	1988–97	2.4	2.6	3.0	2.3	2.8	1.5	2.1	1.9	1.6
	1998–2007	1.0	1.0	2.5	1.9	1.7	1.5	2.3	2.2	2.0
of which Skills accumulation	1978–87	0.1	0.3	0.4	0.3	0.2	0.2	0.0	0.4	0.3
	1988–97	0.5	0.4	0.3	0.4	0.1	0.2	0.1	0.6	0.2
	1998–2007	0.2	0.1	0.1	0.2	0.0	0.2	0.2	0.3	0.2
Total factor productivity (TFP) (excluding skills)	1978–87	1.2	0.4	1.8	1.4	1.0	1.1	0.7	1.4	1.0
	1988–97	0.9	1.8	1.9	0.7	1.7	1.0	1.1	0.8	1.1
	1998–2007	0.5	0.8	2.2	0.9	1.1	0.9	1.8	1.2	1.2
Capital deepening	1978–87	0.8	0.3	0.9	1.5	0.9	0.8	0.4	0.86	0.3
	1988–97	0.9	0.5	0.9	1.2	1.0	0.4	0.9	0.86	0.3
	1998–2007	0.3	0.2	0.2	0.8	0.6	0.4	0.2	0.7	0.6

Notes: Capital deepening is the impact of increased capital per unit of output on labour productivity. Skills effects and TFP excluding skills sum to the productivity residual. Labour input growth is the difference between GDP growth and growth in output per person-hour. Skills are calculated as a Tornquist index using three skill levels and the wages on those skill levels. Over one year the skill level rises when the relative wages (marginal products) of the skilled increase. Over longer periods an increase in the number of people in the skill group will increase skills even when wages remain constant.

Source: R. Barrell, D. Holland and I. Liadze, 'Accounting for UK economic performance', paper presented at Clare College, Cambridge University, 19 September 2013.

contribution to growth than it did in France, Germany and the Low Countries.[8]

The United Kingdom and Finland are the only countries in our small group in which productivity growth (as measured by output per person-hour) was higher than in the United States over the whole thirty-year period. This in part reflects 'catching up', but it also reflects improvements in the operation of both economies. In both the United Kingdom and Finland some of this faster growth came from an increase in the ratio of capital to output (capital deepening), but in both countries underlying total factor productivity growth was also more rapid than in the United States, unlike in the other countries in the table. The reasons for this may lie in the impacts of structural reforms on the economy. They may also be the result of an increased rate of accumulation of skills, as these two countries had experienced revolutions in higher education a decade or so beforehand, when participation rates rose. Skills, as measured in a standard way, rose more rapidly in these two countries in our first decade than they did elsewhere.[9] Indeed, the Conservative radicals of the early 1960s who drove through the Robbins reforms in higher education may have contributed as much to improved performance as did their successors in the 1980s.

The relatively strong growth in TFP growth in Britain in the first decade may be the result of the process of attempting to improve the efficiency of factor use in the country. The privatisation programme, begun in 1984, was based on a belief that private sector ownership was sufficient to ensure that productivity would improve because the threat of takeover, or an actual takeover, would improve productivity, without any concern for the regulatory framework or competition environment in which privatised firms were placed. As a result, private sector monopolies with inflexible pricing rules were set up, and efficiency did not improve as much as might have been expected. The first electricity privatisation, in 1990, was better designed to raise productivity, with some recognition that competition mattered, but it was only with the restructuring of the gas industry, in 1995, that the benefits of privatisation began to become apparent. Indeed, the 2002 OECD report on structural reforms in the United Kingdom suggests that the early UK

---

[8] Capital deepening will depend upon factors other than labour market reform. Nicholas Crafts and Mary O'Mahony suggest that greater macroeconomic stability within the Exchange Rate Mechanism was a major factor encouraging investment. This greater stability, which continued for two decades, was one reason why the radicals, or at least Nigel Lawson, wished to join the ERM in the middle to late 1980s. N. F. R. Crafts and M. O'Mahony, 'A perspective on UK productivity performance', *Fiscal Studies*, 22, 3 (September 2001), 271–306.

[9] B. van Ark, M. O'Mahony and M. P. Timmer, 'The productivity gap between Europe and the United States: trends and causes', *Journal of Economic Perspectives*, 22, 1 (Winter 2008), 64–78.

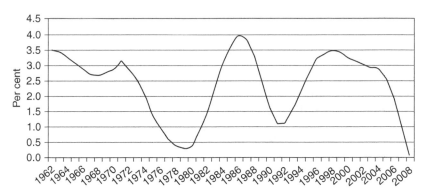

Figure 10.2 Trend growth in the United Kingdom

privatisations were a model for other countries, in that they showed how not to do it.[10] This report, and subsequent work, suggests that it was only once the privatisations began to promote competition in the market that they impacted on overall productivity growth.

UK performance, especially in a comparative context, did improve in the 1980s, but the evidence above suggests that it did not improve much, and that the improvement was only partly sustained in the decade from 1987. Given this, it is important to understand why the radicals thought that the shift in policy evident in the 1981 Budget had changed the trend rate of growth in the economy. There are many ways to look at trend growth, and it is much easier to do so with hindsight, as well as with good statistical tools. In the 1980s economists could have used growth accounting (as above); they could have used sophisticated weighted moving average techniques to make an estimate of underlying trends in sustainable output growth; or they could have utilised the newly proposed Hodrick–Prescott filter.[11] Since then, various other filters have been developed, and in Figure 10.2 I use the Baxter–King band-pass filter to extract trend growth from UK (non-oil basic price) output data. As noted below, it is important to use non-oil output growth over the late 1970s and early 1980s, as the expansion

---

[10] See the 2002 UK issue in the OECD's series 'Reviews of regulatory reform': OECD, *United Kingdom: challenges at the cutting edge* (Paris, 2002).

[11] This filter, commonly used in engineering, is the same as a centred Henderson moving average smoother, and it has significant problems with dealing with breaks of trend towards the end of the data period, and it can be misleading: R. J. Hodrick and E. C. Prescott, 'Post-war US business cycles: an empirical investigation', Northwestern University Center for Mathematical Studies in Economics and Management Science Discussion Paper no. 451 (1980).

of North Sea production was adding to output growth in a way that was largely unrelated to either factor inputs or technology and efficiency factors.

The first thing to note is that trend growth varies over time. This is in part because trend labour input growth varies over time with demographic and other factors. In addition, the utilisable capital stock does not grow at a completely stable rate. The movements in trend growth are much larger than can be explained by these factors, however, and the slow growth in the mid-1970s and the slowdown in the early 1980s to well under 1 per cent are quite noticeable, as is the acceleration in trend growth from the middle of the 1980s to the end of the decade. This increase in trend growth would mean that output could, for a period, grow more rapidly than in the past before inflationary pressures began to mount. When trend growth accelerates to near 3 per cent a year it is not surprising that policy makers claim that their innovations have been successful; nor is it surprising that they acted on the assumption that they had succeeded. Unfortunately, the increase in trend growth probably came from a different source over which they had no control, and which gave only a temporary boost, matching the temporary slowdown that preceded it.

Over the short term, productivity growth will also be influenced by the level of the oil price, as energy is an input into the production process. When oil prices rise in real terms producers slowly change their processes, reducing oil use while increasing the use of other factors of production. This means that, for any given level of labour and capital inputs, the level of equilibrium, or sustainable, output will have been reduced, with the effect being larger the more dependent the economy is on energy use in production. Oil prices gyrated noticeably over the 1970s and 1980s, as we can see from Figure 10.3. In the decade to 2010 it is estimated that a 25 per cent rise in the real oil price (from \$80 to \$100 a barrel) would reduce the level of trend output by 0.5 percentage points, and that this reduction would be spread over three to four years.[12] In 1980 the United Kingdom was twice as energy-intensive as it was in 2010, and hence the impact of a 25 per cent rise in oil prices would have been higher (but not necessarily double).

Using these estimates, the increase in the real oil price between 1973 and 1975 would have reduced trend growth by up to one percentage point a year for four years, while the increase in 1979–80 would have had a

---

[12] See R. Barrell, A. Delannoy and D. Holland, 'Monetary policy, output growth and oil prices', *National Institute Economic Review*, no. 215 (January 2010), F37–43, for a discussion of oil intensity of output and its effects on trend growth.

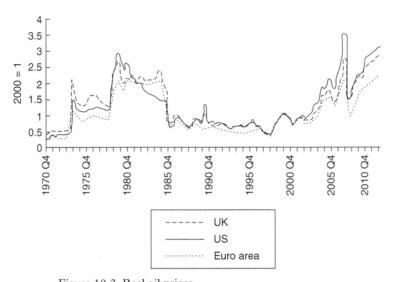

Figure 10.3 Real oil prices
Note: Average of Brent and West Texas Intermediate prices deflated by consumer prices.

smaller impact, reducing trend output growth by about 0.8 percentage point a year for four years. The fall in the real oil price in 1985 will have reversed much of this, and would have added well over one percentage point a year to trend growth for four years. The longer-term tables wash out these effects, and underlying trend growth over the 1980s was probably around 2¼ per cent per year. Policies that were designed on the assumption that it would be higher for a sustained period were likely to be damaging. As Alan Budd discusses elsewhere in this volume, in the early 1970s the Conservative administration of Ted Heath and Anthony Barber was of the opinion that strong demand growth was all that was needed to ensure that Britain grew more quickly, and their policies produced an excess-demand-driven burst of inflation written over a global inflation surge. Margaret Thatcher and Nigel Lawson in the mid-1980s thought that their policies had transformed their world, and based expansionary monetary and fiscal policies on these views. The consequences were not quite as bad as in the early 1970s. Conservative administrations are not the only ones that have fallen foul of acting on the implications of their own mistaken rhetoric. Tony Blair and Gordon Brown from 1997 also based macro-policies on a belief that policies, including 'light touch' macro-regulation, had transformed their world. They were also expensively wrong.

There was a marginal improvement in UK trend growth around the time of the 1981 Budget, and UK relative performance was good from then onwards, at least until the 2008 financial crisis, since when it may have lagged a little. Some of this improvement will have come from the massive expansion in higher education in the 1960s, which had begun to feed through into the skills of the workforce, and hence the efficiency with which it operated. Some of the impact will have come from the reform process, especially from labour market reforms, but these will have been small. The impacts of privatisation and the reduction in the scale of the state were probably more limited in the 1980s than their proponents supposed, and it was only in the new wave of restructuring of previously privatised industries in the 1990s that the impacts began to be felt, with increased competition raising the effectiveness of factor use and hence allowing the economy to reap the benefits. These small changes were swamped by the impacts of changes in the oil price on the trend rate of growth, and politicians had a tendency to attribute some of its impacts to others' failures in the 1970s and their successes in the 1980s.

The impacts of the 1981 Budget

The 1981 Budget was a major affair, and not just because it evinced a strong comment from so many economists. The economy was in recession, reflecting the impacts of both tight monetary policy and the dislocating effects of the significant increase in oil prices in 1979–80. As we can see from Table 10.2, output growth had been negative, and unemployment had risen to a post-war peak. Even with trend growth at around 1 per cent, as is suggested in Figure 10.2, an output gap of more than two percentage points had emerged. Tightening policy at such a time appeared unwise to many, but, given that inflation was proving stubborn, with consumer prices rising at almost 14 per cent at the end of 1980, a further and more reliable reduction in demand seemed necessary. The monetary tightening that had been experienced over the previous two years had not, so far, had the desired effect of reducing inflation significantly. This was perhaps because the monetarists advising ministers had a too simple view of the speed and reliability of the transmission from changes in money to changes in inflation.

The standard textbook treatment of the issue suggested that a tightening of fiscal policy would reduce demand, increasing the output gap.[13] As

---

[13] The IS curve would be shifted in, giving a savings–investment balance at a lower level of output for each interest rate.

Table 10.2 *The United Kingdom in figures, 1979–90*

	Government deficit (% of GDP)	GDP growth (%)	Unemployment (% of workforce)	Inflation (% change)
1979	−3.55	2.17	3.78	13.42
1980	−3.20	−2.01	4.80	16.41
1981	−4.32	−0.97	7.65	11.04
1982	−2.61	2.55	8.98	8.38
1983	−3.34	3.60	9.83	5.37
1984	−3.59	2.37	10.08	5.15
1985	−2.82	3.81	10.28	5.38
1986	−2.56	3.78	10.53	4.29
1987	−2.06	4.38	9.43	4.31
1988	−0.08	4.83	7.55	4.87
1989	0.23	2.34	5.90	6.04
1990	−2.05	1.07	5.45	7.68

Notes: Column 3 is OECD standardised unemployment. Column 4 is the annual rate of change of the consumer price deflator.

a result of the reduction in demand, market interest rates would fall relative to where they would otherwise have been, and the exchange rate would depreciate, partly offsetting the contractionary effects of fiscal policy.[14] The reduction in output would reduce the demand for labour, and this in turn would reduce the real wage rate relative to where it would otherwise have been, once again partly offsetting the contractionary effects of the budgetary tightening. These changes would reduce prices (and inflation) compared to where they would otherwise have been.[15] The reduction in labour demand would raise unemployment, and as a result inflation expectations would be revised down.[16] As real wages adjusted and inflation expectations came down, the economy would begin to recover of its own accord, albeit slowly. Not only was this description of the economy taught in most economics departments in Britain, it was also reasonably well supported by the evidence, and by the mid-1980s formed the core of the numerous macroeconomic models used in the country, including that of the London Business School and that developed by the NIESR (of which more below).

[14] The IS curve moved down the LM curve, and, as we were not in a liquidity trap, interest rates would be lower than they would otherwise have been.
[15] The aggregate demand curve shifted down the aggregate supply curve.
[16] The Phillips curve traced out the short-run inflation unemployment relation but changed when inflation expectations changed. In the long run there was no inflation and unemployment trade-off.

If the impacts of the Budget were well understood, why, then, did so many economists consider it unwise? Any policy making in the economy should be based on a comparison of costs and benefits, and, given the scale of unemployment in 1981, there was at least some debate to be had about the benefits of increasing it further in comparison to the costs of doing so. In part the debate was about the size of the multiplier, or just how contractionary the policy might be. The Conservative radicals claimed that the effects would be small, while extreme Keynesians thought it would be large, and hence there could be genuine disagreement about the short-term impacts. The debate was seldom couched in such balanced terms, however, in part because the economics profession has always had a strong preference for elegant a priori reasoning ahead of boring evidence. It was known to some participants in the debate that UK wages were not set by the market, and it was also known that self-correcting mechanisms were absent. Inflation was known to be a matter of the accumulation of cost pressures that could be controlled. No evidence could be presented to persuade right-thinking people that they were mistaken, and the debate around the 1981 Budget still seems couched in these terms.[17] This habit of preferring a priori knowledge to evidence has continued into the last decade, with 'Balliol man' stressing that tight fiscal policy was the cause of slow growth between 2010 and 2013, and, when growth accelerated, arguing that it could only be because fiscal policy had been surreptitiously loosened.[18]

The level of borrowing had been high in 1980, the amount being equivalent to around 3.2 per cent of GDP. This could partly be explained by the existence of some spare capacity in the economy.[19] Fiscal policy had not been significantly tightened since 1976, however, and it may have been marginally loose.[20] Borrowing had on average been higher by more

---

[17] In his lectures at LSE in the 1970s, Ernest Gellner used the term 'Balliol man' for the people involved in the process whereby knowledge emerged from a discussion amongst the elite without reference to evidence.

[18] The discussion of fiscal policy and the recovery by Chris Giles in the *Financial Times* on 26 September 2013 is particularly relevant: C. T. Giles, 'Economists puzzled by Britain's upswing', *Financial Times*, 26 September 2013.

[19] My estimate would be that the cyclically adjusted deficit was around 2 per cent of GDP. This differs from the commonly used ONS definition. It is common to quote cyclically adjusted deficit figures, as a reduction in output will increase spending and reduce tax revenues. I do not do so in part because the output gap is measured with great uncertainty, but also because the impacts of a shortfall on the deficit are also uncertain. Official UK estimates of the impact of the output gap on the deficit, at around 0.75 per cent, are considered rather high, and 0.5 would be a better estimate.

[20] Britton, *Macroeconomic policy*, 193–226. Given the build-up of output from the North Sea, this was a period when significant taxes on production could have been justified, and the proceeds, which would have induced a public sector surplus, should have been invested in

than 1 per cent of GDP from 1974 to 1976, and, compared to the 2009 and 2010 burst in borrowing to more than 10 per cent of GDP, it was extremely moderate. Thus, in itself, this level of borrowing would not have been particularly worrying if inflation had not peaked at 16 per cent in 1980, with insufficient signs of falling. Clearly, something had to be done, and reductions in spending were an obvious tool to use, especially as they fitted with the preferences of the more radical wing of the administration. The scale of the planned contraction, at just over 1 per cent of GDP, was not excessive, however, especially as compared to the Darling and Osborne Budgets in 2010 and 2011, in which contractionary policies exceeded 2 per cent of GDP.

Some radicals defended the Budget by utilising recent developments in economic theory. Over the previous decade or so the role of expectations had become more prominent in economic theorising, and these developments gave a potential defence for the contractionary policy. Longer-term interest rates for private sector borrowing have always been set by the market, and they are dependent upon what is expected for short-term private sector borrowing rates in the future. The government, through monetary policy, affects these rates, but has direct control only over its own short-term borrowing rate. If governments borrow more, this will drive up short-term public and private sector interest rates. If governments are expected to borrow more in the future, this will drive up expected short-term borrowing costs, and these in turn will affect the costs of longer-term borrowing by both the public and private sector. Hence, a fully credible policy that commits the government to borrow less in future may affect both its cost of borrowing and the costs of private sector borrowing. Indeed, it is possible that the expected reduction in borrowing costs in the future could be so large as to stimulate investment (and consumption) by enough to offset the initial contractionary effects of a reduction in borrowing by the public sector. In addition, but perhaps less plausibly, forward-looking consumers would recognise that a cut in spending and borrowing now meant lower tax payments in future, and hence they could expand their spending now. Equivalently, a rise in taxes now, with less borrowing, could be seen to signal lower taxes in the future, and hence might have no effect on spending.

In the early 1980s the logical possibility of an expansionary fiscal contraction, as the scenario described above is labelled, was well understood. The 'scholastic tradition' in economics can easily change a logical possibility into a probable event. Economists and politicians discuss these

an 'oil fund', much as the Norwegians later did. The UK government chose to use the funds it raised for current purposes, and chose not to tax the companies as much as could have been justified.

matters, and soon become convinced that what was considered a probable event has happened, albeit in another country, such as Ireland or Denmark. Once it is known to all right-thinking people that it has happened elsewhere, it becomes clear to all those involved that it could be happening here. At the next round, all these well-trained scholars come to know that it is happening here, and hence anybody who disagrees is a politically motivated charlatan. This transmogrification of views took place around 1981 in Conservative circles in relation to the contractionary (or expansionary) effects of the 1981 Budget, and it was repeated in relation to the June 2010 Budget of the coalition government. Before we are too critical, their opponents on both occasions used exactly the same scientific process to arrive at their criticisms; it is just that they had trained while members of the Labour Club, and not the Bullingdon.

The literature on expansionary fiscal contractions is a fascinating example of how the economics profession proceeds. By the middle of the 1980s almost all the profession knew that it was possible that we might see such an expansionary fiscal contraction, and Alberto Alesina and Roberto Perotti, and Francesco Giavazzi and Marco Pagano, showed that it had happened in Europe in the run-up to the consolidation of the Exchange Rate Mechanism in the 1980s.[21] It was shown that in the mid-1980s both Ireland and Denmark had clearly undertaken fiscal consolidations, and, as a result of the impacts on expectations, their economies had expanded. The profession was convinced that it had happened there, and hence it could happen (and probably had happened) elsewhere. Only economists in Ireland and Denmark remained puzzled. The Danes were convinced that their expansion, which fiscal policy had moderated, had come from significantly expanding trade with their major trading partner, Germany. The Irish were more puzzled, as they had not observed the expansion caused by their fiscal contraction. Growth had been robust because of trade with the United Kingdom, but it had been markedly slower than had been anticipated without the fiscal package. Some time later Perotti acknowledged that the initial studies had been based on publicly available, but faulty, data for Ireland, and that if the correct national data had been used at the time there would have been no evidence for an EFC in Ireland in the 1980s.[22] That would leave us only the puzzled Danes, who never thought they had had one anyway. Such attention to detailed case studies is not

[21] A. Alesina and R. Perotti, 'Fiscal expansions and adjustments in OECD countries', *Economic Policy: A European Forum*, 21, 2 (October 1995), 207–48; F. Giavazzi and M. Pagano, 'Can severe fiscal contractions be expansionary? Tales of two small European economies', in *NBER macroeconomics annual*, vol. V (Chicago, 1990), 75–111.

[22] R. Perotti, 'The austerity myth: gain without pain', Bank for International Settlements Working Paper no. 362 (2011).

considered good practice in economics, as we know the answers a priori. It was widely thought in some circles in the mid-1980s, however, that the United Kingdom had experienced such a miracle.

Given that the radicals were so wrong, we should ask if their economic (and political) opponents based their case on firmer foundations. Unfortunately, it is clear that they did not. Many of this group thought fiscal multipliers (the impact of an innovation in fiscal policy on the level of output in the economy) were large. It was also thought that the economy, and especially the labour market, did not recover from negative shocks in a reasonable amount of time. Multipliers are easy to understand, and they arise because, when governments spend more, they give people income, who in turn spend more, multiplying the effects of the initial impulse. In addition, firms see output rising and invest to raise capacity, thereby accelerating the impacts of the initial impulse. Some of the increase in consumer and firm spending leaks into imports, however, and raises demand elsewhere, rather than at home, reducing the domestic multiplier. I turn to these issues in the next section.

Growth and the impact of fiscal policy

Although trend growth was low in 1981, at least as indicated by a standard filter, actual growth had been noticeably lower. This was in part because the economy had reached an inflationary peak, with production operating about two percentage points above its capacity output in 1979, and hence some slowdown was inevitable. Between the end of 1979 and the first quarter of 1981 an output gap of some size had opened up, with my estimate, based on the slow trend growth discussed above, suggesting that it was around 2 per cent. This had been driven by a significant tightening of monetary policy, with interest rates being as high as 17 per cent. Although real interest rates (adjusted for inflation) were only around 2.5 per cent in 1981, they had risen by five percentage points since 1979. High nominal rates were perhaps more contractionary than it might at first appear, as many mortgage contracts had flexible rates, which were high at around 15 per cent. Individuals were therefore paying a real rate of return of around 3.5 per cent, and they were also paying back a significant amount of the inflation-adjusted principal, as their debt-to-income ratio would be falling. Given that borrowing constraints were stronger, and remortgaging much more difficult than now, this meant that many individuals were strongly constrained in what they could spend.

Output growth over the period is plotted in Figure 10.4, and we can see that, on average, non-oil output growth was half a percentage point or a little more below the growth rate of overall output because of the strength

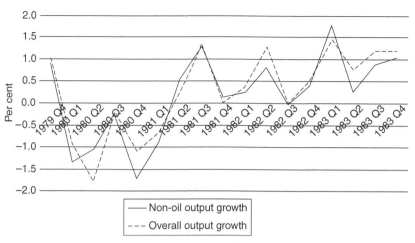

Figure 10.4 Output growth around the 1981 Budget

of oil production growth. Output growth, on both measures, turned positive in the second quarter of 1981, and, on our measure, the output gap was eliminated by mid-1983 and stayed closed until 1987, when expansionary policies drove it up to plus 1½ per cent by mid-1989. Part of the boost to growth came from a fall in market interest rates of three percentage points between the last quarter of 1980 and the second quarter of 1982. The impact would have been quick because the reduction in the 'front-loading' of payments would have been large. If fiscal policy had not been tightened in the spring of 1981, growth would have been faster that year, and the output gap would have closed more quickly. As a result, inflation and inflation expectations would have not fallen as much as they did. The United Kingdom was not experiencing an expansionary fiscal contraction, which would have required a burst to investment driven by a much greater fall in long-term (nominal and real) interest rates than was seen. It would also have required much stronger consumption growth than was seen that year. The recovery into 1982 was led by domestic investment, but the turnaround from a fall in business investment of 7 per cent in 1981 to growth of 4 per cent growth in 1982 might be seen as the normal exit from a recession. These normal reactions were all built into models such as that constructed at the NIESR during the 1980s, and I turn to that next.

Much careful empirical work has gone into the construction of large macro-models such as that produced by the NIESR, and I use Andrew Britton's model-based analysis of fiscal policy during the 1980s as a benchmark. These models contained descriptions of consumption and investment behaviour that were congruent with the data, and Britton's work in 1991 was sufficiently close to the period in question that the model is particularly relevant. When incomes changed, so did consumption, but not necessarily immediately by a large amount, and changes in output would also increase investment, but – again – not by much. They also contain descriptions of the labour market that show a relation between the level of unemployment and the real wage, as well as a description of labour demand. It was clear from the work behind the model that labour markets worked in the textbook way, and would return the economy to an equilibrium, albeit slowly.

Britton set up an experiment, using the NIESR model, in which he kept fiscal policy constant throughout the decade, with government consumption spending rising at a steady rate of 1.4 per cent a year rather than being cut over time. In addition, he assumed that tax rates and the threshold for tax (in real terms) were held constant. Indirect taxes are assumed to be a constant proportion of their bases. The exchange rate was assumed to follow its observed path, and interest rates were adjusted by a feedback rule. Given these assumptions, the fiscal package introduced in 1981 was more contractionary when compared to the Britton baseline than it might at first appear. The cut in government spending in 1981 of almost 2 per cent compares to the counterfactual growth of 1.4 per cent. Compared to Britton's baseline, the fiscal contraction in 1981 represents a 2 per cent of GDP change in the budget deficit. The reduction in output in his scenario was around 1½ per cent.[23] This would mean that, overall, the multiplier used in his analysis was no more than around 0.75 (a £1 cut in spending would reduce GDP by 75 pence in the first year). Over the decade of the 1980s as a whole, changes in fiscal policy, at least in Britton's analysis, had no effect on overall output in the longer term. The self-stabilising properties of the market, as represented by this Keynesian model, were sufficient to offset the contractionary effects of fiscal policy within four years. Of course, if expectations are formed adaptively, taking no account of changes in policy, then the impacts could be larger. Britton concludes that 'the most striking conclusion to be drawn...is the small scale of the policy effects'.[24] The critics of the policy had significantly overestimated its effects, and recovery was under way anyway.[25]

---

[23] Britton, *Macroeconomic policy*, 220.   [24] Ibid.
[25] A comparison between 2010 and 2013 is in order. A number of commentators, including me, thought fiscal policy was too tight in 2010. The effects were not large, however, and it was clear that the economy would recover.

'Why are multipliers small?' we might ask, especially as the 364 authors of the 1981 letter thought the impacts of the Budget would be potentially catastrophic. Clearly, they shared the view, sometimes repeated even today, that the multiplier from a fiscal impulse might be as large as three, and that that impact would be sustained for some years. As a consequence, output growth would have been severely damaged.[26] It is useful to ask what evidence might have persuaded them that these numbers could be so large. Economists agree that consumption does respond to changes in income, and that this is a major part of the multiplier process.[27] Some proportion of consumption leaks into imports, however, and this will reduce the impact of government spending on output.[28] These two factors change over time, and will affect the value of the multiplier. There are many other factors that affect it, however, from the impacts of spending on investment to the effects of crowding out from financial markets.

The factors can be checked against data, and there has been extensive work on the determinants of consumption. Philip Davis and I, for instance, suggest that the marginal propensity to consume out of current income in 1981 was around 0.18, which means that a £1 increase in personal income in Britain would raise spending by 18 pence.[29] If, however, the rise in income were permanent then consumers would increase their spending in line with income, and if the £1 increase were sustained for eight years then consumption spending would rise by 84 pence. This evidence on small responses to current changes in income building up potentially into large changes was commonly available in 1981, and is consistent with the consensus view that the majority of consumers made a

[26] There was much debate around the estimates of the multiplier produced by Christina Romer in 2008 as a partial support for the Obama fiscal package she, as potential chief of the Council of Economic Advisors, was advocating. It has never been clear what model of the US economy she used, or how she used it, but I knew most of them, and did not see how the numbers could be produced. See C. D. Romer and J. Bernstein, 'The job impact of the American recovery and reinvestment plan' (Washington, DC, 2009).

[27] Let consumption be C, G is government spending, a and b are parameters, with b known as the marginal propensity to consume, while income is $Y = C + G$. If $C = a + bY$, then collecting terms equilibrium income is $Y = (1 / (1 - b)) * (a + G)$, with $1 / (1 - b)$ the first-year textbook multiplier. If consumers spent two-thirds of an increase in income, the multiplier would be three (if the world was like this, anyway).

[28] The country exports (X) and imports (M), and these depend on income, $M = cY$. As income is $Y = C + G + X - M$, we can write the multiplier relation as $Y = (1 / (1 - b + c)) * (a + G + X)$.

[29] R. Barrell and E. P. Davis, 'Financial liberalisation, consumption and wealth effects in seven OECD countries', *Scottish Journal of Political Economy*, 54, 2 (May 2007), 254–67.

distinction between transitory and permanent changes in income.[30] The United Kingdom went through a period of financial liberalisation in the 1980s, enabling consumers to align their spending more readily with their perception of their permanent income, unconstrained by the availability of current personal income. Davis and I suggest that, as a result, the short-term marginal propensity to consume had fallen to around 0.09 by 2001, meaning that a £1 increase in personal incomes would lead in the short run to a 9 pence increase in spending, with the rest being saved.[31] As a result, one would expect the multiplier to be noticeably larger in 1981 than in 2000. Over the same period the economy became more open, and the import propensity rose from 0.14 (14 per cent of GDP was imported) to 0.26 in 2001. This rise in leakages also reduced the multiplier, but, together, these effects probably mean that multipliers were only 25 per cent higher in 1981 than they were in 2001 or 2007.

If we look at Table 10.3, we can see estimates of multipliers for the decade up until 2007, and we can see that they vary between countries and between instruments.[32] The thought experiment involves a permanent reduction in the budget deficit, much as the radicals in 1981 proposed. They show, in general, that more open countries have smaller multipliers, that larger levels of wealth as a proportion of income reduce the multiplier and that the estimated short-run propensity to consume affects the multiplier, with an increase in that propensity raising the multiplier. Government spending multipliers are by far the largest, as they impact directly on income, while tax increases have much more limited effects on output, as they are largely absorbed by people changing their consumption.[33] These multipliers apply to the decade to 2008, and I have already discussed why they might have been 25 per cent higher in the United Kingdom in the early 1980s, as the economy was less open, and more consumers were influenced by changes in their current income. Given the package discussed elsewhere in this volume, it would be wise to estimate that the fiscal tightening in 1981 would have reduced output growth in the first year by around three-quarters of a percentage point – slightly lower

[30] This view was consistent with Milton Friedman's permanent income hypothesis and Franco Modigliani's life cycle hypothesis, but not necessarily with the views of more extreme rational-expectations-influenced real business cycle theorists.

[31] Calculations from coefficients in the model and ratios of consumption to income.

[32] These estimates for our small group of countries are abstracted from a more extensive study by Dawn Holland, Ian Hurst and me for the OECD: R. Barrell, D. Holland and A. I. Hurst, 'Fiscal consolidation, part 2: fiscal multipliers and fiscal consolidations', OECD Economics Department Working Paper no. 933 (2012).

[33] In this experiment, I assumed that financial markets were fully forward-looking and that labour market bargains were influenced by expectations. Consumers are not assumed to be forward-looking, however. If they were, multipliers would be less.

Table 10.3 *First-year multipliers from a 1 per cent of GDP permanent consolidation*

	Government spending		Taxes	
	Consumption	Benefits	Indirect	Direct
Belgium	−0.16	−0.04	−0.02	−0.03
Denmark	−0.54	−0.10	−0.02	−0.05
Finland	−0.67	−0.16	−0.05	−0.10
France	−0.65	−0.33	−0.11	−0.26
Germany	−0.46	−0.29	−0.12	−0.25
Netherlands	−0.51	−0.19	−0.05	−0.15
Sweden	−0.40	−0.17	−0.05	−0.13
United Kingdom	−0.55	−0.14	−0.14	−0.08
United States	−0.90	−0.25	−0.27	−0.16

Notes: Budget target shifted by 1 per cent of GDP. Simulations conducted in one country at a time.

than is implied in the Britton analysis.[34] Of course, there is a wide range around either of these estimates, but it is best to base this discussion on the most likely outcome. In neither case does a 1 per cent of GDP change in the budget deficit reduce output by as much as one percentage point, and hence the analyses from 2012 and from 1991 both suggest that the multipliers were, in 1981, less than one.

In this analysis, the longer-run impacts of a change in the level of borrowing are largely absent. The United Kingdom is a small open economy with perfect capital mobility, and has been over the whole period considered here. The impact of a change in government debt in the long term affects the risk premium paid by borrowers, and not the underlying rate of interest, which is much the same as in the rest of the high-grade borrowers in the world. Hence, little crowding out (or in) of private investment, resulting from interest rate changes, is likely to have happened. Economies take time to recover from an unexpected fiscal contraction, but work on labour markets across a range of countries,[35] or including expectations,[36] suggests that a contraction, which would

[34] Britton's counterfactual involves a larger fiscal contraction than was introduced in the Budget, which involved a fiscal contraction of only around 1 per cent, or a little more, of GDP. His counterfactual involves continued spending growth, which was not planned in 1981.

[35] R. Barrell, 'Has the EMS changed wage and price behaviour in Europe?', *National Institute Economic Review*, no. 134 (November 1990), 64–72.

[36] R. Anderton and R. Barrell, 'The ERM and structural change in European labour markets: a study of 10 countries', *Weltwirtschaftliches Archiv*, 131, 1 (March 1995), 47–66.

raise unemployment, would reduce wages compared to where they would otherwise have been, and hence output will slowly recover to around the equilibrium we would have seen without the contraction. Policy makers should have concentrated (and should concentrate) as much on increasing the speed of return to equilibrium as on dealing with the size of any output gap they might think that they see.

Conclusions

The debate around the 1981 Budget was, and remains, a perfect example of the mode of discourse in economics. Strong positions are taken on both sides, and on neither side is evidence used in a dispassionate way. The Conservative radicals claimed that the reduction in the size of the state was central to the transformation of productivity, and they did not concern themselves too much with understanding the limits to the transformation or the role of the state in producing it. Many things affect productivity, and these may be grouped into the efficiency with which factors are used, the level of scientific knowledge available to complement capital and labour, and the skills and training of the workforce. General-purpose technical progress may be a common-pool resource driven by public-good scientific research and general innovation, and it is likely to be similar across countries. Institutions may speed up, or even prevent, the absorption of new ideas, however. The ability to trade enables a country to specialise in more efficient production processes, raising the aggregate growth rate temporarily. There is evidence that increases in competition brought about by the removal of trade barriers raise output, and Barrell, Holland and Liadze draw attention to the European single market programme as a factor affecting EU productivity growth.[37] Some may have been pleased to learn that integration with the European Union, and EU-style legislation, was more important than any part of the Thatcher revolution, but most of the radicals would deny it, whatever the evidence.

The radicals' unwarranted optimism about the world was mirrored by the unjustified pessimism felt by many academic economists about the self-stabilising properties of the economies they inhabited, but did not often observe. A fiscal contraction equivalent to 1 or 2 per cent of GDP (depending upon the baseline adopted) was unlikely to have had much impact on growth, and was unlikely to have had any sustained impact on output. The best estimates suggest that growth would have been between three-quarters and one percentage point higher in 1981/82 without the

---

[37] Barrell, Holland and Liadze, 'Accounting for UK economic performance'.

fiscal package, and equilibrium output would have been attained earlier, albeit with potentially higher inflation expectations. As these ideas were common in macroeconomics textbooks at the time, it is perhaps surprising that so many economists signed the letter objecting to the policy. The 1981 Budget might not have been a good idea, but it was hardly worth the fuss of objecting, and might have done some good – unlike its comparators, the Darling and Osborne Budgets in 2010.

Perhaps we should remind politicians always to be sceptical about their own rhetoric, and academics to be careful with evidence. But the 'scholastic tradition' remains strong in British universities, and evidence-based analysis is not considered a good thing.[38]

---

[38] As Sir Humphrey said to his minister in the mid-1980s, 'We must support the universities. Both of them.'

11 The Keynesian twin deficits in an inflationary context

Robert Z. Aliber

One of my favourite books is John Maynard Keynes' *A tract on monetary reform*.[1] Keynes was a 'monetarist' in the 1920s because he was concerned about the implications of the significant differential increases in national price levels on British competiveness. The book is a marvellously lucid exposition of the relationships between changes in the differential in national inflation rates, interest rates on similar securities denominated in various currencies, forward exchange rates, and changes in the prices of these currencies. Donald Moggridge writes:

> [Keynes] made a strong case for a policy that would aim at stabilising the domestic price level, largely on the ground that the contractual and social arrangements of contemporary capitalism worked best with stable prices. He believed that the Bank of England through its Bank rate policy and its ability to control the reserves of the banking system had the policy instruments available to ensure a modicum of price stability. If the Bank took domestic price stability as its goal, exchange rate policy needed rethinking, for if Britain returned to the gold standard international gold flows would lead her to inflate and deflate at the same rate as the rest of the world.[2]

Keynes thus believed that domestic price stability entailed flexibility in the exchange rate. His model and his policy stance in this book are similar to those of Milton Friedman in 'The case for floating exchange rates'.[3]

In the mid-1930s Keynes presented a new model in *The general theory*, to explain the levels of interest rates in a 'priceless world' – one in which inflation rates were not significantly different from zero, and/or might be declining.[4] He introduced the idea of a 'liquidity trap'. The cliché was that 'you can't push on a string'. The implication was that fiscal policy was the only effective macro-policy instrument if monetary policy was impotent. The irony is that *The general theory* is just a special case of the relation

---

[1] J. M. Keynes, *A tract on monetary reform* (London, 1923).
[2] D. E. Moggridge, *Maynard Keynes: an economist's biography* (London, 1992), 415.
[3] M. Friedman, 'The case for floating exchange rates', in M. Friedman (ed.), *Essays in positive economics* (Chicago, 1953), 157–203.
[4] Keynes, *The general theory of employment, interest and money.*

between the money supply and the price level in a world characterised by excess supply.

In the early 1980s some American economists advocated a 'Keynesian' policy of tax reductions to stimulate economic growth.[5] At about the same time 364 British economists relied on the same Keynesian model as the basis for their criticism that a modest increase in tax rates designed to reduce the British fiscal deficit would lead to a slowdown in the economy.

Both the Americans who wanted a more expansive fiscal policy and the British economists who rallied against the increase in tax rates relied on the same Keynesian model that is at the heart of *The general theory*. But the likelihood that Keynes would have signed the letter to *The Times* in 1981 is less than one in a million. Instead, he would have brought out an updated version of his *A tract on monetary reform*, because of concerns about the implications of the sharp differences in national inflation rates, and the impact of the change in British production of fossil fuels, for the competitiveness of its manufacturing sector.

In 1981 the incoming administration of Ronald Reagan proposed, and then initiated, a reduction in tax rates. US economic growth spurted, and the country's trade deficit soared. The association between the increase in the US fiscal deficit and the increase in the US trade deficit led to the 'twin deficits' hypothesis: that the former was the cause of the latter. The behavioural story was that the reduction in tax rates would lead to a larger fiscal deficit. That in turn would lead to higher interest rates on US dollar securities. Investor demand for these securities would increase, and these purchases would lead to an increase in the price of the dollar. US imports would then increase relative to US exports.

The incontestable facts are that tax rates were reduced, and that interest rates on US dollar securities, the US growth rate and both the US fiscal deficit and the US trade deficit increased. But it is not obvious that the reduction in US tax rates explains the dramatic increase in the US trade deficit. One question is whether the timing is correct. Is the increase in interest rates on US dollar securities better explained by the reduction in tax rates and the change in the fiscal stance of the US government than by the changes in monetary policy? The second question is whether the increase in interest rates on US dollar securities is better explained by the increase in the US fiscal deficit than by some other factors. US Treasury securities then accounted for 20 per cent of total securities in

---

[5] Several Washington types believed that larger fiscal deficits would lead to reductions in government expenditures or the growth of expenditures; they thought that larger fiscal deficits would 'starve the beast' and put downward pressure on the inexorable growth of expenditures.

the hands of the public, and the increase in the US fiscal deficit was only one source of the increase in the supply of securities. The demand for securities was also changing. One aspect of this question is whether the changes in interest rates are better explained by a flow argument (changes in the US fiscal deficit) than by an argument that involves the pricing of a stock.

The next section of this chapter summarises some of the data around 1980. These questions are then answered in the subsequent section.

The US economy around the cusp between the 1970s and the 1980s

The dominant feature of the US economy in the 1970s was accelerating inflation. The inflation rate increased in 1974 and 1975 after the abandonment of the price and wage controls that had been adopted in 1971. The inflation rate declined in 1976 and then accelerated, reaching double digits in 1979. Nominal interest rates were increasing, but less rapidly than the price level, so that real interest rates were declining and becoming negative. The price of the US dollar was declining in both nominal and real terms. The dollar price of gold was soaring; there was a shift into 'hard assets' from financial securities because of the anticipation of accelerating inflation. Economic activity was expanding.

The seminal event in US monetary policy in the late 1970s was the change in the operating procedures of the Federal Reserve in late October 1979 – the 'Volcker shock'. The Fed reversed the independent and the dependent monetary policy variables. Previously the Fed had supplied reserves to limit the upward pressure on US dollar interest rates. Under the new policy, the Fed would manage the growth of the reserves of the banking system, and market forces would determine the level of interest rates. The Volcker shock was reminiscent of the 'Poincaré shock' in France towards the end of 1926: a change in interest rates to position them above the increase in the price level, so as to break the inflationary spiral.

Both nominal and real interest rates on US dollar securities soared for two years. The US dollar price of gold peaked in the third week of January 1980, thirteen weeks after the adoption of the more contractionary policy – a signal that the cycle of accelerating inflation had been busted. The inflation rate peaked in March 1980 and then began to decline. Investors began to move from hard assets into securities. The US economy moved into a severe recession. Most other countries also experienced slowdowns. The sharp increase in interest rates on US dollar securities led to a massive flow of investment funds to the United States. The price of the US dollar surged, and continued to increase until the middle of 1985.

The increase in the price of US bonds and stocks led to a surge in US household wealth. The increase in the US capital account surplus meant that there had to be a correspondingly massive increase in the US current account deficit. The supply of goods available to Americans was increasing, and the 'invisible hands' went to work to ensure that these goods would be absorbed. The increase in the price of the US dollar (the relative price argument) and the increase in US household wealth (the relative income argument) ensured that these resources were absorbed.

Although the reduction in tax rates contributed to the increase in US GDP, its effect was modest compared with the contribution from the increased consumption spending that followed the increase in household wealth.

The US trade deficit continued to increase for two years after the decline in the price of the US dollar, and the interpretation is that household wealth continued to increase.

Why did the US trade deficit increase?

The thrust of the twin deficits story is that the increase in the US trade deficit resulted from the reduction in tax rates, the increase in the US fiscal deficit and the increase in the price of the US dollar. The intermediate argument is that the larger fiscal deficit led to higher interest rates on dollar securities. One shortcoming of the twin deficits story is that the timing of the relationship between the changes in interest rates on US dollar securities and the price of the US dollar is not consistent. Interest rates on dollar securities began to increase sharply after the adoption of the more contractionary US monetary policy in October 1979, and these rates began to trend down about the same time as the reduction in tax rates led to an increase in the US fiscal deficit. The number of months when interest rates increased because of the increase in the US fiscal deficit, and the price of the US dollar increased, is limited to a few months in the latter part of 1981. In the prior months interest rates on US dollar securities were increasing, first because of the increase in the inflation rate, and then because of the more contractive monetary policy. And the price of the US dollar continued to increase from 1982 through the first half of 1985, even though interest rates on dollar securities were decreasing.

The inference from the increase in the price of the US dollar, despite the decline in interest rates on US dollar securities, confirms that changes in interest rates involve the repricing of a stock of securities. In contrast, the twin deficits story is that interest rates are determined by flows. Interest rates are the prices of stocks of debt – government debt, corporate debt, mortgage debt and instalment credit debt. Changes in the fiscal balance have modest impacts on the size of the stock of debt. Instead, interest rates are determined by the demand for these types of debt, and one of the important arguments in household demand is the change in the anticipated inflation rate.

The competing proposition to the twin deficits story is that the increase in the US trade deficit contributed significantly to the increase in the US fiscal deficit. The story is that expenditure switching to less expensive foreign goods led to a decrease in domestic production, employment, profits and the tax base. Expenditure switching from domestic to foreign goods has a multiplier effect. Thus, an increase in demand for foreign goods relative to domestic goods equivalent to 2 per cent of GDP may lead to a decline in GDP of 4 or 5 per cent after recognition of the multiplier effects. The contribution of expenditure switching to the increase in the US trade deficit and the US fiscal deficit almost certainly was larger than the reduction in tax rates.

Keynes and changes in inflation rates and interest rates

The Keynes of the 1920s was a 'monetarist' who analysed the relationships between changes in inflation rates, changes in the prices of currencies and changes in interest rates on similar securities denominated in different currencies. The Keynes of the 1930s focused on the determinants of interest rates in a world of stable or slightly declining price levels. The 1930s might be considered a special case or a limiting case. The likelihood that Keynes would have signed the 1981 letter to *The Times* is trivially small.

1980 was a pivotal year in financial markets. Inflation rates in the United States, Britain and numerous other countries had increased throughout the 1970s. The pattern in the data is that changes in interest rates lag changes in inflation rates, and hence real interest rates decline as the inflation rate accelerates. Interest rates decline as the inflation rate slows, but with a lag, so real interest rates lag and hence increase sharply. The adoption of the more contractive US monetary policy in October 1979 was a seminal event, and explains many of the monetary events of the 1980s. The US dollar price of gold peaked in January 1980, and trended down for the next several decades. Investors sold hard assets to buy securities. The price of the US dollar surged in response to investors' desires to increase the share of securities denominated in the US dollar.

The twin deficits story that the increase in the US fiscal deficit would lead to higher interest rates on US dollar securities is incontestable as a classroom model but, in the context of significant changes in national inflation rates, of limited explanatory power. Changes in the prices of currencies are driven by changes in the anticipated prices of currencies that, in turn, are driven by anticipated changes in the differences in national inflation rates.

12   The long road to 1981: British money supply targets from DCE to the MTFS

Michael J. Oliver

Until the publication of Forrest Capie's monograph on the Bank of England, the history of monetary policy since 1960 was largely told through a number of secondary sources.[1] Capie's account has been written from the perspective of the Bank, and it is expected that in due course a wider account of monetary policy will be written. There is no shortage of archival material on monetary policy for the period, and this should provide the genesis for a stimulating clutch of future PhD theses. In this chapter, I examine one area that will doubtless prove to be of great interest for those seeking to investigate British monetary policy: the evolution of money supply targets between 1968 and 1981.

As the chapter shows, the monetary authorities were very reluctant to take monetary targets seriously in the decade after 1968. The election of a Conservative government in 1979 ushered in a period of economic policy making that has been described as 'monetarist', although the extent and significance of this nomenclature has yet to be fully debated by economic historians. Using official papers from the 1970s and early 1980s, the chapter emphasises three periods in the move to money supply targets. First I examine the late 1960s to 1974, when the authorities seemed to care little about any form of monetary control. The second period can be traced from 1975 to 1979, when the core executive began to take monetary targets seriously to placate financial markets. Finally, I turn to examine 1979 to 1981. Even as the Chancellor was trying to restore fiscal credibility in his 1981 Budget, the adoption of multi-year money supply targets through the Medium-Term Financial Strategy was already in serious trouble, and had little credibility or support from senior Treasury and Bank officials.

---

[1] Capie, *The Bank of England*. The standard accounts for the 1960–74 period are: Tew, 'Monetary policy: part 1'; M. J. Artis, 'Monetary policy: part 2', in Blackaby, *British economic policy*, 258–303; Cobham, *The making of monetary policy in the UK*; and Dimsdale, 'British monetary policy since 1945'. Cobham provides a more technical discussion for the post-1975 period while Dimsdale provides the best overall synthesis of post-war monetary policy to the late 1980s.

1968–74: the struggle to understand

The change in emphasis towards the money supply began shortly after the devaluation of sterling in 1967, when the International Monetary Fund arranged a seminar with the Bank and the Treasury. The seminar was arranged 'to examine the theory of the relationship of financial factors to the national income and balance of payments, and the implications of these relationships for the techniques of economic forecasting', but went beyond these terms of reference.[2] The IMF had been unimpressed with the ability of the UK authorities to control monetary growth prior to the devaluation, and a lot of discussion centred around the amount of importance that should be attached to the money supply. The seminar was uncomfortable for the majority of the officials in the Bank and the Treasury, not least because they were uneasy about accepting sharper and higher movements in interest rates as a trade-off for greater control of the money supply.[3] Although the authorities initially prevaricated on a number of issues, chiefly whether the IMF's preferred definition of the money stock in an open economy – domestic credit expansion – could be applied to Britain, they did acknowledge that they had paid too little attention to monetary policy after 1945 and needed to adopt a clearer position on the money supply.[4]

This manifested itself in two key ways by the turn of the 1970s. First, there was a change in priorities in the gilt-edged market. In the 1960s the authorities had become more concerned with creating an orderly market for gilts, as they wished to prevent higher levels of interest rates. As the authorities came to realise that higher *nominal* interest rates in a period of inflation did not signify higher *real* interest rates, they became more prepared to move interest rates more rapidly. Greater interest rate flexibility was meant to be one of the features of the new method of monetary control, Competition and Credit Control, introduced in 1971, but upward movements became politically unacceptable.[5] Second, in 1969 the then Chancellor, Roy Jenkins, published a Letter of Intent to the IMF stating that he intended to keep DCE within a figure of £400 million in

---

[2] A. H. Lovell, 'Draft report of the UK/IMF monetary seminar October 1968', 2 January 1969, TNA, T326/875.

[3] A paper written by Andrew Britton in the Treasury summarises the position well: A. J. C. Britton, 'Monetary policy and the supply of money', 5 February 1970, TNA, T326/1063. For perhaps the strongest resistance in the Treasury to the IMF's approach, see A. Graham, 'Monetary policy and the IMF', 30 April 1969, TNA, PREM 13/3151.

[4] DCE adjusts the broad money supply (£M3) for the financing of the balance of payments from official reserves.

[5] Capie, *Bank of England*, 508–14.

1969/70. In his April 1970 Budget, Jenkins set a £900 million limit on DCE for 1970/71. It is important to stress that this was not a target for the money supply, although some commentators took this to mean that the Bank of England was assuming a specific money supply target.[6] At this early stage there was no formal commitment by either political party to a target, and when the Conservatives took office in June 1970, led by Ted Heath, they were urged to take a more 'resolute and scientific grip' on the movement of the money supply.[7]

As the briefing paper on monetary policy for the incoming government in 1970 made clear, the new emphasis on money after 1967 'did not represent conversion to Friedmanism, or indeed any greater degree of certainty as to the nature of the relationships between monetary changes and changes in the main components of national income and expenditure'.[8] What it did signify was a gradual realisation by the authorities (via the influence of the IMF) that, if the growth of the money supply was restricted, the domestic economy and the external position could be improved. Thus, while there was no groundswell of officials converted to Friedman, there was a pragmatic acceptance that there should be a more important role for monetary policy.[9] In turn, the work of successive Bank/Treasury Monetary Policy Groups during the 1970s was testament to this, even though the work was steeped in Keynesian demand management, and far too often reverted to tortuous first principles just as it appeared that progress was being made.

From the outset of the 1970s there were misgivings expressed about money supply targets, even down to semantics. As one Treasury official noted, 'Something may depend on the interpretation put upon the word "target". Certainly if it is meant to be something aimed at and hit (and by extension something which would cause concern if missed), then we cannot have "money supply targets".'[10] In October 1970 Treasury officials were asked to supply their Minister of State, Terence Higgins, with a list of objections to having money supply targets for internal use. Noting that they did not want to preclude the discussions of the Treasury/ Bank Group on Monetary Policy (which spent some time discussing this

[6] Batini and Nelson, 'The UK's rocky road to stability', 18–20; 'The empty Budget', *Economist*, 18 April 1970, 13; Tew, *British economic policy*, 247–8.

[7] 'Policy starts at Croydon?', *Economist*, 31 January 1970, 14.

[8] Home Finance Division (HMT), 'General briefing: domestic monetary policy', 17 June 1970, TNA, T326/1062.

[9] B. M. Clift and J. D. Tomlinson, 'When rules started to rule: the IMF, neo-liberal economic ideas and economic policy change in Britain', *Review of International Political Economy*, 19, 3 (August 2012), 495.

[10] R. J. Painter, 'Monetary policy', 28 October 1970, TNA, T326/1255.

in 1971), officials felt that there were a number of theoretical and practical objections.

First, they didn't know enough about the causal relationships between the real economy and the monetary system to know whether it was 'sensible' to have a money supply target. Second, there was 'ignorance' about knowing what the optimum growth of the money supply should be and where the target should be set. Third, the monthly and quarterly figures for the money supply were prone to distortion, and ascertaining any under-lying relationship between money supply growth and a target would be difficult. Fourth, even if sufficient relationships could be established, there would be considerable difficulties in knowing when to tighten mon-etary policy to achieve the money supply target. It was also impractical to 'fine-tune' the money supply.[11]

To this might be added another objection that found its way into policy papers, namely that high interest rates might be required to hit a money supply target. As this is a 'politically and socially sensitive subject...it is unlikely that any government would pursue a true money supply target if there was a chance that nominal interest rates might rise to such levels that institutions normally immune from small changes in rates...may sud-denly be affected'.[12] The paper went on to argue that the Bank of England was concerned that 'violently fluctuating rates would damage the gilt-edged market' – objections that were raised later when it came to the discussions surrounding monetary base control in the early 1980s.

The Treasury knew it had to engage with the wider debate about monetary policy and the interest that this was beginning to have for economists outside government.[13] There was a movement towards accepting that money could play a valuable role in controlling demand and bolstering the reserves, but with the caveats that 'it cannot work miracles' and 'a lax monetary policy creates the sort of flabby environment that frustrates other policies'.[14] This non-technical language was gradu-ally replaced as a younger cohort of more technical economists inside the

---

[11] A. J. C. Edwards, 'Money supply target for internal use', 22 October 1970, TNA, T326/1062.

[12] D. A. Harding, 'Money supply versus interest rates', 3 July 1970, TNA, T338/6.

[13] For example, D. E. W. Laidler, 'The definition of money: theoretical and empirical problems', *Journal of Money, Credit and Banking*, 1, 3 (August 1969), 508–25; G. T. Pepper, 'The money supply, economic management and the gilt-edged market', *Journal of the Institute of Actuaries*, 96, 1 (January 1970), 1–46; D. R. Croome and H. G. Johnson (eds.), *Money in Britain, 1959–1969: the papers of the Radcliffe Report – ten years after* (Oxford, 1970). The work of the Money Study Group and the Manchester Inflation Workshop added to the debate, as did Peter Jay's work in *The Times*.

[14] F. Cassell, 'Monetary policy between now and the Budget', 9 October 1970, TNA, T326/1062.

Treasury and the Bank began to dissect the work of Friedman and others on the relationship of monetary variables to income, output and prices and the practical possibility of monetary control. Generally, the Treasury was slow to accept that there might be an argument for expressing a money supply target as a percentage of annual growth, and was even more reluctant to tie this to a specific time period.[15]

Outside the Treasury and the Bank, financial practitioners, most notably W. Greenwell & Co., were paying attention to the money supply. Greenwell had begun to focus attention on the money supply from the autumn of 1968, and over the next few years conducted a major research project into the use of financial statistics.[16] The significance of this research project was that one of their partners, Gordon Pepper, who had trained as a Keynesian at Cambridge, 'reluctantly' became a monetarist, abandoning Keynesianism after a monetarist forecast for the United Kingdom turned out to be more correct than the Keynesian one.[17] Greenwell was also consulting a network of financial economists in the City, which included John Atkins of CitiBank, Graeme Gilchrist of Union Discount, David Kearn of NatWest Bank, David Tapper of Hambros Bank, Brian Williams of Gerrard and National and Peter Wood of Barclays Bank. It was through Greenwell's *Monetary Bulletin*, however, one of the most widely read monetary publications produced in the United Kingdom, that monetary policy began to be taken seriously by the core executive.

In March 1971 the *Financial Times* proposed that there should be annual targets for the money supply. This attracted the interest of Heath's Chancellor, Anthony Barber, and Frank Cassell in the Treasury conceded that, 'if the target were expressed as an annual rate of increase, the growth of credit through the year would probably be smoother and the authorities might perhaps also have a little more flexibility in adjusting credit policy later in the year'.[18] A little later in the month, however, Cassell was quite happy to draft a speech on the Budget debate for the Minister of State in which he noted that 'by refraining from setting targets here and now for the full financial year we have given ourselves greater

---

[15] Michael Beenstock and Andrew Britton provided the firepower in the Treasury to discuss Friedman and monetarism. In the Bank, the work of Charles Goodhart should be singled out.

[16] G. T. Pepper and R. L. Thomas, 'Cyclical changes in the level of the UK equity and gilt-edged markets', *Journal of the Institute of Actuaries*, 99, 3 (March 1973), 195–247; G. T. Pepper and G. E. Wood, *Too much money? An analysis of the machinery of monetary expansion and its control* (London, 1975).

[17] Pepper, *Inside Thatcher's monetarist revolution*, 11, 139.

[18] F. Cassell, 'Control of bank lending', 5 March 1971, TNA, T326/1254.

flexibility for adjusting the course of the money supply and credit later in the year'.[19] This sort of confusion even led to criticism from government supporters: a leader in the *Yorkshire Post*, a newspaper described by Barber as 'almost a Conservative Central Office news-sheet', professed to being 'baffled' by the Chancellor's views on the money supply.[20] The fear in the Treasury was that announcing or publishing money supply targets would be seen as a 'hostage to fortune', or worse.[21] Things had not improved eighteen months later when, in November 1972, the Financial Secretary to the Treasury, Terence Higgins, cautioned the Chancellor against publishing targets that would be seen to have been missed and 'might be interpreted (quite wrongly) as conversion to the Powell heresy'.[22]

The Heath government never got to grips with the technicalities of monetary policy during its time in office. It was October 1970 before the Chancellor admitted that he needed to do some reading on monetary policy to prepare for a speech, and Treasury officials had to dust off the June 1970 briefing paper.[23] An initial muddle-through on monetary policy became more acute in the two years after October 1971, when the broad monetary aggregate (M3) grew by over 60 per cent. The increase during the first nine months was caused by the growth in bank lending; thereafter it was the rise in the public sector deficit that was the main cause, with only a third of the debt being sold to the non-bank private sector (in other words, the government was borrowing from the banking system). The consequences were asset price inflation (mainly in residential and commercial property), an enormous increase in real domestic demand in 1973 to 7.8 per cent and – as the monetarists had predicted – an increase in inflation after a long and variable time lag (to over 25 per cent in 1975).[24]

In January 1973 Barber told the Cabinet of the increasing disquiet in European circles that the British had not taken more stringent measures to check the growth in public expenditure and to control the growth of the money supply.[25] The view in the Treasury, however, was that European thinking on a money supply target was 'pretty primitive; it appears to take

[19] F. Cassell, 'Monetary policy: draft passage for Minister of State', 29 March 1971, TNA T326/1254.

[20] 'Jobs and wages', *Yorkshire Post*, 26 April 1971; W. S. Ryrie, 'Monetary policy', 27 April 1971, TNA, T326/1254.

[21] A. D. Neale, 'Monetary policy', 30 April 1971, TNA T326/1254.

[22] T. L. H. Higgins, 'Control of the money supply', 7 November 1972, TNA, T233/2513. Higgins was referring to Enoch Powell's enthusiasm for monetarism.

[23] W. S. Ryrie, 'Monetary policy', 5 October 1970, TNA, T326/1062.

[24] T. G. Congdon, *Money and asset prices in boom and bust* (London, 2005), 59–64; Pepper, *Inside Thatcher's monetarist revolution*, 135.

[25] 'Conclusions of a meeting of the Cabinet held at 10 Downing Street', 30 January 1973, CM (73) 4th meeting, TNA, CAB 128/51.

little account of the institutional difference between countries and of the complexities of the linkage between money and income'.[26] However primitive European thought was, the Treasury was completely unaware of the causes of growth in M3, and continued to express the view that money supply targets were difficult to implement and to publish, before conceding that 'the difficulty of formulating a target at the moment stems largely from the obscurity of why money supply has risen so rapidly in the past year'.[27] Admitting to being 'embarrassed' by the rises in M3, and the very big rise in bank lending to the private sector in January 1973, the Minister of State, John Nott, suggested to Treasury officials that 'the more we can play down the importance of M3 and emphasise its fickle nature, as the Bank of England have been doing, the better. I cannot really envisage the M3 figures being a help to us.'[28]

The explosion in monetary growth between 1971 and 1973 was important for the rest of the 1970s for several reasons, not least because several Conservative politicians were determined that an asset price bubble should never be allowed to happened again. When Pepper gave a paper to the Bow Group at the end of March 1974 entitled 'The economic threat to democracy', Geoffrey Howe was sitting in the audience. Pepper's attack on the monetary irresponsibility of the previous Heath government, the Treasury and the Bank of England resonated with Howe, and Pepper was introduced to Sir Keith Joseph and Robert Carr (the Shadow Chancellor).[29] Shortly afterwards Margaret Thatcher became Carr's assistant spokesman on Treasury matters, and Pepper met her. His influence on Thatcher's views on monetary policy, particularly in relation to MBC, was important.[30]

1975–79: playing the game

After 1974 the relationship between the public sector borrowing requirement, the money supply and inflation began to be taken more seriously in

---

[26] F. Cassell, 'Monetary policy', 18 January 1973, TNA, T233/2505.   [27] Ibid.

[28] M. A. Hawtin, 'Press release for January money and banking figures', 14 February 1973, TNA, T233/2513; G. S. Downey, 'Press release for February money and banking figures', 21 March 1973, TNA T233/2513. Capie has shown how the Bank was also struggling to understand monetary policy during this period, and in particular how the newly recruited Executive Director for economics, Christopher Dow, was unsure whether monetary policy was expansionary or not when M3 was growing at an annual rate of over 20 per cent: Capie, *The Bank of England*, 645–8.

[29] See Sir Keith Joseph's speech at Preston in September 1974 entitled 'Inflation is caused by governments', reproduced in K. S. Joseph, *Reversing the trend: a critical re-appraisal of Conservative economic and social policies* (Chichester, 1975), 19–33.

[30] Moore, *Margaret Thatcher*, 344, 524.

some quarters. The Bank was clearly anxious to use money supply targets to control public expenditure. In July 1975 the Permanent Secretary, Sir Douglas Wass, had been informed that the Governor saw 'a need for the enactment in public, and with an element of public drama, of a struggle to keep the [PSBR] figures down'.[31] A few months later Bank Director Kit McMahon suggested that money supply targets would place 'a tighter rope round the Chancellor's neck' to restrain public expenditure'.[32] Although the Home Finance team in the Treasury were critical of the 'accommodating policy' towards the money supply and suggested that the PSBR needed to be cut if the intention was to reduce the growth of the money supply below money GDP, and thus reduce inflation, not everyone in the Treasury supported this line of argument.[33] Gordon Downey urged the Chancellor to recognise explicitly the connection between public expenditure and the control of the money supply in a forthcoming debate on the White Paper *The attack on inflation*, adding: 'I do not possibly see how we can maintain credibility for our monetary objectives by referring to monetary instruments alone.'[34]

By October 1975 Bank officials were noting that they had become 'increasingly anxious about prospective monetary developments... [W]e feel that there is now an urgent need for a review of monetary policy.'[35] Although they did not concede to the monetarist arguments, noting that it was a 'truism' to say that inflation had to be a monetary phenomenon and that 'the short-run relationship between monetary growth and inflation is tenuous at most', they did acknowledge that 'a commitment to restrain the rate of monetary expansion does give confidence over the medium term that inflation *will* be conquered'.[36] The final report of a Treasury/Bank working party reviewing monetary policy went further and recommended that a monetary target should be set, to secure a 'reasonably stable path for growth of the monetary aggregates, particularly M3, in line with the secular growth of income and an "acceptable" rate of inflation'.[37]

---

[31] G. S. Downey, 'Monetary policy group meeting 28 July', 25 July 1975, TNA, T233/2839.

[32] C. W. McMahon, 'Monetary policy', 26 September 1975, BOE, EID 4/200.

[33] J. M. Bridgeman, 'Counter inflationary policy: monetary policy', 25 June 1975, TNA T233/2841. Compare with L. Airey, 'Public expenditure cuts: monetary policy aspects', 27 June 1975, TNA T233/2841; and Wass, *Decline to fall*, 138.

[34] G. S. Downey, 'Chancellor's statement', 10 July 1975, TNA, T233/2841.

[35] Bank of England, 'Monetary policy', October 1975, TNA, T386/274.

[36] Ibid. [emphasis in original]. The paper noted that the views of the advisers in the Bank covered all schools of thought 'with the exception of strong monetarist'. The material in the paper suggests that there was nothing monetarist in the slightest about any of the Bank's views.

[37] 'Review of monetary policy: report of the Treasury/Bank working party', 23 December 1975, TNA, T277/3035.

There was little genuine enthusiasm from either the Bank or the Treasury for any of this, however, and, in some cases, outright hostility to anything that smacked of monetarism. By the beginning of 1976 there was still no consensus on whether a money supply target should be publicly announced. Peter Middleton, a senior Treasury official, felt that this would be a 'dangerous' step, probably for the reasons that had been outlined in the Treasury since the early 1970s.[38] What finally convinced the authorities that they had to take the money supply seriously was the realisation that financial markets were placing importance on the growth of the money supply, and that controlling the monetary aggregates was needed primarily because of the effects 'on the climate of opinion, expectations and attitudes'.[39]

The Chancellor, Denis Healey, also shared this antipathy towards monetary targets.[40] During the sterling crisis of 1976 he announced in July that monetary growth should be around 12 per cent in 1976/77, but this was more a monetary forecast or guideline than a target.[41] Despite the promise to tighten fiscal policy in 1977/78, the Treasury soon learnt that the United Kingdom's attitude towards monetary targets was viewed by a significant part of the financial press, the foreign exchange market, numerous financial institutions, and economists 'as lukewarm, our willingness to stick with them as slight, and the targets themselves as too high'.[42] Ironically, in the months that followed Healey's July announcement the financial markets began to view the 12 per cent figure as a target. By the autumn of 1976 some in the Treasury realised that only a tighter fiscal policy and a lower figure for the growth of the money supply target would placate the financial markets going forward.[43] As the discussions with the IMF for a loan concluded in December 1976 the Chancellor announced DCE targets for the year to 20 April 1977 and the year to 19 April 1978: £M3 was forecast to grow on a banking month basis by between 9 and 13 per cent in 1976/77. In little over a year, through a combination of market pressure, IMF insistence and political pragmatism, the monetary authorities had been forced to make the move and

[38] P. E. Middleton, 'Review of monetary policy' (draft notes), 8 January 1976, TNA, T386/122.

[39] Bank of England, 'Monetary policy', October 1975, TNA, T386/274; Pepper and Oliver, *Monetarism under Thatcher*, 12–15.

[40] Healey, *The time of my life*, 434. There was at least one heated debate in Cabinet on the issue of monetarism: see 'Conclusions of a meeting of the Cabinet held at 10 Downing Street', 7 October 1976, CM (76) 25th meeting, TNA, CAB 128/60.

[41] 'D. W. Healey to G. W. H. Richardson', 22 July 1976, TNA, T386/116. See also Wass, *Decline to fall*, 213; and Capie, *The Bank of England*, 658–9.

[42] S. H. Broadbent, 'Monetary targets', 28 September 1976, TNA, T386/116.

[43] J. M. Bridgeman, 'Monetary target, 1977–78', 4 November 1976, TNA, T386/117.

publicly announce money supply targets. As Wass ruefully commented at the end of 1977, 'It was no longer practical politics to contemplate abandoning monetary targets.'[44]

1979–81: false start and policy confusion

The election of Thatcher's Conservative government in May 1979 ushered in an administration committed to reducing inflation through the control of the money supply. It was the intention of the authorities to select a broad money target (£M3) and to raise interest rates if the growth of the money supply appeared excessive. As part of this strategy, the authorities intended to use fiscal policy as a means of influencing interest rates for a given monetary target: by reducing the PSBR as a percentage of gross domestic product, the money supply would not grow so quickly, and interest rates could be kept low.[45]

During the first two years of this 'monetarist experiment' money supply targets were missed, public expenditure continued to rise and the economy entered a steep recession, accompanied by an overvalued exchange rate.[46] £M3 grew rapidly because of several distortions in the financial system, and the authorities responded to the upward growth by raising Minimum Lending Rate by two percentage points in June 1979, and a further three percentage points in November 1979, when it stood at a post-war high of 17 per cent. Consequently, the early optimism about the monetary strategy expressed by the Chancellor, Geoffrey Howe, to his colleagues soon evaporated, and the evidence from the official papers shows the extent of the frustration within government.[47] Not only did senior ministers have to convince their colleagues that the strategy was on the right path, they also had to demonstrate this publicly.[48]

---

[44] K. V. Watts, 'Note of a meeting held in Sir Douglas Wass' room at 3.15 pm on Wednesday 9 November', 10 November 1977, TNA, T386/269.

[45] *FSBR 1980–81*, 16.

[46] W. H. Buiter and M. H. Miller, 'The Thatcher experiment: the first two years', *Brookings Papers on Economic Activity*, 2 (Fall 1981), 315–79; W. H. Buiter and M. H. Miller, 'Changing the rules: economic consequences of the Thatcher regime', *Brookings Papers on Economic Activity*, 2 (Fall 1983), 305–79.

[47] Compare 'Conclusions of a meeting of the Cabinet held at 10 Downing Street', 30 August 1979, CC (79) 14th meeting, TNA, CAB 128/66, with 'Conclusions of a meeting of the Cabinet held at 10 Downing Street', 13 March 1980, CC (80) 10th meeting, TNA, CAB 128/67, and 'Conclusions of a meeting of the Cabinet held at 10 Downing Street', 3 July 1980, CC (80), 27th meeting, TNA, CAB 128/68. See also 'M. A. Pattison to A. J. Wiggins', 3 September 1980, BOE 7A133/2; and R. E. G. Howe, 'Rolling over the monetary target', 14 November 1980, TNA, PREM 19/180.

[48] At one point the Cabinet Secretary appeared to strengthen the resolve of the Prime Minister with the suggestion that she should impress upon her colleagues that there was

The launch of the Medium-Term Financial Strategy in March 1980 provided a framework for the government's economic strategy. The intention was to provide financial objectives for fiscal and monetary policy. Charles Moore has suggested that Margaret Thatcher was always 'nervous' about the MTFS, and she later admitted that she didn't believe the strategy was needed.[49] The move away from discretion to rules was an essential break from the policy making that had characterised the British economy since 1945, however.[50] Unfortunately, if the rules were broken then the MTFS had limited value, and, with the overshooting of the money supply targets, the government faced a very difficult task in maintaining its economic credibility.

The £M3 target for June 1979 to April 1980 was 7 to 11 per cent, and the outturn over the target period was 9.6 per cent; the outturn over the financial year was 12.5 per cent, however, largely as a result of increased money growth in April and May 1979. The target range for £M3 from February 1980 to April 1981 was the same as the previous year, but the outturn overshot considerably for both the target period and the financial year, at 19.1 per cent and 18.5 per cent, respectively. There is not the space here to conduct a full counterpart analysis, but David Cobham has suggested that the main reason for the overshoot in 1979/80 was above-target growth in the PSBR, and increased bank lending to the private sector, which was not totally compensated for by public sector debt sales to the private sector. In 1980/81 there was a very large overshoot of the PSBR (which the 1981 Budget intended to address), and a smaller overshoot on bank lending (owing to post-'corset' reintermediation and the squeeze on the corporate sector), which were only partly offset by higher than planned debt sales.[51]

The difficulties with achieving the monetary targets added urgency to an overall review of monetary policy.[52] Soon after taking office the Prime Minister expressed her dissatisfaction with the target range for the money supply and pressed hard for a system known as monetary base control, which she believed would lead to greater control of inflation and lower

---

'no acceptable alternative to the strategy which the Government has set its hand': R. T. Armstrong, 'Public expenditure and the economic outlook', 23 January 1980, TNA, PREM 19/164.

[49] Moore, *Margaret Thatcher*, 505; Michael Oliver and Gordon Pepper interview with Lady Thatcher, 21 May 1999.

[50] Lawson, *The view from No. 11*, 67.

[51] The supplementary special deposit scheme (the 'corset') was introduced in December 1973 to constrain the growth of the banks' interest-bearing liabilities: Cobham, *The making of monetary policy*, 44.

[52] See *Monetary control*, Cmnd 7858, and the third report from the Treasury and Civil Service Committee, *Monetary control*, HC 713, 1979–80 (London, 1980).

interest rates.[53] Pepper and other monetarists had influenced her thinking on this; she found limited support for this option in the Treasury, however, and hostility in the Bank.[54] She later complained that officials had 'thrown sand in her eyes' about MBC.[55] The Prime Minister's economic adviser, Alan Walters, was a strong supporter of MBC in principle, and he was actively sending material to the No. 10 Policy Unit to be passed on to Thatcher even before he took up his position.[56] Walters was instrumental in the decision to get Jürg Niehans, the distinguished Swiss monetary economist, to prepare a study on UK monetary policy.[57] Niehans' conclusion, that monetary policy had been too tight and should be loosened quickly, was also followed with a recommendation that the money supply target should be expressed in terms of the monetary base instead of £M3.[58]

The head of the No. 10 Policy Unit, John Hoskyns, claims that Niehans' conclusion surprised both the No. 10 Policy Unit and the Treasury.[59] It should not have come as a surprise to anyone. Although the Prime Minister was clearly irritated with an article by Pepper in *The Observer* in August 1980 in which he argued that monetary policy was too tight, W. Greenwell & Co. had been arguing on these lines since May 1980 in the *Monetary Bulletin*, copies of which went to the Chancellor and the Prime Minister.[60] Walters records that he had said at a seminar and briefing in the United States in October and November 1980 that he judged monetary policy to be too tight, as had Tim Congdon (Chief Economist at L. Messel & Co.), who was no supporter of narrow money.[61] The conclusions of monetary economists who monitored the situation closely were very different from the impression given by the behaviour of the published data for £M3 relative to its target.

---

[53] T. P. Lankester, 'Note for the record', 16 May 1979, TNA, PREM 19/29. On Thatcher's interest in MBC just for 1979, see, for example, T. P. Lankester, 'Note for the record', 18 May 1979, TNA, PREM 19/183; M. A. Hall, 'Monetary seminar', 3 July 1979, TNA, PREM 19/33; and T. P. Lankester, 'Note for the record', 25 July 1979, TNA, PREM 19/33.

[54] A more detailed discussion of MBC can be found from Pepper and Oliver, *Monetarism under Thatcher*, 63–86.

[55] Oliver and Pepper interview with Thatcher, 21 May 1999.

[56] See, for example, 'A. A. Walters to J. A. H. L. Hoskyns', 6 November 1980, Churchill, HOSK 2/205, and 'J. A. H. L. Hoskyns to M. H. Thatcher', 9 December 1980, Churchill, HOSK 2/221.

[57] 'A. Sherman to R. G. Puttick', 14 November 1980, Churchill, THCR 2/11/3/1.

[58] Niehans, 'The appreciation of sterling'.   [59] Hoskyns, *Just in time*, 256–7.

[60] G. T. Pepper, 'Barometric pressure', *Observer*, 12 August 1979; 'Gordon Pepper: M for money supply', 20 August 1979, Churchill, HOSK 2/23; *Greenwell Monetary Bulletin*, 105 (May 1980).

[61] Walters, *Britain's economic renaissance*, 145; T. G. Congdon, *Messel's Weekly Gilt Monitor*, 2 January 1981.

Taking stock at the end of 1980, the Chief Economic Adviser to the Treasury, Terry Burns, admitted that the reputation of £M3 had suffered during the last twelve months.[62] This was a huge understatement. The rapid growth of broad money, and the slow growth of narrow money (M1), coupled to the strong exchange rate, were not what the Thatcher government had foreseen at the start of the year. Moreover, monetarists had repeatedly argued that velocity was stable in the medium run and that any monetary expansion, after a lag, would be inflationary. The non-appearance of inflation following the rapid monetary growth in 1980 was therefore puzzling to policy makers. Burns suggested that there were two interpretations of events. There was the optimistic version, in which rapid growth of broad money affected inflation only when it led to a weak exchange rate and an increase in aggregate demand. In a recession, with a high exchange rate and low growth of M1, an acceleration of inflation in the future was unlikely to occur. The alternative, and more pessimistic, interpretation was that a rapid growth of broad money would lead to a weak exchange rate and a faster growth of narrower aggregates. Once interest rates fell and the economy began to recover, the exchange rate would fall sharply and the excess liquidity would cause inflation.

The problem facing the authorities was whether they should make allowance for the behaviour of M1 and the exchange rate when deciding the monetary target for 1981/82 and how much (if any) of the monetary overshoot it was possible to claw back. For Burns, it had reached the point at which a more flexible approach was needed for the short-run monetary targets while maintaining anti-inflationary financial discipline over the medium term. By the turn of the year Middleton, now Deputy Secretary in the Treasury, was prompted by Burns' note of 22 December to instigate a series of papers on the behaviour and significance of the narrow aggregates; to review the use of the wider aggregates as a guide to fiscal policy and interest rates; and to explore the significance of other indicators, particularly the exchange rate. He conceded that the danger with this work would be that 'everything provides some relevant information without providing a guide to policy'. The key for Middleton was to produce work that should 'revive the monetary strategy and express it in a way which increases its credibility rather than make it so diffuse that it becomes meaningless'.[63]

The Bank and the Treasury spent some time considering various monetary aggregates. Intellectually, many in the Bank were inclined towards M1 as a target, insofar as they even accepted the importance of the money

---

[62]   T. Burns, 'Monetary aggregates and all that', 22 December 1980, TNA, T388/186.

[63]   P. E. Middleton, 'Monetary aggregates and all that', 30 December 1980, TNA, T388/186.

supply.[64] The Bank's Chief Adviser, Charles Goodhart, recognised the enormous difficulties that financial innovation could have for the monetary aggregates; the Bank undertook a study of a new M2 monetary aggregate, both from the statistical aspect and from a conceptual economic viewpoint.[65] The Treasury became impatient with the length of time it was taking the Bank to define M2: Rachel Lomax, a senior economic adviser, told Nick Monck, who was liaising with the Bank, that 'what they need from us, now, is a shove. No more meetings until we see some action.'[66] What the Treasury wanted to see was the removal of wholesale deposits from £M3, as there were shifts in and out of £M3 in response to relative interest rates, which had little or no economic significance. The Treasury felt that M2 would be more stable in relation to expenditure, nominal income and prices than £M3, and might be used as a control variable in a mandatory MBC system.[67]

Although £M3 had been given pride of place at the launch of the MTFS, it began to have less importance in the monetary strategy over the next six months. Senior Treasury officials urged a reduction in MLR, but this could not be justified on the grounds of success in hitting the £M3 target, which was breached by a considerable amount.[68] Conscious of this, Howe was keen that the government should not appear to be abandoning its monetary strategy with this interest rate cut.[69] The damage was done, however: the two percentage point reduction in MLR in the 1980 Autumn Statement was a clear indication to markets that changes in £M3 did not appear to have much influence on interest rate decisions. Effectively, from this point the government gave priority to the presentation of policy, which led to considerable difficulties in trying to reconcile this with monetarist theory. There were three developments leading up to the 1981 Budget that demonstrate the significant relaxing of the 'monetarist experiment'.

First, despite the robust defence of the government's monetary strategy by the Financial Secretary, Nigel Lawson, in a speech to the Zurich Society of Economists in January 1981, Treasury officials had finally reached the point at which they did not see £M3 as an adequate measure of monetary conditions in the economy. Even Lawson had admitted in Zurich that

---

[64] C. W. McMahon, 'Towards a Bank view on monetary policy', 25 January 1980, BOE, 6A/221.

[65] C. A. E. Goodhart, 'An M2 series', 9 December 1980, TNA, T388/186.

[66] J. R. Lomax, 'M2', 16 December 1980, TNA, T388/186.

[67] J. R. Lomax, 'Draft letter to Charles Goodhart', 16 December 1980, TNA, T388/186.

[68] C. W. McMahon, 'Treasury thinking on economic policy', 25 September 1980, BOE, 7A134/16.

[69] 'T. P. Lankester to A. J. Wiggins', 13 November 1980, TNA, T388/199.

PSL1 was a better measure of broad money growth than £M3 (PSL1 captured the unwinding of the 'corset'), and, although Treasury officials favoured PSL2, Andrew Britton argued that £M3 should be abandoned when M2 was in place and running in tandem with a PSL number.[70] Now echoing Niehans, Middleton was more minded to focus on the narrow aggregates, which, he argued, displayed a better relationship to the final objective of reducing inflation; £M3 could have a role as a medium-term objective to be achieved over the whole MTFS period.[71]

Second, officials were doubtful whether the £M3 growth target for 1981/82 (6 to 10 per cent) could be achieved, how the missed targets might be explained and how the monetary strategy should be presented. Howe's Private Secretary, John Wiggins, asked Middleton: 'How good a story can we tell based on stock adjustment models?' He also asked: 'Can we argue that personal sector holdings of £M3 are below an "equilibrium" level?' In what was pure spin, Wiggins suggested:

If there is anything in this line of argument, we should in effect be saying that the MTFS looked mainly at prospective flows, on the assumption that the world remained much as it had been in the 1970s: now, having seen that we were in a rather different world, with a larger personal sector surplus and a larger company sector deficit, we were re-specifying the numbers which seemed likely to be consistent with given inflation objectives. If this sort of argument will run, can we use it to explain a reasonably high 'expected increase' (not a target) in M1 as well as, say, 10 per cent for £M3 in 1981–82?[72]

At a meeting with the Prime Minister and senior officials on 10 February, Howe acknowledged that, for the 'sake of credibility of the strategy', the £M3 target could not 'simply be abandoned' in the Budget speech, but said that he would indicate that the authorities 'would be moving as fast as they sensibly could in the direction of monetary base control' (Thatcher was clearly unhappy with this, and wanted Howe to announce a 'concrete plan' for moving to MBC).[73]

The setting of interest rates was the third area that vexed the authorities in the weeks leading up to the Budget. After initially ruling out a reduction in MLR in the Budget because of worries about a high figure for the PSBR, the Chancellor concluded that, while £M3 would retain 'primacy in the presentation of monetary policy' in setting interest rates, 'other

[70] A. J. C. Britton, 'Presentation of the monetary aggregates', 6 February 1981, TNA, T388/199; Lawson, 'Thatcherism in practice', MTFW 109506.

[71] P. E. Middleton, 'Interest rates', 16 February 1981, TNA, T386/551.

[72] A. J. Wiggins, 'Monetary targets and monetary control', 15 February 1981, TNA, T386/551.

[73] T. P. Lankester, 'Note for the record', 10 February 1981, Churchill, WTRS 1/4.

factors' needed to be taken into account.[74] At this stage the other factors were not defined, but Lawson argued that short-term interest rates should be determined by M0 and real interest rates and there should merely be a 'regard' to £M3.[75] The problem for policy makers was that, apart from the exchange rate, all the other monetary indicators suggested that interest rates needed to be increased. In a draft of a note to the Prime Minister, Middleton conceded that it was 'not easy' to construct a case for a sustained fall in interest rates based on the projected growth of the monetary aggregates; Thatcher was seeking a one percentage point reduction – 'no more than that' – on Budget day.[76]

Officials met with the Chancellor on 19 February to consider monetary targets and monetary control. Various opinions were given. Middleton argued that a PSBR of £11¼ billion with a reduction in MLR would put at risk the £M3 target of 8 to 10 per cent, and it was unlikely that growth would be within the 6 to 10 per cent range during the first few months of 1981/82.[77] He suggested that either the target should be qualified or the range extended. Howe wanted to reduce MLR because of the 'psychological and practical effectiveness', and to keep the PSBR as low as possible in pursuit of the monetary target in the MTFS. Lawson argued that the markets were already expecting the monetary target to be overshot in the early months of 1981/82 and wanted some reduction in interest rates as part of the Budget. In discussion, it was noted that the markets had to be given 'sufficient assurance' that the authorities were trying to control monetary growth and that the target range could be widened if monetary growth was at the top of the range and the exchange rate was rising. The meeting concluded that, in pursuit of the monetary target and in determining nominal interest rates, 'the authorities would also have regard to movements in the narrower monetary aggregates, in real interest rates and in the exchange rate'.[78]

The Governor admitted that he was 'relieved' when he was told by Wass on the same day as the Chancellor's meeting that the existing monetary target was going to be qualified with reference to other variables, as he had felt that the Treasury had locked itself 'in too unqualified a manner' to

---

[74] Ibid; A. J. Wiggins, 'Note of a meeting held in No. 11 Downing Street at 5.15 pm on Friday, 13 February 1981', 18 February 1981, TNA, T386/551.

[75] N. Lawson, 'Changes in the banks' money market operations and policy for short-term interest rates', 13 February 1981, TNA, T386/551.

[76] P. E. Middleton, 'Interest rates', 16 February 1981, TNA, T386/551; 'T. P. Lankester to A. J. Wiggins', 19 February 1981, TNA, T386/551.

[77] A. J. Wiggins, 'Note of a meeting held in the Chancellor of the Exchequer's room, House of Commons, at 4.45 pm on Thursday, 19 February 1981', 20 February 1981, TNA, T386/551.

[78] Ibid.

£M3.[79] On 23 February Gordon Richardson expressed anxiety about the quantification of the MTFS and the general thrust of the economic strategy. In particular, he felt that the growth prospect was 'wishful thinking' in relation to public expenditure and that there was incompatibility between the fiscal and monetary figures.[80] He argued that the MTFS was now seen as less attractive than in 1980, that credibility was much harder to sustain with the new numbers and that the original idea of the MTFS (a progressive strengthening of expectations of lower inflation) had not been met. Lawson retorted that there was 'no escape' from providing new figures for the MTFS.[81]

On 27 February Middleton suggested a two percentage point reduction in MLR on 10 March, but warned that £M3 would grow more rapidly and on the basis of present forecasts, and two percentage points was as much as could be managed in the entire year. The alternative was to cut by one percentage point, with the expectation of doing another percentage point cut later in the year. The advantage of this course of action was that the prospects of further interest rate falls might help to maintain favourable expectations in the gilts market. Middleton eventually came down on the side that a two percentage point cut in MLR was a 'necessary ingredient to give a proper balance to the budget'.[82] Noting that this was going to be a 'pretty harsh budget', the Second Permanent Secretary, William Ryrie, concurred with Middleton in a note to Howe, arguing that there should be some 'tangible benefit apparently flowing from the harsh measures you are taking'.[83] On 2 March the Financial Secretary and Chief Secretary both supported the reduction of two percentage points, as did the Governor on 4 March.[84]

Surprisingly, Wass was unconvinced by the argument for reducing interest rates, and supported the change only on political grounds, telling the Chancellor that 'without a significant move on MLR the budget will be greeted with dismay by the industrial lobby; indeed many of your own supporters will be pretty upset too'.[85] He urged the interest rate cut to be firmly linked to monetary objectives, warning that, without this, the defence of an interest rate cut 'could look particularly weak under cross-examination from for instance the Select Committee and even more from

---

[79] 'D. W. G. Wass to Chancellor of the Exchequer', 19 February 1981, TNA, T386/551.
[80] A. J. Wiggins, 'Note of a meeting held at No. 11 Downing Street on Monday, 23 February, 1981 at 2.30 pm', 23 February 1981, TNA, T386/551.
[81] Ibid.
[82] P. E. Middleton, 'MLR in the Budget', 27 February 1981, TNA, T386/552.
[83] W. S. Ryrie, 'MLR in the Budget', 2 March 1981, TNA, T386/552.
[84] A. J. Wiggins, 'Monetary affairs', 5 March 1981, TNA, T386/552.
[85] D. W. G. Wass, 'MLR in the Budget', 2 March 1981, TNA, T386/552.

some of our monetarist critics'.[86] At a meeting with Howe and Richardson on 4 March, Wass thought it might be safer to go for a cut of only one percentage point.[87] In this, he echoed Walters, who would have preferred no cut in MLR at all.[88] Walters' position was viewed by Leon Brittan, the Chief Secretary, as 'quite extraordinary in view of his other public views'.[89] For Brittan, a one percentage point reduction 'could be so disastrous politically that it ought not be to be contemplated unless *all* the economic evidence pointed in its favour'. Since there was not the evidence, the Chief Secretary supported a two percentage point reduction.[90]

Conclusions

The story of the evolution of money supply targets in the United Kingdom is long and tortuous, and a short chapter cannot possibly do justice to the twists and turns in the authorities' thinking after 1968. The reluctance to engage with monetary targets, unless they were forced to do so by external influences such as the IMF or the financial markets, was the most significant characteristic of monetary policy until 1979 and symptomatic of the Keynesian mindset that dominated most official thinking. As this chapter has suggested, a distinction might be drawn in the pre-1979 period from 1968 to 1974 and from 1975 to 1979. In the former period the sometimes bellicose stance of the authorities only really altered after the 1971–73 monetary explosion and its consequences. Between 1974 and 1979 there was a conversion to monetarism by some in the Conservative Party, and an acceptance by the Labour Party that money supply targets made for good politics with the markets and the IMF. There was no enthusiasm among senior officials in the Treasury or the Bank for anything that appeared to be Friedmanite monetarism.

There was clearly a determination on the part of several senior Conservative politicians to make monetarism work upon entering office in 1979. As has been argued elsewhere, however, 'political monetarism' dominated, and the number of 'genuine monetarists' in the core executive remained in the minority.[91] Although Lord Howe has disputed such a

---

[86] Ibid.   [87] Wiggins, 'Monetary affairs', 5 March 1981, T386/552.

[88] 'A. A. Walters to D. W. G. Wass', 26 February 1981, TNA, T386/552.

[89] T. F. Matthews, 'MLR in the Budget', 3 March 1981, TNA, T386/552.

[90] Ibid. [emphasis in original].

[91] 'Political monetarism' refers to individuals who are in favour of monetary targets but who do not accept the argument that the money supply should be controlled as an intermediate target for controlling nominal GDP. 'Genuine monetarists' advocate that the money supply should be controlled as an intermediate target for controlling nominal GDP. See Pepper and Oliver, *Monetarism under Mrs Thatcher*.

characterisation he also concedes that he did not believe in monetarism.[92] As this chapter has shown, the shift in focus away from £M3 began within six months of the launch of the MTFS, and the substance of the discussions surrounding monetary policy in the weeks before the 1981 Budget illustrates the extent of the pragmatism that had set in. A month after the Budget Nick Monck was forced to admit that monetary control was 'rather bare' and officials were now in an 'uncomfortable situation... [W]e all seem to be agreed that the existing and emerging systems of control are weak and unreliable.'[93] For its supporters, there was always monetary base control, which, as soon as the ink was dry on the 1981 Budget, Walters wished to pursue, again with Thatcher's support.[94] Clearly, the story about monetary targets in the United Kingdom does not end in 1981, and, in time and with more space, a more detailed account will be able to explore the post-1968 period in more depth.

---

[92] R. E. G. Howe, 'Can 364 economists all be wrong?', in H. J. Davies (ed.), *The Chancellors' tales: managing the British economy* (London, 2006), 105–6; Moore, *Margaret Thatcher*, 504, 531, 628.

[93] N. J. Monck, 'Monetary control', 13 April 1981, TNA T388/191.

[94] A. A. Walters, 'Monetary base control', 12 March 1981, TNA, T388/191.

List of names

Allen, Douglas A. V. (later Lord Croham), Department of Economic Affairs: Deputy Under Secretary, 1964–66; Second Permanent Under Secretary, May–October 1966; Permanent Under Secretary, 1966–68. HM Treasury: Permanent Secretary, 1968–74. Bank of England: Adviser to the Governor, 1978–83.

Armstrong, Robert T., Radcliffe Committee: Secretary, 1957–59. Prime Minister's Principal Private Secretary, 1970–75. Cabinet Secretary, 1979–87.

Ball, R. James, London Business School: Professor of Economics, 1965–97; Principal, 1972–84.

Biffen, W. John, Chief Secretary to the Treasury, 1979–81.

Bridgeman, J. Michael, HM Treasury: Under Secretary, 1975–81.

Brittan, Samuel, Department of Economic Affairs: Adviser, 1965. *Financial Times*: economic columnist, 1966–present; Assistant Editor, 1978–95.

Britton, Andrew J., HM Treasury: Under Secretary, 1980–82. National Institute for Social and Economic Research: Director, 1982–95.

Burns, Terence, HM Treasury: Chief Economic Adviser, 1980–91.

Callaghan, L. James, Chancellor of the Exchequer, 1964–67. Prime Minister, 1976–79.

Cassell, Frank, HM Treasury: head of Monetary Policy Division, 1971–74; head of Medium-Term Policy Analysis, 1976–83.

Couzens, Kenneth E., HM Treasury: Deputy Secretary (Incomes Policy and Public Finance Division), 1973–77; Second Permanent Secretary (Overseas Finance Division), 1977–82.

Crockett, Andrew D., Bank of England: Economics Department and Cashier's Department, 1966–72.

Dell, Edmund E., HM Paymaster General, 1974–76. Secretary of State for Trade, 1976–78.

Dicks-Mireaux, Leslie A., Bank of England: head (Economic Section), 1969–81.

Dow, J. Christopher R., Bank of England: Executive Director (Economics Division), 1973–81; Adviser to the Governors, 1981–84.

Downey, Gordon S., HM Treasury: Under Secretary, 1972–76; head of Central Unit, 1975; Deputy Secretary, 1976–81. Central Policy Review Staff: Deputy Head, 1978–81.

Sources: Hacche and Taylor, *Inside the Bank of England*, 259–70; *Who's Who*. These notes give details of the positions and roles of the key individuals named in this volume and are mainly restricted to the period under examination.

Evans, Arthur M. (Moss), Transport and General Workers Union: General Secretary, 1978–85.

Fforde, John S., Bank of England: Chief Cashier, 1966–70; Executive Director (Home Finance Division), 1970–82; Adviser to the Governors, 1982–84.

Friedman, Milton, University of Chicago: Professor of Economics, 1948–82. Nobel Memorial Prize in Economics, 1976.

George, Edward A. J., Bank of England: Adviser on international monetary questions, 1974–77; Deputy Chief Cashier, 1977–80; Assistant Director (Gilt-Edged Division, 1980–82; Executive Director (Home Finance Division), 1982–90; Deputy Governor, 1990–93; Governor, 1993–2003.

Gilmour, Ian H. J. L., Secretary of State for Defence, 1974. Lord Privy Seal, 1979–81.

Goodhart, Charles A. E., Department of Economic Affairs: Economic Adviser, 1965–67; Bank of England: Monetary Adviser, 1969–85; Chief Adviser, 1980–85.

Healey, Denis W., Chancellor of the Exchequer, 1974–79.

Hoskyns, John A. H. L., No. 10 Policy Unit, 1979–82.

Howe, R. E. Geoffrey, Chancellor of the Exchequer, 1979–83.

Joseph, Keith S., Secretary of State for Social Services, 1970–74; Secretary of State for Industry, 1979–81.

Lankester, Timothy P., HM Treasury: Prime Minister's Private Secretary for Economic Affairs, 1978–81.

Lawson, Nigel, opposition spokesman on economic affairs, 1977–79. Financial Secretary to the Treasury, 1979–81. Chancellor of the Exchequer, 1983–89.

Littler, J. Geoffrey, HM Treasury: Under Secretary 1972; Deputy Secretary, 1977; Second Permanent Secretary (Overseas Finance Division), 1983–88.

McMahon, Christopher W., Bank of England: Adviser, 1964; Adviser to the Governors, 1966–70; Executive Director (Economics Division), 1970–73; Executive Director (External Finance Division), 1973–80; Deputy Governor, 1980–85.

Middleton, Peter E., HM Treasury: Press Secretary, 1972–74; head (Monetary Policy Division), 1975; Under Secretary, 1976; Deputy Secretary, 1980–83; Permanent Secretary, 1983–91.

Monck, Nicholas J., HM Treasury: Assistant Secretary, 1971; Principal Private Secretary to Chancellor of the Exchequer, 1976–77; Under Secretary (Nationalised Industries, Home Finance Division), 1977–84.

Niehans, Jürg, Johns Hopkins University: Professor of Economics, 1966–77; Visiting Professor of Economics, 1981–88. University of Berne: Professor of Economics, 1977–81.

Pepper, Gordon T., W. Greenwell & Co.: Partner, 1962; Joint Senior Partner, 1980–86.

Prior, James M. L., Secretary of State for Employment, 1979–81.

Richardson, Gordon W. H., Bank of England: Governor, 1973–83.

Ryrie, William S., HM Treasury: Assistant Secretary (International Monetary Affairs Division), 1966–69; Principal Private Secretary to Chancellor of Exchequer, 1969–71; Under Secretary (Public Sector Group), 1971–75; Economic Minister, Washington, and UK Executive Director, International Monetary

Fund and International Bank for Reconstruction and Development, 1975–79; Second Permanent Secretary (Domestic Economy Division), 1980–82.

Thatcher, Margaret H., leader of the Conservative Party, 1975–90; Prime Minister, 1979–90.

Walker, David A., Bank of England: Chief Adviser, then Chief (Economics Intelligence Department), 1977; Assistant Director, 1980–81; Executive Director, 1981–88.

Walters, Alan A., London School of Economics: Professor of Economics, 1968–76. Chief Economic Adviser to Prime Minister, 1981–84, 1989.

Wass, Douglas W. G., HM Treasury: Second Permanent Secretary, 1973–74; Permanent Secretary, 1974–83.

Chronology of events

18 November 1967	Sterling devalued from \$2.80 to \$2.40 against US dollar.
23 November 1967	Outgoing Chancellor, James Callaghan, pledges that 'the growth of the money supply will be less in 1968 than the present estimate for 1967' when applying for an IMF loan.
15 October 1968	Chief Cashier, John Fforde, calls for 'thorough review' of monetary policy within the Bank of England, prompting formation of the internal Money Supply Group.
16–18 October 1968	Monetary policy seminar with IMF officials.
22 May 1969	Chancellor, Roy Jenkins, commits to a £400 million domestic credit expansion ceiling (including a £250 million target) in IMF Letter of Intent.
June 1970	'The importance of money' published in the *Bank of England Quarterly Bulletin*.
18 June 1970	General election: Ted Heath (Conservative) elected with a thirty-one-seat majority, embarks upon a strategy of rapid economic growth.
30 March 1971	Budget: Chancellor, Anthony Barber, states that 'there would be dangers for liquidity and employment if we sought immediately to reduce the growth of money supply to much below 3 per cent per quarter'.
17 May 1971	Government Broker withdraws liquidity in gilts of more than twelve months' maturity to facilitate control of the money supply.
28 May 1971	Bank of England Governor, Leslie O'Brien, announces that 'we have increasingly shifted our emphasis towards the broader monetary aggregates – to use the inelegant but apparently unavoidable term: the money supply'.
15 August 1971	US President, Richard Nixon, suspends convertibility of US dollar into gold.

23 August 1971	Sterling floats.
16 September 1971	Competition and Credit Control becomes operational. Clearing bank cartel dissolved.
18 December 1971	Sterling fixed at $2.60.
14 February 1972	Three-day week begins.
21 March 1972	'Dash for growth' Budget: Barber announces 5 per cent real GDP growth target and agrees to unpublished 20 per cent M3 target.
28 April 1972	United Kingdom repays outstanding IMF debts.
1 May 1972	Sterling enters the European currency 'snake'; fluctuations limited to 2.25 per cent.
23 June 1972	Sterling exits the 'snake' and floats.
31 July 1972	United Kingdom draws $630 million (equivalent) from IMF gold tranche to repay central banks for failed sterling support in June.
9 October 1972	Minimum Lending Rate replaces Bank Rate.
1 January 1973	United Kingdom joins European Economic Community.
October 1973	OPEC raises price of oil following Yom Kippur War.
7 November 1973	Stage 3 of Heath's incomes policy becomes effective: wage rises indexed to inflation.
17 December 1973	Barber unveils the 'corset' in his mini-Budget.
21 December 1973	Bank launches the 'Lifeboat' operation to rescue the secondary banks.
1 January 1974	Three-day week begins (again).
28 February 1974	General election produces hung parliament.
4 March 1974	Harold Wilson forms minority Labour government.
8 March 1974	Three-day week ends.
26 March 1974	First Budget of new Chancellor, Denis Healey, implies M3 growth 'below money GDP growth'.
10 October 1974	General election: Wilson wins a three-seat majority.
11 February 1975	Margaret Thatcher wins Conservative Party leadership election.
15 April 1975	Budget: Healey 'abandons' Keynesianism, raises basic rate of income tax by two percentage points to 35 per cent.
5 June 1975	'Yes' vote on continued UK membership of EEC.
11 July 1975	Reintroduction of incomes policy prompts monetary policy review within the Bank.

August 1975	RPI growth peaks at 26.9 per cent.
7 November 1975	Healey applies to IMF for remaining gold tranche, first credit tranche and oil facility loan.
20 November 1975	Government announces that more than 50 per cent of public spending will be constrained by cash limits.
31 December 1975	IMF board agrees to UK loans.
5 March 1976	Sterling falls below $2 for the first time.
5 April 1976	James Callaghan succeeds Wilson as Prime Minister.
7 June 1976	Consortium of central banks announces $5.3 billion loan for United Kingdom.
22 July 1976	Healey announces 12 per cent M3 target.
28 September 1976	Healey's 'about-turn' at Heathrow. Further IMF application announced the next day.
15 December 1976	Healey's mini-Budget announces PSBR and DCE ceilings and £M3 target range of 9 to 13 per cent.
3 January 1976	IMF board agrees to $3.9 billion stand-by credit.
23 March 1977	The Labour government forms a pact with the Liberals after a series of parliamentary defeats.
15 September 1977	Bank concludes that 'there is no obvious simple, single equation, demand for M3 balances'.
26 October 1977	Sterling uncapped, rises 5 per cent versus dollar; exchange controls relaxed.
1 January 1978	Callaghan reveals 5 per cent earnings target in New Year broadcast.
11 April 1978	Budget: Healey lowers £M3 target range to 8 to 12 per cent, reaffirms £8.5 billion PSBR ceiling.
6 September 1978	TUC conference rejects 5 per cent wage guideline, precipitating the 'winter of discontent'.
28 March 1979	Callaghan government loses confidence vote.
3 May 1979	General election: Margaret Thatcher elected with forty-three-seat majority.
12 June 1979	Sir Geoffrey Howe's first Budget cuts incomes tax, raises VAT to 15 per cent, further relaxes exchange controls, lowers £M3 target range to 7 to 11 per cent (annualised and applied from June 1979 to April 1980) and raises MLR by two percentage points to 14 per cent.
23 October 1979	Howe abolishes remaining exchange controls.
15 November 1979	MLR raised to 17 per cent.

26 March 1980	Budget: Howe launches MTFS; four-year series of declining £M3 target ranges and PSBR ceilings.
18 June 1980	'Corset' abolished.
3 July 1980	MLR lowered by one percentage point to 16 per cent to ease pressure on the corporate sector, despite £M3 growth above target range.
10 July 1980	Cabinet agrees to cut public expenditure by £2 billion.
8 September 1980	'Difficult' meeting between Thatcher and senior Bank officials on monetary policy (MTFW 113138); Annualised £M3 growth at 26 per cent.
22 September 1980	HM Treasury meeting discusses 'the possibility of a package of measures as "cover" for a reduction in interest rates' (MTFW 128330).
10 October 1980	Thatcher tells Conservative Party conference that 'the lady's not for turning'.
20 October 1980	Thatcher asks Sir Douglas Wass 'to explore ways of mitigating the adverse conditions in which British industry is operating, so that good and viable companies like ICI should not be driven to the wall'.
24 October 1980	Sterling peaks at $2.4645 against US dollar.
4 November 1980	Cabinet reneges on agreement to cut public expenditure by £2 billion.
5 November 1980	Wass suggests a 'modest' two percentage point cut in MLR (MTFW 113271).
11 November 1980	CBI Director General threatens 'bare-knuckle fight' with the government.
12 November 1980	Thatcher agrees to cut MLR by two percentage points (MTFW 113270).
20 November 1980	£M3 target taken 'out of action' until 1981 Budget (MTFW 113205).
24 November 1980	Autumn Statement: Howe raises employees' National Insurance contributions, imposes a supplementary petroleum duty and £1 billion of spending cuts to reduce PSBR estimate for 1981/82 from £11 billion (4½ per cent of GDP) to £9 billion (versus implied MTFS ceiling of £7½ billion) and lowers MLR two percentage points to 16 per cent despite M3 growing by annualised 20 per cent.
6 January 1981	Alan Walters joins No. 10 Policy Unit.

7 January 1981	Jürg Niehans' 'bombshell': tight monetary policy rather than North Sea oil is the cause of the strong pound.
17 January 1981	Howe reveals updated £11 billion PSBR estimate for 1981/82 at Chequers meeting; Thatcher 'not amused'.
25 January 1981	Roy Jenkins, David Owen, Bill Rogers and Shirley Williams announce intention to leave the Labour Party and form the forerunner of the Social Democratic Party.
27 January 1981	HM Treasury meeting concludes that the Budget should reduce the PSBR estimate for 1981/82 by a minimum of £1½ billion, to around £10 billion (MTFW 127452).
10 February 1981	Howe informs Thatcher that the PSBR estimate for 1981/82 has risen to £13 billion while ruling out spending cuts in the Budget.
13 February 1981	Tim Lankester informs Thatcher that the PSBR estimate for 1981/82 has risen to £13¾ billion (MTFW 114003); Howe suggests that a PSBR below £11 billion is not 'politically feasible'.
17 February 1981	Thatcher willing to contemplate an increase in the basic rate of income tax to achieve a PSBR of less than £11 billion.
24 February 1981	Thatcher presses Howe for a PSBR of £10½ billion to justify lowering MLR before agreeing to £11¼ billion; Walters excluded from meeting.
25 February 1981	HM Treasury meeting agrees to a £10½ billion PSBR estimate for 1981/82, by freezing the income tax allowances, and a two percentage point cut in MLR (MTFW 127482); Walters describes freezing the allowances as 'stupid politically, indefensible morally and economically' (MTFW 128829).
26 February 1981	Walters complains that the final Budget measures are 'too little and the wrong kind' (MTFS 114026).
5 March 1981	Treasury and Civil Service Committee criticises government's monetary policy.
10 March 1981	Budget: Howe raises taxes and lowers MLR from 16 per cent to 14 per cent. £M3 growth in 1980/81 overshoots by eight percentage points.

30 March 1981	364 economists' letter reported in *The Times*.
15 June 1981	Financial Secretary, Nigel Lawson, recommends UK membership of the Exchange Rate Mechanism.
9 October 1981	Polls show Thatcher to be the most unpopular Prime Minister since records began.
9 March 1982	Budget: Howe relaunches MTFS by raising £M3 targets.
14 June 1982	Argentine surrender ends Falklands War.
9 June 1983	General election: Thatcher wins 144-seat majority.
17 October 1985	Chancellor, Nigel Lawson, suspends £M3 target.
18 March 1986	Lawson reintroduces £M3 target.
February 1987	Lawson begins shadowing the deutschmark.

Official sources

Employment policy, Cmnd 6527 (London, 1944).

Radcliffe Committee on the working of the monetary system, Cmnd 827 (London, 1959).

The attack on inflation, Cmnd 6151 (London, 1975).

Financial Statement and Budget Report 1979–80 (London, 1979).

Monetary control, Cmnd 7858 (London, 1980).

Financial Statement and Budget Report 1980–81 (London, 1980).

Third report from the Treasury and Civil Service Committee: monetary policy (London, 1981).

Financial Statement and Budget Report 1981–82 (London, 1981).

Financial Statement and Budget Report 1987–88 (London, 1987).

Economic trends annual supplement (London, 1994).

Bibliography of secondary sources

Alesina, A., and R. Perotti, 'Fiscal expansions and adjustments in OECD countries', *Economic Policy: A European Forum*, vol. 21, no. 2 (October 1995), 207–48.

Allen, W. A., 'Recent developments in monetary control in the United Kingdom', in L. H. Meyer (ed.), *Improving money stock control: problems, solutions, and consequences* (Boston, MA, 1983), 97–123.

Allsopp, C. J., 'Macroeconomic policy: design and performance', in M. J. Artis and D. P. Cobham, *Labour's economic policies, 1974–1979* (Manchester, 1991), 19–37.

Anderton, R., and R. Barrell, 'The ERM and structural change in European labour markets: a study of 10 countries', *Weltwirtschaftliches Archiv*, vol. 131, no. 1 (March 1995), 47–66.

Artis, M. J., 'Monetary policy: part 2', in F. T. Blackaby (ed.), *British economic policy, 1960–74* (Cambridge, 1978), 258–303.

Axilrod, S. H., 'Monetary policy, money supply, and the Federal Reserve's operating procedures', in P. Meek (ed.), *Central bank views on monetary targeting* (New York, 1982), 32–41.

Bank of England, 'Economic commentary', *Bank of England Quarterly Bulletin*, 17, 1977, 137–61.

'Bank of England notes', *Bank of England Quarterly Bulletin*, 18, 1978, 359–64.

'The monetary base: a statistical note', *Bank of England Quarterly Bulletin*, 11, 1981, 59–65.

'The supplementary special deposits scheme', *Bank of England Quarterly Bulletin*, 22, 1982, 74–85.

'The role of the Bank of England in the money market', *Bank of England Quarterly Bulletin*, 22, 1982, 86–94.

Barrell, R., 'Has the EMS changed wage and price behaviour in Europe?', *National Institute Economic Review*, no. 134 (November 1990), 64–72.

'Fiscal consolidation and the slimmer state', *National Institute Economic Review*, no. 215 (January 2011), F4–9.

'Fiscal policy in the longer term', *National Institute Economic Review*, no. 217 (July 2011), F4–10.

Barrell, R., and E. P. Davis, 'Financial liberalisation, consumption and wealth effects in seven OECD countries', *Scottish Journal of Political Economy*, vol. 54, no. 2 (May 2007), 54–67.

Barrell, R., A. Delannoy and D. Holland, 'Monetary policy, output growth and oil prices', *National Institute Economic Review*, no. 215 (January 2010), F37–43.

Barrell, R., D. Holland and A. I. Hurst, 'Fiscal consolidation, part 2: fiscal multipliers and fiscal consolidations', OECD Economics Department Working Paper no. 933 (February 2012).

Barrell, R., D. Holland and I. Liadze 'Accounting for UK economic performance', paper presented at Clare College, Cambridge University, 19 September 2013.

Barrell, R., D. Holland, I. Liadze and O. Pomerantz, 'Volatility, growth and cycles', *Empirica*, vol. 36, no. 2 (May 2009), 177–92.

'The impact of EMU on growth in Europe', in M. Buti, S. Deroose, V. Gaspar and J. Nogueira Martins (eds.), *The euro: the first decade* (Cambridge, 2010), 607–37.

Barrell, R., and S. Kirby, 'UK fiscal prospects', *National Institute Economic Review*, no. 213 (July 2010), F66–70.

Batini, N., and E. Nelson, 'The UK's rocky road to stability', Federal Reserve Bank of St Louis Working Paper no. 2005–020A (March 2005), 1–114.

Beenstock, M., and A. Longbottom, 'The statistical relationship between the money supply and the public sector borrowing requirement', London Business School Centre for Economic Forecasting, *Economic Outlook*, vol. 4, no. 9 (June 1980), 27–31.

Bernanke, B. S., T. Laubach, F. S. Mishkin and A. Posen, *Inflation targeting: lessons from the international experience* (Princeton, NJ, 1999).

Beveridge, W. H., *Full employment in a free society* (London, 1944).

Biffen, W. J., *Semi-detached* (London, 2013).

Blackaby, F. T., 'Comments on Michael Foot's paper "Monetary targets"', in B. Griffiths and G. E. Wood (eds.), *Monetary targets* (London, 1981), 54–61.

Boleat, M., *National housing finance systems: a comparative study* (London, 1985).

Brittan, S., *The Treasury under the Tories* (Harmondsworth, 1964).

Steering the economy: the role of the Treasury (Harmondsworth, 1971).

The role and limits of government: essays in political economy (London, 1983).

Britton, A. J. C., *Macroeconomic policy in Britain, 1974–87* (Cambridge, 1991).

Browning, P., *The Treasury and economic policy, 1964–1985* (London, 1986).

Bryan, L. L., *Breaking up the bank: rethinking an industry under siege* (Burr Ridge, IL, 1988).

Budd, A. P., 'The development of demand management: comments', in F. A. Cairncross (ed.), *Changing perceptions of economic policy* (London, 1981), 52–6.

'Fiscal policy in the United Kingdom', in I. McLean and C. Jennings (eds.), *Applying the dismal science: when economists give advice to governments* (London, 2006).

Budd, A. P., and M. Beenstock, 'Tightening the fiscal and monetary controls', London Business School Centre for Economic Forecasting, *Economic Outlook*, vol. 5, no. 5 (February 1981), 21–7.

Budd, A. P., and T. Burns, 'Economic viewpoint: how much reflation?', London Business School Centre for Economic Forecasting, *Economic Outlook*, vol. 2, no. 1 (October 1977), 7–11.

'Should the PSBR be cut next year?', London Business School Centre for Economic Forecasting, *Economic Viewpoint*, vol. 3, no. 11 (August 1979), 1–4.

Budd, A. P., and G. R. Dicks, 'The budget, the PSBR and the money supply', London Business School Centre for Economic Forecasting, *Economic Outlook*, vol. 4, no. 5 (February 1980), 13–17.

'The Medium-term Financial Strategy', London Business School Centre for Economic Forecasting, *Economic Outlook*, vol. 4, no. 9 (June 1980), 12–15.

'Bringing counter-inflation policy back on course', London Business School Centre for Economic Forecasting, *Economic Outlook*, vol. 5, no. 1 (October 1980), 17–22.

'The 1981 budget', London Business School Centre for Economic Forecasting, *Forecast Release*, vol. 5, no. 6 (March 1981), 1–4.

Buiter, W. H., and M. H. Miller, 'The Thatcher experiment: the first two years', *Brookings Papers on Economic Activity*, no. 2 (Fall 1981), 315–79

'Changing the rules: economic consequences of the Thatcher regime', *Brookings Papers on Economic Activity*, no. 2 (Fall 1983), 305–79.

Campbell, J., *Margaret Thatcher*, 2 vols. (London, 2000, 2003).

Capie, F. H., *The Bank of England: 1950s to 1979* (New York, 2010).

Chamberlin, G., 'Output and expenditure in the last three UK recessions', *Economic and Labour Market Review*, vol. 4, no. 8 (August 2010), 51–64.

Clarida, R. G. J., J. Gali and M. Gertler, 'The science of monetary policy: a New Keynesian perspective', *Journal of Economic Literature*, vol. 37, no. 4 (December 1999), 1661–707.

Clift, B. M., and J. D. Tomlinson, 'Negotiating credibility: Britain and the International Monetary Fund, 1956–1976', *Contemporary European History*, vol. 17, no. 4 (November 2008), 545–66.

'When rules started to rule: the IMF, neo-liberal economic ideas and economic policy change in Britain', *Review of International Political Economy*, vol. 19, no. 3 (August 2012), 477–500.

Cobham, D. P., *The making of monetary policy in the UK, 1975–2000* (Chichester, 2000).

Congdon, T. G., *Monetary control in Britain* (London, 1982).

Money and asset prices in boom and bust (London, 2005).

Crafts, N. F. R., 'Recent European economic growth: why can't it be like the Golden Age?', *National Institute Economic Review*, no. 199 (January 2007), 69–81.

Crafts, N. F. R., and M. O'Mahony, 'A perspective on UK productivity performance', *Fiscal Studies*, vol. 22, no. 3 (September 2001), 271–306.

Croome, D. R., and H. G. Johnson (eds.), *Money in Britain, 1959–1969: the papers of the Radcliffe Report – ten years after* (Oxford, 1970).

Darling, A. M., *Back from the brink: 1,000 days at Number 11* (London, 2011).

Davies, A., 'The evolution of British monetary targets, 1968–79', University of Oxford Discussion Paper in Economic and Social History no. 104 (2012).

Dimsdale, N. H., 'The Treasury and Civil Service Committee and the British monetarist experiment', in M. L. Baranzini (ed.), *Advances in economic theory* (Oxford, 1982), 184–5.

'British monetary policy since 1945', in N. F. R. Crafts and N. W. C. Woodward (eds.), *The British economy since 1945* (Oxford, 1991), 89–140.

Donoughue, B., *Downing Street diary: with James Callaghan at No. 10* (London, 2009).

Dow, J. C. R., and I. D. Saville, *A critique of monetary policy: theory and British experience* (Oxford, 1988).

Foot, M. D. K. W., C. A. E. Goodhart and A. C. Hotson, 'Monetary base control', *Bank of England Quarterly Bulletin*, 19, 1979, 149–59.

Fforde, J. S., 'Setting monetary objectives', *Bank of England Quarterly Bulletin*, 13, 1983, 200.

'Setting monetary objectives', in Bank of England, *The development and operation of monetary policy 1960–1983: a selection of material from the Quarterly Bulletin of the Bank of England* (Oxford, 1984), 65.

Friedman, M., 'The role of monetary policy', *American Economic Review*, vol. 58, no. 1 (March 1968), 1–17.

'Memoranda on monetary policy', *Treasury and Civil Service Committee*, HC 720-11 (London, 1980)

Giavazzi, F., and M. Pagano, 'Can severe fiscal contractions be expansionary? Tales of two small European economies', in *NBER macroeconomics annual*, vol. V (Chicago, 1990), 75–111.

Gilmour, I. H. J. L., *Dancing with dogma: Britain under Thatcherism* (London, 1992).

Goodhart, C. A. E., 'Problems of monetary management: the UK experience', Reserve Bank of Australia Paper in Monetary Economics no. 1 (1975).

Money, information and uncertainty (London, 1975).

(ed.), *Monetary theory and practice: the UK experience* (London, 1984).

'The conduct of monetary policy', *Economic Journal*, vol. 99 (June 1989), 324–5.

'The Bank of England over the last 35 years', in *Bankhistorisches Archiv*, supplement 43, *Welche Aufgaben muß eine Zentralbank wahrnehmen? Historische Erfahrungen und europäische Perspektiven* (Stuttgart, 2004), 44.

Goodhart, C. A. E., and A. D. Crockett, 'The importance of money', *Bank of England Quarterly Bulletin*, 10, 1970, 159–98.

Goodhart, C. A. E., and A. C. Hotson, 'The forecasting and control of bank lending', in C. A. E. Goodhart (ed.), *Monetary theory and practice: the UK experience* (London, 1984), 139–45.

Goodhart, C. A. E., and P. V. Temperton, 'The UK exchange rate, 1979–81: a test of the overshooting hypothesis', paper presented to the Oxford Money Study Group, 6 November 1982.

Gordon, C., *The Cedar story: the night the City was saved* (London, 1993).

Greider, W., *Secrets of the temple: how the Federal Reserve runs the country* (New York, 1987).

Griffiths, B., 'Resource efficiency, monetary policy and the reform of the UK banking system', *Journal of Money, Credit and Banking*, vol. 5, no. 1 (February 1973), 61–77.

Hacche, G., 'The demand for money in the United Kingdom: experience since 1971', *Bank of England Quarterly Bulletin*, 14, 1974, 284–305.

Hacche, G., and C. Taylor (eds.), *Inside the Bank of England: memoirs of Christopher Dow, chief economist 1973–84* (Basingstoke, 2013).

Hay Davison, I. F., and M. Stuart-Smith, *Grays Building Society: investigation under section 110 of the Building Societies Act, 1962*, Cmnd 7557 (London, 1979).

Healey, D. W., *The time of my life* (London, 1989).

HM Treasury, *Economic Trends* (August 1970).

Hewitt, M. V., 'Financial forecasts in the United Kingdom', *Bank of England Quarterly Bulletin*, 17, 1977, 188–95.

Hodrick, R. J., and E. C. Prescott, 'Post-war US business cycles: an empirical investigation', Northwestern University Center for Mathematical Studies in Economics and Management Science Discussion Paper no. 451 (1980).

Hoskyns, J. A. H. L., *Just in time: inside the Thatcher revolution* (London, 2000).

Hotson, A. C., 'British monetary targets 1976 to 1987: a view from the fourth floor of the Bank of England', London School of Economics and Political Science Financial Markets Group Special Paper no. 190 (2010).

Howe, R. E. G., *Conflict of loyalty* (London, 1994).

'Can 364 economists all be wrong?', in H. J. Davies (ed.), *The Chancellors' tales: managing the British economy* (London, 2006), 76–112.

Howe, R. E. G., K. S. Joseph, J. M. L. Prior and D. A. R. H. Howell, *The right approach to the economy* (London, 1977).

Howson, S., 'Money and monetary policy since 1945', in R. C. Floud and P. A. Johnson (eds.), *The Cambridge economic history of modern Britain*, vol. III, *Structural change and growth, 1939–2000* (Cambridge, 2004), 134–66.

Johnson, C., *The economy under Mrs Thatcher, 1979–1990* (London, 1991).

Joseph, K. S., *Reversing the trend: a critical re-appraisal of Conservative economic and social policies* (Chichester, 1975).

Kaldor, N., *The scourge of monetarism* (Oxford, 1982).

Keegan, W. J. G., *Mrs Thatcher's economic experiment* (London, 1984).

Mr Lawson's gamble (London, 1989).

Keynes, J. M., *A tract on monetary reform* (London, 1923).

The general theory of employment, interest and money (London, 1936).

How to pay for the war: a radical plan for the Chancellor of the Exchequer (London, 1940).

King, M. A., 'No money, no inflation: the role of money in the economy', *Bank of England Quarterly Bulletin*, 42, 2002, 162–77.

'Monetary policy: practice ahead of theory', Mais lecture, *Bank of England Quarterly Bulletin*, 45, 2005, 226–36.

Krugman, P. R., 'Who was Milton Friedman?' *Journal of Monetary Economics*, vol. 55, no. 4 (May 2008), 835–56.

'Response to Nelson and Schwartz', *Journal of Monetary Economics*, vol. 55, no. 4 (May 2008), 857–60.

Kydland, F. E., and E. C. Prescott, 'Rules rather than discretion: the inconsistency of optimal plans', *Journal of Political Economy*, vol. 85, no. 3 (June 1977), 473–92.

Laidler, D. E. W., 'The definition of money: theoretical and empirical problems', *Journal of Money, Credit and Banking*, vol. 1, no. 3 (August 1969), 508–25.

Monetarist perspectives (Oxford, 1982).

Lawson, N., *The view from No. 11: memoirs of a Tory radical* (London, 1992).

Leigh-Pemberton, R., 'Some aspects of UK monetary policy', *Bank of England Quarterly Bulletin*, 24, 1984, 474–81.

London Business School Centre for Economic Forecasting, 'The lessons of the Mansion House', *Forecast Release*, vol. 3, no. 2 (November 1978).

'Forecast summary', *Economic Outlook*, vol. 5, no. 9 (June 1981).

Ludlam, S., 'The gnomes of Washington: four myths of the 1976 IMF crisis', *Political Studies*, vol. 40, no. 4 (December 1992), 713–27.

Middlemas, R. K., *Power, competition and the state*, vol. III, *The end of the post-war era: Britain since 1974* (Basingstoke, 1990).

'Margaret Thatcher, 1979–1990', in V. B. Bogdanor (ed.), *From new Jerusalem to new Labour: British prime ministers from Attlee to Blair* (Basingstoke, 2010).

Moggridge, D. E., *Maynard Keynes: an economist's biography* (London, 1992).

Moore, C. H., *Margaret Thatcher: the authorized biography* (London, 2013).

Morgan, K. O., *Britain since 1945: the people's peace* (Oxford, 1991).

Needham, D. J., 'Fentiman Road: drawing the Conservative fiscal policy threads together in 1978' (June 2011), available at www.academia. edu/2431227/Fentiman_Road_drawing_the_Conservative_fiscal_policy_ threads_ together_in_1978.

'Britain's money supply experiment, 1971–73', Cambridge Working Paper in Social and Economic History no. 10 (2012.

UK monetary policy from devaluation to Thatcher, 1967–1982 (London, 2014).

Needham, D. J., M. J. Oliver and A Riley, 'The 1981 Budget: facts and fallacies', transcript of witness seminar held at Lombard Street Research, 27 September 2011, available at www.chu.cam.ac.uk/archives/exhibitions/ Witness_ seminars.php.

Niehans, J., *The appreciation of sterling: causes, effects, policies* (Rochester, 1981).

OECD, *United Kingdom: challenges at the cutting edge* ('Review of regulatory reform') (Paris, 2002).

Pepper, G. T., 'The money supply, economic management and the gilt-edged market', *Journal of the Institute of Actuaries*, vol. 96, no. 1 (January 1970), 1–46.

Inside Thatcher's monetarist revolution (London, 1998).

Pepper, G. T., and M. J. Oliver, *Monetarism under Thatcher: lessons for the future* (Cheltenham, 2001).

Pepper, G. T., and R. L. Thomas, 'Cyclical changes in the level of the UK equity and gilt-edged markets', *Journal of the Institute of Actuaries*, vol. 99, no. 3 (March 1973), 195–247.

Pepper, G. T., and G. E. Wood, *Too much money? An analysis of the machinery of monetary expansion and its control* (London, 1975).

Perotti, R., 'The austerity myth: gain without pain', Bank for International Settlements Working Paper no 362 (2011).

Pliatzky, L., *The Treasury under Mrs Thatcher* (Oxford, 1989).

Price, L. D. D., 'The demand for money in the United Kingdom: a further investigation', *Bank of England Quarterly Bulletin*, 12, 1972, 43–55.

Prior, J. M. L., *Balance of power* (London, 1986).

Riddell, P. J. R., *The Thatcher government* (Oxford, 1983).

Romer, C. D., and J. Bernstein, 'The job impact of the American recovery and reinvestment plan' (Washington, DC, 2009).

Stephens, P. F. C., *Politics and the pound: the Tories, the economy and Europe* (London, 1997).

Tew, J. H. B., 'Monetary policy: part 1', in F. T. Blackaby (ed.), *British economic policy, 1960–74* (Cambridge, 1978), 219–57.

Thain, C., 'The education of the Treasury: the Medium-Term Financial Strategy 1980–84', *Public Administration*, vol. 63, no. 3 (autumn 1985), 261–85.

Thatcher, M. H., *The Downing Street years* (London, 1993).

Tucker, P. M. W., 'Managing the central bank's balance sheet: where monetary policy meets financial stability', *Bank of England Quarterly Bulletin*, 44, 2004, 359–82.

Treaster, J. B., *Paul Volcker: the making of a financial legend* (Hoboken, NJ, 2004).

Trundle, J. M., and P. V. Temperton, 'Recent changes in the use of cash', *Bank of England Quarterly Bulletin*, 22, 1982, 519–29.

Van Ark, B., M. O'Mahony and M. P. Timmer, 'The productivity gap between Europe and the United States: trends and causes', *Journal of Economic Perspectives*, vol. 22, no. 1 (winter 2008), 64–78.

Volcker, P. A., 'The role of monetary targets in an age of inflation', *Journal of Monetary Economics*, vol. 4, no. 2 (April 1978), 329–39.

Walsh, C. E., *Monetary theory and policy* (Cambridge, MA, 2010).

Walters, A. A., *Britain's economic renaissance: Margaret Thatcher's reforms 1979–84* (Oxford, 1986).

Wass, D. W. G., *Decline to fall: the making of British macro-economic policy and the 1976 IMF crisis* (Oxford, 2008).

Woodford, M. D., *Interest and prices: foundations of a theory of monetary policy* (Princeton, NJ, 2003).

'How important is money in the conduct of monetary policy?', *Journal of Money, Credit and Banking*, vol. 40, no. 8 (December 2008), 1561–98.

Young, H. J. S., *One of us: a biography of Margaret Thatcher* (London, 1989).

Index

Allen, Douglas, 154, 157
Allsopp, Christopher, 149
Armstrong, Robert, 165
Atkinson, Fred, 5

Ball, James, 53
bank deposit levy (1980), 15, 16, 26, 71
Bank of England
  'practical monetarism', 92, 94
  and exchange controls, 60
  and Geoffrey Howe, 121
  and gilt-edged bonds, 213
  and inflation, 83
  and Margaret Thatcher, 121
  and Milton Friedman, 214, 227
  and monetarism, 83, 158
  and monetary targets,
    M1, 136, 174, 177, 222
    M2, 223
    M3, 59, 61, 80, 149, 155, 212, 216, 217
    £M3, 62, 83, 162, 167, 172
  and sterling, 99
  and the MTFS, 20, 82, 83, 84, 86, 93, 98,
    150, 172
  Money Supply Group (1968–70), 153
Barber, Anthony, 38, 40, 122, 154, 190, 215
Beckett, Terence, 168
Benn, Tony, 74
Berrill, Kenneth, 165
Beveridge, William, 8
Biffen, John, 21, 22, 115, 128, 165
Blair, Tony, 8, 144, 190
Bridgeman, Michael, 136, 177
British Steel Corporation, 30
Brittan, Leon, 22, 227
Brittan, Samuel, 84, 146, 168
Britton, Andrew, 167, 169, 173, 197, 198,
  201, 224
Brown, Gordon, 144, 190
Bruce-Gardyne, Jock, 41
Brunner, Karl, 104, 117, 167

Budd, Alan,
  and the MTFS, 53, 68, 164
Building Societies Association, 138, 139,
  140
Burns, Terry,
  and Alan Walters, 12
  and the 1981 Budget, 222
  and the MTFS, 53, 68, 164, 222
  and the November 1980 mini-Budget,
    106, 107
  and the PSBR in 1981, 21, 32
  appoined Chief Economic Adviser at
    HM Treasury, 46
  appointed Permanent Secretary at
    HM Treasury, 55
  London Business School, 43, 44, 45
  pre-Budget meetings in 1981,
    17 January, 24
    10 February, 26
Burns–Middleton hypothesis, 16

Cairncross, Alec, 5
Callaghan, James, 60, 64, 91, 92, 124, 131,
  152, 160
Cambridge University, 4, 74, 214
Campbell, John, 11
Capie, Forrest, 153, 210
Carr, Robert, 216
Carter, Jimmy, 131
Clarke, Kenneth, 55, 144
Clegg Commission on Pay Comparability,
  63–5, 66, 85
Cockfield, Arthur, 21, 173, 178
Competition and Credit Control (CCC),
  39, 81, 129, 132, 153–6, 176, 177,
  211
'concerted action' (*Konzertierte Aktion*),
  130, 131, 145, 160
Confederation of British Industry (CBI), 16,
  69, 156, 168, 170
Congdon, Tim, 41, 221

Conservative Research Department, 62, 174
credit counterparts, 133, 145, 147, 151, 157, 158, 177
Cripps, Francis, 74
Cropper, Peter, 22, 35
cyclically-adjusted budget balance, 6, 52, 75, 77

Darling, Alistair, 181, 194, 203
Domestic Credit Expansion (DCE), 42, 44, 61, 145, 150, 152, 153, 158, 211, 218
Dow, Christopher, 83, 84, 86, 105, 149, 179
Downey, Gordon, 217

Economic Reconstruction Group (ERG), 128–30, 131, 137, 143
Emminger, Otmar, 99
European currency 'snake', 56, 80
European exchange rate mechanism (ERM), 54, 80, 143, 177, 179, 195
exchange controls, 18, 60, 68, 80, 137, 166
expansionary fiscal contraction, 124–5, 181, 194, 195, 196, 197

Fforde, John, 84, 86
Friedman, Milton,
    'macroeconomic charlatan', 2, 3, 4
    and fiscal policy, 135
    and HM Treasury, 212
    and inflation, 132, 146, 148, 155
    and Keynes, 204
    and monetarism, 7, 128, 131, 134
    and the Bank of England, 153
    and the vertical Phillips Curve, 40
    and the natural rate of unemployment, 2, 8

George, Eddie, 84, 86, 144, 145
Gilmour, Ian, 128, 142, 164
gilt-edged bonds, 17, 71, 84, 86, 117, 124, 130, 155, 158, 163, 164, 211, 213, 226
Godley, Wynne, 41, 42, 74
Goodhart, Charles, 84, 86, 105, 153, 156, 158, 164, 172, 177, 223
Griffiths, Brian, 128, 129, 154

Hahn, Frank, 1, 2, 4
Hall, Robert (Lord Roberthall), 5
Healey, Denis
    'practical monetarism', 45
    'Sod-off Day', 58, 59
    1976 IMF loan, 58
    and incomes policy, 130, 131, 157
    and monetary targets, 149, 157, 158, 159, 162, 177, 218

and Nigel Lawson, 48
and the London Business School, 45
and the November 1980 mini-Budget, 17, 57, 108
success as Chancellor, 1977–79, 159
Heath, Edward, 69, 91, 124, 126, 128, 129, 155, 156, 176, 190, 215, 216
Higgins, Terence, 157, 212, 215
Hopkin, Bryan, 5
Hoskyns, John
    and David Wolfson, 15
    and Geoffrey Howe, 34, 72
    and Keith Joseph, 31
    and Margaret Thatcher, 14, 26, 27, 28, 29, 30, 98, 176
    and the 1981 Budget, 11, 12, 13, 33, 34, 35, 118, 171, 176
    and the MTFS, 179, 221
    and the PSBR in 1981, 20, 23, 24, 30, 72, 100
    and HM Treasury, 118
    pre-Budget meetings in 1981
        17 February, 28
Howe, Geoffrey,
    and Alan Walters, 27
    and capital controls, 106, 109, 110, 112
    and 'concerted action', 130, 160
    and corporate distress, 110
    and Douglas Wass, 111
    and exchange controls, 166
    and fiscal policy, 18, 27
    and Gordon Richardson, 119
    and John Hoskyns, 27
    and Leon Brittan, 22
    and Margaret Thatcher, 11, 12, 13, 15, 25, 28, 29, 35, 105, 163, 224
    and monetarism, 95, 227
    and monetary policy, 121
    and monetary targets, 103, 162, 163, 166, 175, 179
    and Nigel Lawson, 22, 179
    and retaining Healey's monetary framework, 126
    and sterling, 18, 143
    and the 1979 Budget, 97, 159, 161
    and the 1981 Budget, 10, 11, 12, 13, 35, 51
    and the 364 economists, 1
    and the Bank of England, 25, 162, 165, 216
    and the Economic Reconstruction Group, 128, 129, 130, 131, 143
    and the monetary policy U-turn, 167, 169, 223
    and the MTFS, 47, 126, 148, 165

Howe, Geoffrey (cont.)
  and the November 1980 mini-Budget,
    17, 18, 19, 107, 111, 112, 113,
    114, 169
  and the personal income tax allowances,
    116
  and the PSBR in 1981, 25, 29, 30, 31, 32
  approach to decision-making, 13, 20, 22,
    72, 115
  economic policy in opposition, 61
  pre-1981 Budget planning, 21
  pre-Budget meetings in 1981,
    17 January, 24, 170
    27 January, 25
    10 February, 26
    13 February, 27
    17 February, 24, 28, 29
    24 February, 29, 30
    25 February, 31, 32, 34
Howell, David, 128

Ibbs, Robin, 24
Imperial Chemical Industries (ICI), 24, 98,
    110, 168, 169
International Computers Ltd, 98
International Monetary Fund (IMF),
  1976 loan, 12, 42, 43, 58, 59, 61, 62, 99,
    158, 159, 160, 218, 227
  and Britain in the 1960s, 133, 152, 153,
    211, 212
  and the Bretton Woods system, 57

Jay, Peter, 41, 130
Jenkins, Roy, 69, 152, 211, 212
Joseph, Keith
  and the Bank of England, 129
  and Geoffrey Howe, 31
  and Gordon Pepper, 216
  and incomes policy, 128, 131
  and Margaret Thatcher, 115, 127, 128
  and monetarism, 2
  and the 1981 Budget, 116, 126
  and the Economic Reconstruction
    Group, 128

Keegan, William, 11, 170
Keynes, John Maynard, 1, 204, 205, 208
  A tract on monetary reform, 204
  How to pay for the War, 1
  *The General Theory of Employment, Interest
    and Money*, 1, 204, 205
Keynesian economics, 1–2, 8, 11, 41, 57, 67,
    93, 94, 108, 123, 124, 129, 141, 145,
    146, 147, 193, 198, 205, 214, 227
King, Mervyn, 145

Laidler, David, 128
Lamont, Norman, 55, 144
Lankester, Tim, 163
Lawson, Nigel,
  and 'crowding out'
    contemporary views, 23, 171
    current views, 22, 124, 171
  and Denis Healey, 48
  and Douglas Wass, 106
  and exchange controls, 60
  and Geoffrey Howe, 22, 23, 32, 72, 108,
    109, 121
  and inflation, 97, 126
  and Jürg Niehans, 172
  and Margaret Thatcher, 23
  and monetarism, 178
  and monetary policy in opposition,
    126, 159
  and monetary targets, 137, 174, 179,
    225
  and shadowing the Deutschmark, 143,
    180
  and sterling, 86, 109, 115
  and the 1981 Budget, 10, 11, 12, 13,
    175, 176
  and the Exchange Rate Mechanism,
    179
  and the 'Lawson Boom', 100
  and the MTFS, 22, 53, 159, 163, 164,
    165, 167, 178
  and the mythology of the 1981 Budget,
    101
  and the personal income tax allowances,
    170
  and the PSBR in 1981, 22
  monetary policy as Chancellor, 142, 143
  pre-Budget planning in 1981, 21
  views on academics, 37
  views on freezing the income tax personal
    allowances in 1981, 32
  Zurich speech (1981), 142, 223
Leigh-Pemberton, Robin, 143
London Business School
  and the PSBR, 45

Major, John, 144
McMahon, Kit, 19, 83, 84, 86, 103, 105,
    106, 111, 112, 158, 217
Meade, James, 5
Medium-Term Financial Strategy
    (MTFS)
  and London Business School, 46–50, 51
  failure of, 16–17, 20, 21, 67–9, 117,
    141, 145, 163–8, 176, 210, 220,
    223, 226

launch, 67, 103, 126, 148, 220
opposition to, 22
origins, 21, 22, 58, 159, 160
success, 78–80
Middleton, Peter
and Alan Walters, 12
and Jürg Niehans, 172
and MLR, 225, 226
and monetary policy, 180, 222
and monetary targets, 218, 222, 224,
225
and the 1981 Budget, 117
and the MTFS, 126, 173, 174, 179
and the PSBR in 1981, 21, 32
Moggridge, Donald, 204
monetarism
'crude monetarism', 12
'practical monetarism', 162, 227
and inflation, 40
as a veil for deflation, 8
criticisms of, 2, 4, 123, 191, 222
disagreements amongst Conservative
Party advisers, 61–2
'international monetarism', 42
'sado-monetarism', 99
the retreat from monetarism, 100, 167,
173
monetary aggregates
monetary targets
M0, 20, 61, 131, 133, 136, 221
M1, 20, 132, 133, 134, 140, 156
M3, 132, 154
£M3, 17, 20, 44, 50, 51, 61, 80, 85, 92,
99, 104, 108, 126, 127, 132, 133,
134, 148, 162, 167, 219, 220
monetary base control, 136
Moore, Charles, 11, 12, 13, 14, 28, 30, 35,
101, 118, 220

National Coal Board, 30
National Economic Development Council
(NEDC), 74
National Insurance, 17, 18, 114, 169, 170
Niehans, Jürg, 20, 99, 100, 117, 137, 170,
171, 172
No. 10 Policy Unit, 11, 14, 18, 19
North Sea oil, 58, 59, 85, 86, 99, 123, 164,
170, 171
Nott, John, 126, 128, 157, 216

oil shock
1973, 2, 40, 184, 189
1979, 56, 66, 97, 123, 169, 191
Oppenheim, Sally, 128
Osborne, George, 101, 181, 194, 203

Parkin, Michael, 128
Pepper, Gordon, 154, 214, 216, 221
personal income tax allowances, 16, 32
Phillips Curve, 3, 39, 40
Pliatzky, Leo, 101
Prior, James, 98, 128
Public Sector Borrowing Requirement
(PSBR)
discussions ahead of the 1981 Budget,
15, 28, 29, 30, 32, 33, 170
IMF ceilings, 42
MTFS objectives, 19
Treasury forecasts for 1981/82, 19, 27, 34

Radcliffe Report, 151, 153, 180
Reagan, Ronald, 32, 100, 205
Rees, Peter, 21
Richardson, Gordon
and 'concerted action', 130
and Geoffrey Howe, 25
and Margaret Thatcher, 13, 163, 165
and monetary policy, 99
and monetary targets, 103, 149
and North Sea oil, 86
and sterling, 87
and the 1981 Budget, 25, 36
and the monetary policy U-turn, 167,
225, 226
and the MTFS, 164
Ridley, Adam, 21, 32, 35
Ridley, Nicholas, 41
Ryrie, William, 18, 19, 20, 31, 106, 107,
111, 112, 116, 226

Savings and Loan Associations (SLAs),
141
Sherman, Alfred, 117, 170
Shore, Peter, 74
Social Democratic Party, 69, 178
Savings and Loan Associations (SLAs),
141
sterling
after the 1981 Budget, 36
and Bretton Woods, 152
and North Sea oil, 99, 170
and the 1967 devaluation, 38, 211
and the 1976 IMF loan, 130
and the 1981 Budget, 24, 114, 124
and the Exchange Rate Mechanism,
144, 145
and the MTFS, 17, 85, 104, 117, 124,
166, 170
and the November 1980 mini-Budget,
18, 119
Bank of England views, 85, 119

Supplementary Petroleum Duty, 15, 26, 34, 71, 169
Supplementary Special Deposits (the 'corset'), 133, 137, 156, 166

Thatcher, Margaret,
　1979 election victory, 2, 131
　and Alan Walters, 14, 15, 26, 27, 28, 29, 30, 31, 32, 36, 41, 118, 171
　and capital controls, 113
　and 'concerted action', 130
　and 'crowding out', 23
　and David Wolfson, 14, 15, 31, 32
　and Douglas Wass, 110, 111, 112
　and financial deregulation, 147
　and fiscal policy, 27, 124, 145, 150, 178
　and Geoffrey Howe, 12, 13, 22, 28, 30, 31, 35, 36, 100, 115, 170
　and Gordon Pepper, 216, 221
　and Gordon Richardson, 104, 105
　and HM Treasury, 11, 16
　and inflation, 98, 123, 145, 147
　and John Hoskyns, 14, 27, 28, 30, 32
　and Karl Brunner, 104, 167
　and Keynesian economics, 148
　and monetarism, 2, 14, 134, 145
　and monetary targets, 117, 122, 179
　and Robin Ibbs, 24
　and sterling, 18, 24, 105, 110, 119
　and the 1981 Budget, 10, 11, 12, 36, 119, 123
　and the Bank of England, 163, 172, 176
　and the Exchange Rate Mechanism, 144
　and the inheritance in 1979, 97
　and the monetary policy U-turn, 113, 167, 179
　and the MTFS, 143, 220
　and the mythology of the 1981 Budget, 10, 15, 30, 97, 103, 176
　and the No. 10 Policy Unit, 16, 26, 35, 113
　and the November 1980 mini-Budget, 19, 113, 114
　and the PSBR in 1981, 16, 30, 134
　and monetarism, 2
　approach to decision-making, 10, 13
　criticism of, 81
　economic policy in opposition, 61, 127, 128
　pre-Budget meetings in 1981,
　　17 January, 24
　　10 February, 26
　　13 February, 27
　　17 February, 28, 29

　　24 February, 29
　　25 February, 32, 34
　social philosophy, 8
　unpopularity, 10
The Right Approach to the Economy, 44
Trades Union Congress (TUC), 59, 66
trades unions, 2, 7, 19, 39, 57, 59, 60, 64, 65, 66, 69, 79, 83, 91, 143, 156, 160, 184, 185
Treasury, Her Majesty's (HMT),
　and Milton Friedman, 214, 227
　and monetary targets, 61, 80, 149, 162, 214, 222
　and No. 10 Downing St, 11, 12, 13, 15, 20, 118
　and sterling, 99
　and the Bank of England, 136
　and the MTFS, 82
　and the PSBR in 1981, 19, 20, 21, 98, 99

Unwin, Brian, 20, 31
US Federal Reserve, 8, 119, 131, 178, 206

Value Added Tax (VAT), 29, 65, 67, 73, 85, 123
Volcker, Paul, 8, 119, 131, 178, 206

Walker, David, 85
Wallich, Henry, 9
Walters, Alan,
　and Brian Griffiths, 128
　and Geoffrey Howe, 27, 28, 33, 34, 72
　and HM Treasury, 14, 36
　and Jürg Niehans, 117, 170, 221
　and Keith Joseph, 128
　and Leon Brittan, 227
　and Margaret Thatcher, 14, 15, 20, 26, 27, 28, 29, 30, 31, 33, 100, 171, 176
　and monetarism, 14, 21, 41, 221
　and monetary policy, 20, 171, 228
　and Peter Middleton, 12, 33, 35
　and sterling, 77, 99, 101, 117
　and Terry Burns, 12, 35
　and the 1981 Budget, 11, 12, 33, 34, 35, 36, 119, 227
　and the Bank of England, 14
　and the Barber boom, 122
　and the monetary policy U-turn, 100, 137, 221
　and the mythology of the 1981 Budget, 13, 28, 30, 33, 34, 77, 78, 100, 103
　and the PSBR in 1981, 21, 23, 24, 25, 26, 30, 72, 100, 182

pre-Budget meetings in 1981
   10 February, 26
   13 February, 27
   17 February, 28
Wass, Douglas
  and Alan Walters, 33, 118
  and capital controls, 112
  and fiscal policy, 103
  and Geoffrey Howe, 110
  and Margaret Thatcher, 110, 112
  and monetarism, 20
  and monetary policy, 158, 168, 226, 227
  and monetary targets, 149, 217, 219,
    225
  and Nigel Lawson, 106
  and Peter Middleton, 21
  and sterling, 111
  and the monetary policy U-turn, 101,
    112, 113, 168, 169

and the November 1980 mini-Budget, 18,
   106
and the personal income tax allowances,
   32, 116
and the PSBR in 1981, 20, 32
pre-Budget meetings in 1981
   10 February, 26
   24 February, 29, 30
   27 January, 25
Whitmore, Clive, 31
Wiggins, John, 20, 224
Wolfson, David
  and Margaret Thatcher, 15, 26, 31,
    176
  and the PSBR in 1981, 23, 30, 100
  pre-Budget meetings in 1981
    10 February, 26

Young, Hugo, 11